PLANT-DRIVEN DESIGN

*Creating gardens that honor plants,
place, and spirit*

PLANT-DRIVEN DESIGN

Creating gardens that honor plants, place, and spirit

Scott Ogden & Lauren Springer Ogden

TIMBER PRESS
Portland · London

FRONTISPIECE *Tanacetum cinerariifolium, Stipa pennata, Oenothera macrocarpa, O. fremontii, Fallugia paradoxa, Nassella tenuissima, Sideritis scardica, Dianthus alpinus, Agastache rupestris,* authors' garden, Fort Collins, Colorado.

RIGHT A May meadow bursts forth in spring hues of pale yellow, white, and fresh green. Daffodils, *Thermopsis lupinoides, Euphorbia epithymoides, Malus sargentii* 'Tina', *Deschampsia caespitosa,* authors' garden, Fort Collins, Colorado.

OVERLEAF This free-spirited dryland garden, planted primarily in western natives, evokes the untamed feel of the region. *Forestiera neomexicana, Pinus aristata, Eschscholzia californica, Nassella tenuissima, Penstemon* spp., *Phlox nana, Agastache rupestris,* authors' garden, Fort Collins, Colorado.

Copyright © 2008 by Scott Ogden and Lauren Springer Ogden. All photographs by the authors. All rights reserved.

Published in 2008 by
Timber Press, Inc.

The Haseltine Building
133 S.W. Second Avenue, Suite 450
Portland, Oregon 97204-3527
www.timberpress.com

2 The Quadrant
135 Salusbury Road
London NW6 6RJ
www.timberpress.co.uk

Printed in China
Designed by Susan Applegate

Library of Congress Cataloging-in-Publication Data

Ogden, Scott.
    Plant-driven design: creating gardens that honor plants, place, and spirit/by Scott Ogden and Lauren Springer Ogden.—1st ed.
        p. cm.
    Includes index.
    ISBN-13: 978-0-88192-877-8
        1. Gardens—Design. 2. Landscape design. 3. Plants, Ornamental.
I. Ogden, Lauren Springer. II. Title. III. Title: Plant driven design.
IV. Title: Creating gardens that honor plants, place, and spirit.
    SB472.45.O33 2008
    712—dc22
                                                    2008002791
A catalog record for this book is also available from the British Library.

CONTENTS

FEATURES AND PLANT LISTS

PREFACE
Gardens are for plants

Every plant has fitness
and must be placed in its proper surroundings
so as to bring out its full beauty.
Therein lies the art of landscaping.

JENS JENSEN (1860–1951)
Danish-American landscape architect

THIS BOOK IS FOR lovers of plants, nature, and gardens—in particular those who are inspired by this love to make wonderful gardens. The ideas and opinions filling the pages that follow arise from one premise: gardens exist because of gardeners, not designers. And yet this is a book about garden design. In it we aim to unite the often disparate roles of designer and gardener, and the work of creating and planting.

A troublesome gap exists between those who tend gardens and those who design them. Certainly some people do both these things with joy and ease, but most do not. Perhaps this results partly from natural tendencies: those who gravitate toward growing may have one set of innate preferences and abilities, and those who tend toward visual artistry, another. Mostly the schism seems to stem from a lack of confidence on the part of those who find themselves in an unfamiliar realm. So you'll hear many exceptional gardeners and specialist growers protest that they can't design themselves out of a hole in the ground and see them show signs of serious intimidation when confronted by the process, with more self-deprecation forthcoming or even out-and-out refusal to try. Designers are often more circum-spect about admitting their discomfort. Many simply avoid intimacy with plants or any depth of plantsmanship and rely instead on a limited, proven palette and series of plant combinations that they trot out like familiar dinner recipes, again and again.

True to its title, this book differs from other design books in that it begins with the assumption that plants come first, not style or architecture. What it is not is a cookbook for garden design. You'll find no simple how-to, no formulaic step-by-step, no hard-and-fast rules, no lofty principles. Instead you'll meet with ideas, options, approaches, and plants from the world over. So, more specifically, this book is for gardeners who want the confidence to design, and designers who want the confidence to plant.

The single most essential element in any garden is not some particular object, plant, or tool. What's vital is a gardener who loves it. Unfortunately, much of what is promoted as or called a garden in North America is nothing

OPPOSITE *Echinacea pallida, Monarda fistulosa, Salvia sclarea, Festuca mairei, Koeleria macrantha,* authors' garden, Fort Collins, Colorado.

more than a landscape installation. Love has nothing to do with it. This sad reality is furthered by our culture's ever-shrinking attention span and ever-growing demand for material things. The garden has become a product, a home-improvement project, a look. No wonder home decor and plants often share space at retail outlets—they're being billed as one and the same. Statues, gazing globes, finials, and whatnot proliferate alongside plants. This is not to suggest that incorporating objects into the garden is a bad thing (though there ought to be some creativity, relevance, and personal expression in their selection and/or placement), but the implication that they should get equal billing with the plants is absurd.

Gone, then, is the ongoing process and relationship gardeners seek and enjoy, as gardening becomes a goal-driven activity with the desired end product a garden that once installed should be maintained with a minimum of effort and involvement. How can a novice gardener learn from such a model? How can a designer create a real garden this way? Maintenance may occasionally be tedious, but most of the time it's simply gardening, and that's what many of us love to do. The reality is, a person who dislikes gardening but wants to possess a garden will never have one that can honestly be called his or her own, no matter how much money or hired staff is thrown at it.

Maintenance also implies a static state for the garden. Plants and gardens change thanks to time, erratic weather, and people's desires. Inherent change, lack of complete control, and the ongoing relationship between plant and gardener all give gardening a special allure that sets it apart from other passionate activities for those of us so smitten; otherwise we would spend that time rebuilding engines, painting faux finishes on walls, or embroidering chair seats. Plants are the element that sets gardening apart from other arts or crafts, which have no such relationship with anything alive. Making plants the main focus of design returns gardenmaking to being about a relationship between plants and people. That relationship should be a happy one. Why not invite plants into the garden not as surrogates for paint chips, curtains, carpets, or chairs, but rather as living beings that attract us, pique our curiosity, and encourage interaction?

There's an ongoing argument whether gardens and gardenmaking are art or belong to the supposedly lowlier realms of hobby, craft, or skill. The answer depends on how one defines art. Stimulating to the senses? Definitely. Able to profoundly affect those who experience it? Resoundingly so. An original result of a person's combined creativity, skill, and effort? Only in part. Perhaps cooking shares the most similarities, as there's a big dollop of spontaneity and lack of control involved in the making of both great food and great gardens. Whether gardening is an art or not, gardeners garden because they love plants—alive, growing, and thriving. We want to look at them, nurture them, arrange them, watch them respond. We may differ slightly in why we garden and what we want from a garden, but love—love of plants, love of beauty, love of the natural world—surely holds us strongly and tenderly in its grasp.

Since childhood, that's what has inspired the two of us to spend as much time as possible outside, to venture into natural places wherever and whenever possible, and to surround ourselves with plants, indoors and out. We both came to gardening and design from a broad perspective and breadth of experience based on ecology, natural history, and simple observation of nature. This combined knowledge gives us a different view of plants' cultural and aesthetic attributes than that of many others who come either from a more narrow training in the applied science of horticulture or a background in the visual arts. Scott spent his youth hunting for fossils, wading up and down the neighborhood creek turning over rocks, and helping his mother in the garden, and then went on to study geology and paleontology before launching into a career as nurseryman, horticultural consultant, and garden designer. As a child Lauren collected houseplants, and she poked around nearby woods and hiked in the Alps each summer, obsessing about wildflowers and learning their names and habitats. A career in forestry and park management beckoned before she chose to garden professionally, earn a master's degree in horticulture, and design gardens.

As adults we've spent most of our waking hours either gardening or exploring wild places. The gardens we've made for ourselves and for others have been primarily in Texas and Colorado, both regions with exacting, unforgiving soil and climate, forcing us long ago to embrace careful plant selection and placement before all other design considerations. Over the three decades of our professional involvement with plants, gardens, and garden design, we've seen increasingly outward-directed, shallow, overdesigned spaces promoted and idolized in the popular horticultural press and on television. Our frustration at this galvanized us to write this book, as did our sadness at seeing natural areas, agricultural land, and older neighborhoods relentlessly devoured by a voracious mass of man-made generic spaces and architecture from coast to coast. Plants and gardens have been made second-class citizens and yet they remain one of the next generation's few hopes for communion with living things and the fascinating beauty intrinsic to the natural world. By reclaiming gardens as a home first to plants, above all other elements, desires, and vanities, we return a life-affirming vitality to gardens and garden design.

As fashion and politics ebb and flow, the discipline of landscape architecture periodically gives lip service to regionality, site sensitivity, and the ideal of a sense of place. Yet the plant-deprived, homogeneous curricula offered by most landscape architecture departments at American universities and the majority of landscapes churned out by their graduates attest to it not being much more than that. We would like to suggest that students read this book before embarking on a career that so greatly affects how we experience our surroundings. When we allow plants rather than architecture to run the show and when we learn about choice and placement to honor them, unlimited possibilities emerge for reconnection with the natural world, resonance with one's region, recognition and expression of the uniqueness of a site, ecological attunement and preservation of diversity, and celebration of the beauty inherent in plants and plant-driven design.

The following pages will take you on an exploration of these possibilities. You'll see how they derive from relationships between plant and region, plant and site, plant and plant, and plant and person, and how these relationships can be harnessed by design and used as its starting point and driving force. In this book we hope to inspire and enable you to design with what you love—plants.

Acknowledgments

Thanks first and foremost to Timber Press executive editor and friend Tom Fischer for his enthusiasm regarding this book and his support, or at least forbearance, for our often unconventional ideas. His humor, intelligence, and grace make time with him, whether at work or at play, a pleasure.

Thanks to Lorraine Anderson for cleansing our unclear prose, catching our bad grammar, and for being the rare talented editor who sees both forests and their trees. She truly understands the meaning of Emerson's quote, "A foolish consistency is the hobgoblin of small minds."

Thanks are due to our designer, Susan Applegate. Having been taken by Susan's stunning work for Timber Press, we asked her to design our book. Thankfully she agreed, creating a visual feast from our images and prose. And for the interminable final details, many thanks to Mike Dempsey for his help and good humor.

Last, our gratitude goes to the plantspeople whose work inspires us; who have shared their time, knowledge, and plants with us; and most of all, along our lives' plant-strewn paths, whom we have had the good fortune to come to know personally as friends.

ABOUT THE PHOTOGRAPHS

The images in this book, with the exception of our portrait on the jacket, were photographed by us. We are fortunate to live lives that take us to amazing places, and no less fortunate to possess the time and temperament to enjoy exploring our own native haunts and home gardens with equal fervor and curiosity.

Lauren took the majority of the photographs in this book. She used her twenty-one-year-old manual Nikon FM2 35 mm camera and its 55 mm Nikkor lens, and shot exclusively with Fuji Velvia ISO 50 professional film. She put a sky filter on the lens on all but the dreariest days, mainly for cleanliness. Impatient and always moving, she defies tripods, knowing from miserable attempts with them that she would give up photography were she forced to use one. Luckily a steady hand allows her to shoot clearly down to a fifteenth of a second and a limber body gets her in the most difficult spots and positions for a shot. Bottom line, her photography is all about eye and no gadgets. We find our own road.

PUTTING PLANTS FIRST
A different approach to designing gardens

THIS BOOK APPROACHES garden design from a perspective that places plants, nature, and horticulture on equal footing with art and architecture. Such a view grows from the conviction that a garden first and foremost is a place to cultivate, be among, and experience plants. A garden engages the senses with beauty; it also nurtures a person's fascination with the green world. A landscape that doesn't allow plants to do this can hardly be called a garden.

How we feel toward plants—our sense of their presence in a garden—reflects our response to their innate character and also their context, placement, and varied capacities to touch us by bringing to mind past experience and association. Gardens are as much emotional constructs as aesthetic compositions. A tiny emerging crocus bud, the mysterious fragrance of a sweet olive seeping from its hidden flowers onto the night air, or the anticipation of spring blossoms not yet open may weigh as heavily on our experience as shade cast by a mature oak. Being near and among plants moves us, for in their presence we hold the wonder and beauty of nature close at hand. It is this connection with the growing world that compels most of us to create gardens, so it seems that these places should be designed to consider and celebrate their green inhabitants before all else.

Formal plantings with linear beds alongside walls and walkways; informal areas with meandering paths edging curved beds, swales, and berms; naturalistic landscapes with romantic streams, rock outcrops, woods, and meadows; modernist designs with strong forms, open spaces, and starkly juxtaposed elements; even constrained areas such as patios, decks, rooftops, hellstrips, and medians along busy roads: all of these can be gardens if they include plants in generous, thoughtful ways. By considering plants at the start of the design process, gardeners help them assume their rightful places as the driving experiences of a composition. For the creation of gardens rather than mere landscapes, putting plants first is crucial. Yet, as with other human constructs, gardens frequently bend to desires, vanities, prejudices, and impulses that frustrate this goal.

How plants came to be last

Architects generally think of gardens as outdoor extensions of houses, and many texts repeat this as a primary canon of design. It is an idea with a long history and grows from a natural desire to make house and garden into complementary

OPPOSITE Architecture, whether mundane or beautiful, is enhanced by plants that receive equal billing. A romantically overgrown walled garden offers a glimpse through a gate shrouded in rampant vines and cascades of blossoming coral blow. *Russelia coccinea, Parthenocissus* sp. 'Hacienda Creeper', *Sophora secundiflora, Muhlenbergia lindheimeri, Chamaerops humilis, Bauhinia macranthera*, Austin, Texas, Ogden design.

experiences. As usually set forth, however, this architecture-first approach puts consideration of plants at the end of the design process. Consequently gardens often lose much of their natural power to touch the human spirit, the very reason we are drawn to create them in the first place.

Born into the arid landscape of the Middle East, the gardens of ancient Egypt grew by necessity alongside water-filled canals serving residences. These oasis plantings were enclosed by their owners to protect plants from browsing animals and may have begun as simple collections of desirable flora brought near for enjoyment. Descriptions recount the sweet fragrances of narcissi, roses, lilies, and jasmines, shady retreats created by tall sycamores and cypresses, and succulent fruits of grapes, figs, pomegranates, and dates. Today, echoes of this type of garden can still be seen in the walled patios of Spain and other Mediterranean countries.

As civilization spread, gardens followed, adopting mostly linear forms from the canals. Over time this became codified in the foursquare formality shared by gardens in ancient Rome, the Islamic empire, and Renaissance Europe. While common people continued to cultivate herbs and flowers in simple enclosures, nobility imposed axial grids upon the surrounding landscape, extending the geometry of their houses and dividing planting spaces into rectangular plots, with plants serving architectural purposes as hedges, patterned ornaments, or masses of color.

In China and Japan gardens developed from more naturalistic models, perhaps as an outgrowth of the lush, plant-friendly environment and romantic, hilly terrain common to these countries. Styled after idealized wild landscapes, oriental gardens nevertheless reflected carefully controlled designs extending from the residences of the elite. Workers diverted and dammed streams to create lakes, and upended rocks and boulders as statuary or for grottoes. Symbolic gates and shaped windows framed views and played with light and shadow; plants were sheared, trained, or contorted to represent abstract mountain scenes and windswept vistas.

In both Asia and the West, gardeners selected plants for improved ornamental qualities, introducing new peonies, roses, flowering trees and shrubs, bulbs, and perennials. But in the precisely designed gardens of the gentry, these played within rigid schemes. At the end of the Victorian era the influential British garden designer Gertrude Jekyll articulated a dilemma: "The first purpose of a garden is to give happiness and repose of mind, which is more often enjoyed in the contemplation of the homely border . . . than in any of the great gardens where the flowers lose their identity, and with it their hold on the human heart, and have to take a lower rank as mere masses of colour filling so many square yards of space" (*Wall and Water Gardens*, 1903.)

While she extolled the unique beauty of individual plants in her prose, Jekyll nonetheless followed strict artistic principles in her design partnership with architect Edwin Lutyens, who set forth defined, usually formally styled outdoor rooms backed by walls or hedges. She then filled these preset spaces with seemingly informal masses of plants. Constrained by architecture, the billowing flora poetically conveyed some of the natural spirit and abundance of wildflower meadows, although Jekyll imposed her painter's eye to orchestrate careful color schemes. As with elite gardens everywhere, these demanded continual care to achieve desired effects; gardeners who were left to make this happen had little say in the designs.

Jekyll's life (1843–1932) coincided with an especially prosperous era for horticulture. Expanding world trade and industrialization had brought innumerable plants into gardens and nurseries, and diverse plant collections became popular among a newly wealthy merchant class. To accommodate their plant acquisitions, estates often combined traditional formal gardens extending from the main house with extensive adjacent "wild" gardens planted in the picturesque style advocated by Jekyll's contemporary William Robinson.

Following the Great Depression and World War II, gardens evolved around smaller private residences and their adjacent outdoor living spaces. Working in the sunny, perpetually mild climate of California, Thomas Church created landscapes to support a casual outdoor lifestyle. In

ABOVE Exuberant greenery—
bromeliads festooning tree
branches, filling urns and flower
beds—envelops this house,
merging garden with architecture.
Jesse Durko garden, Davie,
Florida.

LEFT A traditional garden
enclosure reenergizes with
novel planting; bold flowers
and foliage mingle, standing
up to the architectural setting.
Kniphofia 'Alcazar', bear's breech
(*Acanthus mollis*), windmill palm
(*Trachycarpus fortunei*), clockvine
(*Thunbergia alata*), Royal
Horticultural Society Garden
at Wisley, Surrey, England.

ABOVE A linear rill fed by splashing fountains and arching jets of water—a design made famous in the courtyard of the Generalife next to the Alhambra in Spain—is an oft-copied feature in formal gardens. The unswervingly straight lines derive from ancient Persian and Egyptian gardens alongside irrigation canals. Colossal stone pots filled with tree beargrasses (*Nolina nelsonii*) provide vertical definition in lieu of walls. San Antonio Botanical Garden, Jim Keeter design.

RIGHT Oddly shaped karst boulders (taihu stones) and plants of Asian ancestry give a sense of oriental nature. Daylilies and dwarf mondo grass carpet the ground beneath an unusual tree-sized variegated holly-leaf osmanthus. *Hemerocallis* sp., *Ophiopogon japonicus* 'Nanus', *Osmanthus heterophyllus* 'Variegatus', Classical Chinese Garden, Portland, Oregon.

LEFT Hollyhocks, clary sage, and self-seeding larkspur frame a rustic arbor in a cottage garden planting. *Alcea rosea*, *Salvia sclarea*, and *Consolida ajacis*, Wave Hill, Bronx, New York, Marco Polo Stufano design.

BELOW This perennial border showcases the profusely floral English style popularized by Gertrude Jekyll and her contemporaries. *Papaver somniferum*, *Delphinium* cvs., *Campanula* spp., *Lychnis coronaria*, *Phlox paniculata*, Jim Reynolds garden, Butterstream, Trim, Ireland.

Gardens Are for People (1955) he advocated functional outdoor rooms filled with amenities such as swimming pools, barbecues, and decks. Plants were called upon only to decorate occasional nooks or flowerpots as horticultural treats, serve as ground cover to hold and unite a slope, provide shade, or create leafy frames to enclose space and show off distant views. Designed to require minimal maintenance, these convenient landscapes were no longer gardens in the original sense. The plants fostered little interaction with their human cohabitants, in spite of Church's understanding that a home landscape also needed to fulfill "the primary function of being a garden in the true sense of providing trees and flowers, fruits and vegetables, a place where man can recapture his affinity with the soil, if only on Saturday afternoons."

How structure-driven gardens fall short

What Church missed in his approach to gardens, and what most architecture-first approaches miss in one way or another, is that entirely taming plants or wholly directing a landscape to human purposes obliterates the opportunity for people to become immersed. What gives gardens their potency is that they represent idealized natural spaces whose living components, while retaining individual qualities and spirits, sum into a greater whole. Recognizing that we belong to this living kingdom remains one of the few moments of transcendence left in modern life, reminding us of our place in nature. The opportunity for a personal relationship with the natural world is essential to a garden but may be lost simply by failing to include plants in a way that celebrates their inherent character and natural power. Gardens are certainly for people, but to actually be gardens, they must be created with plants first in mind.

This is not to say that architecturally driven landscapes can't be beautiful. They often are, in the same way that well-proportioned buildings are beautiful. But if their fixed geometry goes too far, so that the composition rests only on the static beauty of paving, walls, sheared hedges, massed bedding flowers, and repeated lines and beds of matching trees, shrubs, and other architectural subjects, there is lit-

tle to love save architecture. In these kinds of landscapes nature has been utterly defeated. The results, visible everywhere along public streets, in malls, and beside commercial buildings as well as in many professionally designed residential "gardens," are spaces that give people few reasons to pause or contemplate their place in the world.

Abandoning formal style for curvilinear shapes and asymmetrical balance won't rescue a garden from this bullying. Avant-garde designs that require plants to perform as living sculptures or swaths of paint, such as those of the oft-copied Brazilian designer Roberto Burle Marx, can be as overpowering to plantings as any formal style. There is little opportunity for change and growth in plants or in people's responses when a design requires the plants to submit to wholly architectural roles. What happens instead is the gradual development of a series of blobs comprised of shrubs, flowering plants, ground covers, panels of ornamental grass, even trees. All lose their unique qualities over time as they grow together in similar masses or are hacked, sheared, or mowed. Such landscapes demand that plants stay in near suspended animation to fulfill the designer's vision and often impose an unrealistic burden on their owners for upkeep.

Unfortunate things happen to a garden when the importance of plants and their individual characters are diminished. At the outset the landscape loses complexity. What's left is often so obvious to look at that the scene hardly merits a second glance. Remove natural diversity and we feel no invitation to explore further. There is no reason even to get out of the car.

The error usually made by designers of these spaces is assuming that a garden is a place or a thing. As any gardener knows, what's missing from this view is the sense of process. The noun *garden* only comes into being when it is also a verb:

gar·den *verb:* to care for and cultivate plants in a plot of ground or enclosure; to lay out or work in a garden; to make into a garden

At its heart a garden is a relationship, an ongoing dialog between people, plants, and the place in which they both

Not simply chores, weeding and editing sustain and renew a garden's design and at the same time nurture fascination and connection for the gardener. Lauren fills a bucket with weeds and flopping seed heads in the steppe garden. Authors' garden, Fort Collins, Colorado.

frustrates the chance to create a meaningful design. It also cuts short the enjoyment of gardening just as tyranny sabotages any relationship.

Plants as partners

You can't have a garden without gardening. And you aren't likely to do very well designing one without getting your hands dirty. This is simply because gardens change over time. The gardenmaker becomes both author and editor, entering a relationship of observation, enjoyment, and thoughtful intervention.

A tree grows up and what once was sun becomes shade. Perennials that thrived in the early, sunny days of the garden struggle for light. Different shade-loving flowers might replace these original plants so that blooms again fill the garden. However, these replacements may need renewal themselves in a few years as the garden continues to evolve.

Solutions to such shifting challenges won't be evident at the outset of a garden's design; they come about through observing and responding to plants over many seasons and depend in equal measure on the horticultural and visual abilities of the gardenmaker. Some plants will succeed beautifully in their initial positions. Others will die outright or turn in only mediocre performances. More than a few will be overly successful, aggressively crowding neighbors. Several will call for more effort to maintain than their beauty warrants.

Oriental poppies offer spectacular blooms in vibrant colors, tempting prominent placement. However, their leafy clumps become entirely dormant in early summer, leaving ugly vacancies unless they have been carefully hidden in the background. A designer fortunate enough to know the bad habits of the poppies can anticipate their premature retreat and place them accordingly. One who discovers their maddening lapses later will need to confess the weaknesses of initial designs and relocate or, at times, ruthlessly send on to the compost heap such previously cherished plants.

For gardenmakers this willingness to rethink plantings is likely to prove as useful as any reference on horticulture or garden design. Over time, revising, redirecting, and

live and grow. What separates gardenmaking from architecture, sculpture, and other arts is that this living creation is not something we will into being by ourselves. Plants and nature are our partners; our relationship with them is what builds a garden. As with a marriage, it is by observing idiosyncrasies, respecting needs, and envisioning potential of our partners (plants in this instance) that gardeners gather the background information needed to create a lasting relationship. Simply dominating the plants from the outset squanders the opportunity for this to evolve and restructuring become as vital to a plan as any initial vision. Moreover, these processes nurture the essence of the garden: its continuing relationship with the gardener. Architects may orchestrate essentially fixed landscapes; gardeners passionately involved in process succeed in designing the living organism that is a garden.

A robust star magnolia (*Magnolia stellata* 'Royal Star') has been growing more strongly than expected for several years near a flagstone path along the north side of our home in Colorado. In a year or two it may impinge on people walking by. What to do then? Prune the offending branches away? Dig the tree up and move it elsewhere? Realign and reset the path? These questions need to be answered by someone with knowledge of and experience with this plant—in other words, someone who has a relationship with this tree.

Star magnolias are generally slow-growing, with shallow, fleshy roots that resent disturbance; their large, snowy blossoms appear from tips of bare branches in early spring, making a lively show. The beauty of this floral event depends not only on the flowers but also on the graceful scaffolding provided by the tree's branches and on a dark background to give contrast. In this instance an effective backdrop is supplied by a gray-green wall, several dark-needled conifers, and leafy semi-evergreen ground covers of wild ginger, sedge, epimedium, and Christmas rose. Native to damp hills and streamsides on the island of Honshu in Japan, star magnolias appreciate a cool, moist root run as may be found along our north foundation. This partly shaded, cooler position also discourages the magnolia's flowers from emerging too early in the year when they might be spoiled by hard frost.

We treasure this small tree and its spring display. We know that it would be a tremendous hardship for the plant

Watery blue sheets of naturalized chionodoxa spread beneath the white, lilylike flowers of a star magnolia in early spring. *Scilla luciliae*, *Magnolia stellata*, Chanticleer, Wayne, Pennsylvania.

(and, to a lesser extent, for us as diggers) to transplant it; it would also be difficult to find a better site in our garden to show off the charms of the magnolia's flowers. The bed near our north foundation is the best place we can offer to satisfy the magnolia's cultural needs, display its character, and celebrate its special beauty. Thoughtful pruning may stall the impending walkway problem for a season or two, but hacking branches from the path could ultimately spoil the shape of the tree and the beauty of its spring display. When the time comes we will almost certainly elect to move the path.

Only a gardener with a relationship to and an understanding of this plant would likely come away with such a solution. An affectionless designer whose prejudices incline toward architecture would be more likely to make a choice in keeping with advice once offered us by a French landscape designer while we were working on a joint project: "Don't let the trees stop you."

Thoughtful formality

This is not to imply that formal or architectural gardens can't be respectful of plants. They can be. If we had better anticipated the vigor of our star magnolia and made our path wider so people could still pass by, there would be no reason not to allow the magnolia to continue in its present position, extending its branches to transgress just a bit over the paving. This kind of gentle overgrowth, with plants slightly overtaking the architecture or burgeoning beyond their original placements and patterns, lies at the heart of many seemingly formal or architectural designs whose structure is actually intended to serve as backdrop for exuberant planting.

The poetic contrast of billowing plants against strong

Framing a river view, the otherwise stiff balustrade and columns of a formal pergola succeed as counterpoints to lush summer vines and effusive potted plants. This is architecture meant for planting. *Hydrangea macrophylla*, *Hakonechloa macra* 'Aureola', *Phormium* cvs., *Codiaeum variegatum*, *Celastrus* sp., Wave Hill, Bronx, New York, Marco Polo Stufano design.

Walls imbue garden borders with structure, textural contrast, and unifying color.

RIGHT An English classic—a border backed by a ruddy aged brick wall—takes a new twist with rich plantings artfully orchestrated in a nontraditional red theme. *Papaver somniferum*, *Crocosmia* 'Lucifer', *Achillea millefolium*, *Foeniculum vulgare* 'Purpureum', roses, Hadspen House, Somerset, England, Nori and Sandra Pope design.

BELOW Filled with sun-loving, lush yet xeric plantings, this western border plays against pale masonry walls that double as seating for Maurice the cat. *Phlomis russeliana*, *Penstemon pinifolius* 'Mersea Yellow', *Fallugia paradoxa*, *Eremurus* 'Cleopatra', *Salvia sclarea*, *Stachys byzantina* 'Silver Carpet', *Allium christophii*, northern Colorado, Ogden design.

architecture became an essential theme of gardens created by Gertrude Jekyll and many of her contemporaries, as well as innumerable other designers in the English style. Blowsy roses and lush perennials are often featured in these plantings, creating contrast with the fixed lines of stone walls, shaped boxwoods, perfect lawns, and dark yew hedges. The loose plantings do much to soften the otherwise rigid forms of these classic gardens. Over time even paving, urns, and stonework soften under patinas of moss and lichen, assuming a mellower, organic presence.

What gives these architectural gardens spirit is that some of the plants have been allowed, at least partly, to have their own way. Even a composition as heavily manipulated as a knotted herb garden still takes on a lively air when its precisely clipped inhabitants are permitted to swell and list a bit, playfully veering from the formal patterns originally

LEFT A slightly listing sundial, imperfectly sheared boundary hedges, and bulging santolina along the paths impart vitality and individual character to this formally quartered garden. Cranborne Manor, Dorset, England.

BELOW The strong geometry of this boxwood-anchored herb garden is softened by self-sowing, spreading, and otherwise effusive plants. *Allium tuberosum*, *Pelargonium graveolens* 'Variegatum', *Salvia officinalis*, *Buxus sempervirens*, *Thymus* sp., Duck Hill, Page Dickey garden, North Salem, New York, sculpture by Kim Dickey.

intended. Somehow, plants in these gardens have been empowered and seem no longer wholly under human direction. Likewise, a vast architectural opus like Versailles, blurred by a few centuries of growth from its trees, acquires a more natural grace. A garden's design needn't go into disarray, but somewhere it does need to bend to acknowledge the will and spirit of the plants. It needs to share power.

So what are the qualities that give an outdoor space the feeling of a garden? There are many answers to this question, perhaps as many as there are gardeners. One is that a garden reflects the respectful, genuine affection of the gardenmaker for the plants. It shows this in spaces thoughtfully created to encourage pleasurable experience with them. As H. E. Bates eloquently argued in *A Fountain of Flowers* (1974), "That, in fact, is what true gardens are made of. Not wholly of professional skills or tomes of encyclopedic knowledge or even of green fingers: but love."

Landscape installations and exterior decor

When the designer of New York's Central Park, Frederick Law Olmsted, wrote about landscape architecture in the early twentieth century, he envisioned a utopian blend of disciplines: art and architecture would join with biology, geology, urban planning, and the gardener's applied science of horticulture to create a better world, all directed and facilitated by the landscape architect. The discipline has grown since Olmsted's time so that landscape architects presently work in park planning, urban design, site development, environmental mitigation, historical restoration, and other areas of specialization in addition to the design of gardens. For many in the profession it is the creation of exterior architecture, popularly known as hardscape, rather than planting design that drives their work. This is hardly surprising given the emphasis in North American universities, where landscape architecture curricula often focus on designing paving, walls, water features, and other outdoor structures; manipulating drainage; and creating drawings, reports, and presentations to support land development and master planning for public and commercial projects.

Nevertheless, landscape architects determine plantings for most public and commercial projects, so it may come as a surprise—especially considering the enormous sums spent on plants specified by these professionals—that in several states landscape architects may obtain degrees and become licensed without demonstrating any plant knowledge whatsoever. When they do pursue expertise in horticulture, students of landscape architecture learn plants common to the region in which they are studying. A degree taken in the Midwest assures no competence for a designer practicing in California, New Mexico, or Florida. In these very different climates new flora and new horticultural techniques need to be mastered.

Some landscape architects have natural affection for and interest in plants, nature, and gardens. As designers they overcome shortcomings in their academic training through experience. If they are conscientious practitioners, they also learn to set aside their own prejudices so that they can help create plantings tailored to their clients' predilections, engaging them and drawing them into daily experience with their gardens. They collaborate with contractors and garden staff, and remain available as consultants to periodically adjust a design as changes in plants and the desires of the client dictate over time.

Yet many landscape architects are not so inclined. By divorcing the process of gardenmaking from garden design, landscape architecture has attracted designers who are not gardeners themselves. In practice these well-dressed professionals remain sequestered in offices creating drawings instead of interacting with plants. One consequence of this separation becomes apparent in British landscape architect Sylvia Crowe's 1958 treatise, *Garden Design*: "There are two attitudes to plants in gardens. One is that the purpose of a garden is to grow plants, the other is that plants are one of the materials to be used in the creation of gardens." The author's words introduce a chapter entitled "Plant Materials," leaving little doubt about her feelings, or more aptly, her absence of feelings toward plants. From a sterile ivory tower has come the presumption that plants are items to be manipulated rather than living beings to be cherished.

Plants have their way with human designs.

ABOVE Sprawling shrubs and probing vines invade an open window in a ruin garden. *Corylopsis pauciflora*, *Tulipa* 'White Elegance', *Asarum splendens*, *Athyrium nipponicum* 'Pictum', *Osmunda cinnamomea*, *Schizophragma hydrangeoides* 'Moonlight', *Tiarella* 'Ninja', visible through window *Acer palmatum* 'Bloodgood', *Ulmus parvifolia* 'Frosty', Chanticleer, Wayne, Pennsylvania, Laurel Voran and Chris Woods design.

RIGHT In the staid courtyard of a former estate, red-leafed Abyssinian banana, reedy horsetail, and other bold plantings upstage the erstwhile formal mood of the architecture. *Ensete ventricosum* 'Maurelii', *Equisetum hyemale*, Chanticleer, Wayne, Pennsylvania, Dan Benarcik design.

The troubling aspect of this perspective is that it perpetuates a myth, one convenient for designers not inclined to horticulture, that the general organization, hard lines, and built features of a garden (its so-called bones) can be laid out independently of the intended planting. While it is certainly possible to design a garden in this way (and this is a method pursued by many trained designers), ignoring individual needs and qualities of plants until after the architecture has been drawn has consequences.

If a designer hopes to show off close-up features of a particular plant, perhaps its showy bark or fragrance, a path will be needed nearby; laying out a design without setting aside this position might hamstring a composition or leave only poor options for the garden. Failure to consider a suitably spare backdrop for an architectural plant or the potential effect of the direction and interplay of light on felted foliage or translucent flowers might also diminish a planting. Daffodils often face southeast toward the spring sun and usually show best in a position north or west of an observer; peculiarities such as this need to be accommodated in a design at the outset. Not actually choosing specific plants, instead designating "a large tree here" or "a small evergreen there" might protect a designer from an overt horticultural mistake, but it also disregards the importance of individual plants and plantings and their impact on a garden. Worst of all, with these banished from primary roles in a composition, little is left to breathe life into a design. Architecture and spatial treatments, whether beautiful or banal, may then be imposed without regard to site or climate, creating a monotonous sameness in designs. Plants and structural design both lose in this scenario.

The term *landscape architecture*, originally borrowed from an 1828 monograph on Italian landscape painting, is itself at odds with gardens, as it implies a static quality. Olmsted addressed this incongruity in *Landscape Architecture* (December 5, 1911): "A normal healthy-minded architect rebels at the necessity of waiting for growth in landscape work. He is impatient to 'get his effect' at once, and he wholly fails to grasp that the aim in most landscape work is not a single fixed 'effect' conceived as immutable, but in reality only instantaneous."

The impatient, "healthy-minded" architect Olmsted apologizes for has the ring of a familiar caricature: the imperious designer. Despite admonitions about the need for process and change, it is easy to predict the garden such an arrogant person will create. Obelisks, sculpture, pergolas, grand water features, and plants relegated to perpetually subordinate roles seem likely, along with a good deal of labor to keep it all swept up. Such an overmanipulated garden won't change in the course of time as it will when plants are allowed their own identities. The experience of visiting will always be the same one predetermined by the designer, with little room for individual response or interpretation.

As professionals, landscape architects generally operate in a hierarchy that places the designer at the top, dictating specifications. A contractor then installs plants, walkways, and other aspects of a garden, while a third party, usually the owner or a landscape service, adopts and manages the completed design. This "install and maintain" model allows for competitive bidding but often dissociates gardeners from the design process; it can paralyze "finished" landscapes instead of encouraging their evolution and

Many people use the terms *landscape* and *garden* interchangeably, but a garden is foremost a place in which to grow plants, while a landscape may have other goals. Designing a garden or plant-driven landscape begins with taking into account each plant's unique qualities and how people might best enjoy them. Ideally this precedes architectural layout.

OPPOSITE TOP Long-nosed blooms of early daffodils face toward spring sun (southeast in the Northern Hemisphere). Designers need to anticipate this and place paths and other positions for viewing accordingly. *Narcissus* cvs. with *Chaenomeles japonica* and *Abeliophyllum distichum*, Chanticleer, Wayne, Pennsylvania.

OPPOSITE BOTTOM Feathery grass blossoms, felted foliage, and potted cacti armed with shimmering spines line a path along a western exposure, glowing each afternoon in the late-day sunlight. *Stipa pennata*, *Nassella tenuissima*, *Helictotrichon sempervirens*, *Stachys byzantina*, *Cleistocactus aureus* (syn. *Hildewintera aurea*), northern Colorado, Ogden design.

redesign over time. With this approach a garden begins life as a drawing and the architect is often not present to adjust the design at installation. The resulting landscapes may succeed on a coarse scale easily represented on paper yet miss human-sized details important for creating an experience on the ground.

So why would people accept this as an approach to gardenmaking? Worship of style and the creation of reputations are common reasons. Seeing an intended vision installed and pronouncing it finished seduce with an alluring if false measure of one's own power and perfection. For some designers (and the clients who participate in the illusion with them), celebrating the brilliance of their own intentions is more important than developing an ongoing relationship with plants and nature.

Elevation of style over substance is also glorified by makeover shows on television, where audiences celebrate the transformation of a barren slate into instant verdure. This is credited wholly to the vision of a heroic designer who departs, check in hand, before the inevitable oversights

become apparent. Remarking on these shallow approaches to garden design, British gardener and BBC host Nigel Colburn laments, "I have watched with increasing frustration my beloved hobby, my chosen way of life, the thing I love most hijacked by what seems to me to be a gang of interior decorators and installation artists" (Royal Horticultural Society Bicentenary Debate, January 2004, www.rhs.org.uk).

Plants themselves—without architecture or artifact—can create beautiful gardens.

BELOW *Penstemon* 'Rondo' hybrid, *P. hirsutus*, other penstemons, *Seriphidium filifolium*, *Pinus edulis*, *Forestiera neomexicana*, *Eriogonum umbellatum*, authors' garden, Fort Collins, Colorado.

OPPOSITE TOP In the light shade of a palo verde, clustering torch cacti and fiercely armed agaves make an intriguing

desert vignette. *Parkinsonia* sp., *Echinopsis huascha* (syn. *Trichocereus huascha*), *Agave* sp. Felipe Otero (syn. *Agave* sp. Sierra Mixteca), Arizona-Sonora Desert Museum, Tucson, Arizona.

OPPOSITE BOTTOM A meadow of late-blooming members of the daisy family, all North American natives, make themselves at home in central Europe. *Helenium autumnale*, *Rudbeckia* spp., *Solidago* sp., *Coreopsis verticillata*, Weihenstephan Garten, Freising, Germany.

COTTAGE GARDENS The unselfconscious garden

Cottage gardens evolve when untrained gardeners gather plants they admire. These simple, casual plantings—common property of paupers everywhere—feature easily grown and propagated plants shared at minimal cost: roses struck from cuttings (often first set in water steeped with willow branches to enhance rooting), perennials that divide effortlessly with a spade, reseeding annuals, and especially bulbs, as described by Martha the maid in Frances Hodgson Burnett's 1911 book *The Secret Garden*: "They're things as helps themselves. That's why poor folk can afford to have 'em. If you don't trouble 'em, most of 'em'll work away underground for a lifetime an' spread out an' have little 'uns." In the cottage tradition, such flowery passalongs mingle with fruiting plants, herbs, and vegetables, sharing common ground. Offered benign but only casual attention, these undesigned gardens take on the appearance of a natural plant community as more aggressive plants spread or seed throughout, repeating form and flower. Often a well-adapted garden results, with a sense of charm found missing in many designed plantings. Here are some classic cottage garden denizens.

Trees, shrubs, and vines
Chaenomeles speciosa, flowering quince
Clematis terniflora (syn. *C. dioscoreifolia*),
   C. ×*jackmanii*, clematis
Ficus carica, fig
Hibiscus syriacus, rose of Sharon
Hydrangea macrophylla, hydrangea
Lagerstroemia indica, crape myrtle
Malus spp., crabapple
Nerium oleander, oleander
Osmanthus fragrans, sweet olive
Philadelphus coronarius, mock orange
Prunus persica, peach
Punica granatum, pomegranate
Rosa spp. and cultivars, rose
Syringa vulgaris, lilac
Vitex agnus-castus, chaste tree
Wisteria floribunda, *W. sinensis*, wisteria

Herbaceous perennials and succulents
Agapanthus praecox subsp. *orientalis* (syn.
   A. africanus), lily-of-the-Nile
Agave spp., century plant
Alcea rosea, hollyhock
Aloe vera, aloe
Antirrhinum majus, snapdragon
Canna spp., canna lily
Convallaria majalis, lily-of-the-valley
Dianthus barbatus, sweet William
Dicentra spectabilis, bleeding heart
Echeveria spp., *Graptopetalum paraguay-*
   ense, *Sempervivum* spp., hen and chicks
Hemerocallis fulva, daylily
Hemerocallis lilioasphodelus, lemon lily
Hosta plantaginea, plantain lily
Hylotelephium spectabile, stonecrop
ice plants, *Carpobrotus*, *Lampranthus*, and
   others
Iris albicans, *I. germanica* hybrids, *I. pallida*,
   bearded iris

Iris orientalis, white flag
Mirabilis jalapa, four o'clock
Opuntia compressa, *O. ellisiana*,
   O. englemanii, *O. ficus-indica*,
   O. sp. 'Old Mexico', prickly pear
   cactus (thornless selections)
Paeonia lactiflora, *P. officinalis*, peony
Papaver orientale, poppy
Phlox paniculata, summer phlox
Sedum ×*luteolum*, stonecrop
Viola spp., violet

Annuals
Consolida ajacis, larkspur
Lathyrus odoratus, sweet pea
Papaver somniferum, opium poppy
Tropaeolum majus, nasturtium
Viola tricolor, Johnny jump-up

Bulbs and corms
Amaryllis belladonna, naked ladies
Crinum spp., crinum lily
Galanthus nivalis, snowdrop
Gladiolus byzantinus 'Cruentus', Byzantine
   gladiolus
Hippeastrum ×*johnsonii*, Saint Joseph lily
Hyacinthoides hispanica, Spanish bluebell
Leucojum aestivum, snowflake
Lilium lancifolium, tiger lily
Lycoris radiata, spider lily
Lycoris squamigera, surprise lily
Muscari spp., grape hyacinth
Narcissus spp., daffodil

OPPOSITE Loving care, or sometimes benign neglect, and always a host of self-reliant plants meet in the unselfconscious profusion of cottage gardens.

ABOVE LEFT Loose-petaled heirloom roses relax among long-blooming herbaceous flowers and casually mingled silver foliage. *Artemisia absinthium* 'Lambrook Silver', *Stachys byzantina* 'Silver Carpet', *Aquilegia chrysantha*, *Antirrhinum* 'Dulcinea's Heart', *Digitalis thapsi*, *Salvia nemorosa* 'Blue Hill' ('Blauhügel'), *Rosa* 'Lawrence Johnston', *Rosa* 'Stanwell Perpetual', *Rosa* 'Ghislaine de Feligonde', *Helictotrichon sempervirens*, authors' garden, Fort Collins, Colorado.

ABOVE Old favorites lilacs and Darwin hybrid tulips combine colors unabashedly. *Syringa* ×*chinensis* 'Saugeana', northern Colorado, Ogden design.

LEFT An unpainted porch pairs with untended plants: red spider lily (*Lycoris radiata*), river fern (*Thelypteris normalis* var. *lindheimeri*), and English ivy. New Braunfels, Texas.

The so-called conceptual garden advocated by a few modern designers seems the ultimate tyranny of style, for these aren't gardens at all but instead essentially plantless installations based on a designer's concept. Working without the natural partnership supplied by living plants, the creators of these spaces resort to obscure references to give meaning to their schemes, enshrining historical, literary, or artistic elements to impress their clients. In a cynical nod to "sustainability," these nongardens often feature artificial turf chipping greens, outdoor fireplace-kitchens, spas, and other lifeless amenities, supposedly to help eliminate upkeep for clients whose "active lifestyles" prohibit activities like weeding. Were such compositions presented honestly as art installations, as is the popular plant- and nature-inspired work of Scotsman Andy Goldsworthy, they might be judged on their merits, but what these pillow pickers present as gardens are really just exercises in exterior decor.

Horticultural zealotry

While overly architectural approaches rob gardens of spirit and life, it is equally possible to err by not including enough commonsense design. Single-mindedness or obsession with plantings can overwhelm a garden's larger aesthetic and emotional effects as surely as unbridled imposition of style. An all-powerful affection for plants can be nearly as troublesome to a garden as its absence.

The most familiar blind plant passions belong to the horticultural specialist. Plantings by these focused individuals often have more in common with albums of stamp collectors than gardens. If their interests are truly narrow and they appreciate only a particular genus or family of plants, their gardens may come to resemble a small cemetery, filled with evenly spaced daylilies, roses, conifers, cacti, hostas, or other select treasures, each with its own discrete marker. These monocultures usually offer a fair display during the flowering season of the favored genus, but their restricted palette eventually becomes tiresome. They often have little to offer at other times of the year.

When a collector's passion is less myopic, as with a rock garden or pond planting, a more natural composition can evolve. However, these areas of special interest still need careful consideration if they are to merge well with a larger garden. In many instances it is a plant's obscurity or rarity that is held in high regard by the collector, not its actual beauty. Creating an aesthetic experience with such curios is challenging. Only when gardenmakers moderate their passion for the individual plant, allowing companions for their favorites and repeating plants in effective groups, does it become possible to create a scene resonant for someone other than the collectors themselves.

The impulse to acquire plants also finds a less-focused expression, one we sometimes succumb to ourselves. This variant of the collector gene gives gardeners a magpie's instinct, driving them to bring home any variety that catches their eye. Plantings that spring from this acquisitive tendency risk looking like overstuffed attics filled with gaudy clothing and old knickknacks. In this case the collector's desires develop a bric-a-brac palette too broad rather than too narrow and the restless-looking garden that results feels filled with plant divas competing for attention. Well-known nurseryman and plant collector Tony Avent wryly describes this as designing in "sweeps of one."

Such a patchwork approach to planting begins to form a garden composition only after the gardener slows the acquisition of plants. Surviving varieties that have thrived and increased then begin to shape the planting themselves by creating natural clusters of varied form. Cottage gardens—classically a mix of tried-and-true perennials, shrub roses, and reseeding annuals—derive from just such a process: the original impulse to collect is tempered by time and benign neglect while the most successful plants spread and reproduce themselves, setting up a rhythm of repeated textures and colors. Under these conditions a community of garden plants evolves almost as in nature.

New horticultural varieties appear regularly in nursery offerings, hyped with catchy names and colorful packaging. Likewise, older heirloom plants are lovingly proffered by specialists along with romantic titles—often multisyllabic French—wistfully recalling gardens of former eras. Even

LEFT Horticulturists on safari give rapt attention to a mesmerizing Cape bulb in full flower. Gardens can be enriched by such novelties, but an assemblage of curios is likely to appeal only to collectors. Left to right, Cameron McMaster of African Bulbs, Laurel Voran of Chanticleer, Dan Johnson of Denver Botanic Gardens; standing, Ellen Hornig of Seneca Hill Nursery. *Brunsvigia radulosa*, Eastern Cape, Republic of South Africa.

BELOW LEFT This novel rock garden features a cherished collection of dwarf cacti, penstemons, and other small dryland plants suited to high elevations; these blend more readily into their surrounding landscape— semiarid northern New Mexico— than similar gardens dedicated to traditional alpines. *Echinocereus triglochidiatus* var. *inermis*, *E. triglochidiatus*, *Escobaria sneedii*, *Opuntia fragilis* 'Alberta Sunset', *Penstemon teucrioides*, *Lesquerella* sp., David Salman garden, Santa Fe, New Mexico.

when these turn out to be beauties as advertised, both the old-fashioned and newfangled varieties promise a happy result only if they also prove adaptable to local conditions and aspects, and mingle well with other garden denizens.

A designer creating a garden around an old home or estate may want to honor the period of the architecture with historical plantings; this attention to the past can add charm and cohesion to a landscape. But if taken too far, history can also get in the way of a garden. Old plant varieties and landscape plans are worth repeating only if they also complement modern interests and the affections of people who will live in and visit the garden. Antique notes, plant lists, and drawings preserved from a previous designer's work include mistakes and failures as well as successes; restoring them without critical modification hardly makes sense. As with any garden, historic plantings also need to move forward over time. Expecting them to remain frozen in an idealized moment of the past risks sacrificing their value in the present and their potential in the future.

Native and exotic plants

People generally obtain plants for their gardens from nurseries and from other gardeners who share them, yet the ultimate source for garden flora has always been nature. Concerning the introduction of new varieties, Thomas Jefferson expressed the feelings of a progressive gardener of his era in a memorandum composed around 1800: "The greatest service which can be rendered any country is to add a useful plant to its culture." This welcoming attitude toward new plants can also be found in botanical treatises and floras where introduced species that become part of local flora have traditionally been said to "naturalize."

Of course, not all such changes improve on nature. In some instances spontaneous or, as they are scientifically known, adventive plants become weeds, and in recent decades alarm over this possibility has brought forth a new terminology. Many varieties previously described as naturalizing are now labeled invasive. This language says as much about changing attitudes toward plants, nature, and the responsibilities of people as it does about the specific plants themselves, and it frames a current debate over the role of native and introduced plants in gardens.

It's essential first to recognize that while gardens connect us to nature, they are not natural in the romanticized use of that word. They are very much products of human desires, actions, and interventions. But if we can comfortably see ourselves as part of nature, not separate from or antipathetic to it, then in a general sense gardens are natural, even though not a part of what we refer to as nature and the natural world, meaning where human hands haven't made a large mark. This may all sound like a bad case of semantics, but the words *nature* and *natural* get bandied about a great deal of late, often with much pretense and self-righteousness, so some distinctions are in order for the sake of this argument.

Gardeners create plantings with an unspoken assumption that people are a part of nature. Enjoyment of both gardening and simply being in a garden often grows from a sense of losing oneself among plants. The earthly Edens we create are indeed poetic realms in which we are able to forget our modern-day divorce from the natural world. This renewal of our relationship with nature is the very essence of garden experience.

Yet the possibility of making emotional connections may find itself stifled when a garden is directed by an opposing view, that nature is pure unto itself and that people's actions diminish its perfection. This is a tacit assumption made by some advocates for native plants who regard typical garden flora as threatening alien vegetation. Putting potential environmental issues aside for the moment, let us look at how this attitude affects gardens.

While it is certainly conceivable that a gardener might develop affections only for native flora, we haven't met any so narrowly smitten. Love for plants, like any honest affection, is blind to such details. Instead, people respond most directly to plants they knew in childhood; in our mobile society these are rarely species indigenous to a garden's immediate vicinity. More likely they are plump lilacs and rosy peonies like the ones that flowered along a friend's fence, colorful crape myrtles like those that filled old neighborhoods with big trusses of summer bloom, or sweet-scented Japanese honeysuckle vines laden with nectar-filled blossoms like those that smothered a wall on the walk back from grade school—never mind that these were also choking several native dogwoods.

If our emotions naturally attract us to such introduced flora, why would we want to have gardens filled only with less familiar, less beloved indigenous plants? Advocates for native plant gardens argue that indigenous species are best adapted to local conditions, more attractive and beneficial to wildlife, and more in keeping with the regional spirit of a garden's setting. The difficulty with such rationales is that nature is rarely so simple.

Unless one defines *native* in terms of geology, regional climate, and specific habitat rather than by the boundaries of local geography, this label has little bearing on a plant's adaptability. For instance, species indigenous to sandy, acid understories might grow with abandon in gardens with similar soil and shade hundreds or thousands of miles away but perish in clay soil on alkaline, sunny prairies nearby. Other plants seem miraculously indifferent to both climate and site: rusty blackhaw (*Viburnum rufidulum*) and yaupon (*Ilex vomitoria*) commonly inhabit acid swamps and shaded woodlands in the humid Southeast but also grow on dry limestone hillsides in the sunny Southwest, thriving in near-desert conditions. Go figure.

Plants often give their best garden performances outside

Romantic beauties or invading weeds? Thomas Jefferson and other gardeners of his generation would have been pleased by such successful introductions, as would many gardeners in the present.

ABOVE Naples onion creates a white cascade in rocky, disturbed woods. *Allium neapolitanum*, Austin, Texas.

RIGHT Pristine white summer snowflakes—natives of Europe and Turkey—join indigenous skunk cabbages in a damp woodland. *Leucojum aestivum*, *Lysichiton americanus*, near Greenville, Delaware.

People are part of nature; gardeners know this. *Prunus* sp., Mount Auburn Cemetery, Cambridge, Massachusetts.

native ranges. For instance, several species of wild indigo (*Baptisia* spp.) inhabit prairies of the Gulf states and southern Great Plains, offering showy blooms above handsome foliage. Yet in these hot climates flowers hardly last a week and leaves scorch brown by midsummer. Transplanted to East Coast or Pacific Coast gardens, or to gardens in the upper Midwest or Intermountain West, these same species remain in bloom almost a month and keep healthy foliage the entire summer.

While certain indigenous plants show unique, specific relationships with wildlife, most creatures are not particular and happily make use of introduced garden flora. Hummingbirds native to the Western Hemisphere eagerly sip nectar from flowers of African aloes and kniphofias in American gardens, although these are customarily visited only by sunbirds in their homeland. Many introduced plants couldn't naturalize if wildlife didn't pollinate flowers and distribute fruits and berries. In regard to leaf-eating insects, a particular type of wildlife ordinarily judged detrimental to gardens, introduced plants may retain a distinct advantage, having left such pests behind in their land of origin. Including such pest-free exotics in a garden can preserve aesthetics while distracting from seasonally disfigured natives left to feed local bugs, if this is deemed important.

It's true that mature native trees, specimen shrubs, and other distinctive plants tie a garden to its site and give a sense of relationship to the surrounding countryside; adding these plants to a new landscape is one of the surest ways to make a garden feel settled and also help create a more naturalistic design if such is desired. But native plants don't own this role exclusively, for similar climates around the world produce similar-looking plants. For garden purposes the rustic twisted branching of a Mediterranean olive can convey much the same spirit as indigenous California madrones and manzanitas; a hardy Austrian pine simulates the effect of western ponderosas; an African aloe or Australian *Xanthorrhoea* easily fills in for American yuccas or agaves; while hybrid rhododendrons of Himalayan ancestry with their evergreen lushness offer much the same landscape appearance as native Appalachian rhododendrons or mountain laurels (*Kalmia latifolia*).

If native plants cannot be declared inherently better, either practically or aesthetically, what about the larger environmental implications of gardening with native versus exotic plants? Here, too, nature offers no clear-cut answers. Where plants grow today they didn't always occur in the past, for climates and habitats have changed many times, and are changing now under the pressure of human

Gardens devoted to native plants convey regionality and a strong sense of place when created with artistry and cared for with affection.

ABOVE An eastern American woodland garden revels in its finest season with unbridled spring bloom. *Phlox divaricata, Senecio aureus, Cornus florida, Rhododendron* sp., *Fothergilla major*, Mount Cuba Center, Greenville, Delaware.

LEFT Desert envelops an adobe building with century plant, beargrass, and creosote bushes. *Agave americana, Nolina bigelovii, Larrea tridentata*, Arizona-Sonora Desert Museum, Tucson, Arizona.

development. For example, large-leaf magnolias (*Magnolia macrophylla*), presently native to a few rich, wooded ravines in the Southeast and, in the subspecies *dealbata,* to certain cloud forests in mountain valleys of eastern Mexico, also once grew plentifully in Idaho, as testified to by well-preserved fossil leaves that appear there as carbon films delicately pressed between layers of stone. DNA recovered from these fossils shows that little about this species has changed in twenty million years, yet where this plant grows has changed dramatically.

In the Northern Hemisphere many plants presently restricted to eastern Asia formerly grew also in Europe and North America, a reality made possible by land bridges that periodically linked continents across the North Atlantic and the Bering Sea. The absence of these varieties from Europe and North America today is a result of global cooling that began about five million years ago, recently by geological standards. Spreading sheets of ice forced plants to retreat southward, sometimes to their deaths; in the case of especially hard-hit areas like Great Britain, Canada, and many of the states adjacent to the Great Lakes, glaciers simply wiped the slate clean, covering the earth in frozen whiteness.

The ice retreated about fifteen thousand years ago, exposing bare soil. Plants considered native to ravaged places like the British Isles have recolonized since that time. When the now-famous English garden tradition had its beginnings it was understood that garden plants came from abroad, for that country had inherited only a sparse native flora. North America and the rest of Europe also lost species during the ice ages, although many survived in refuges along the

The world is a small place; wildlife makes use of introduced as well as native flora.

ABOVE LEFT Strong stalks of *Agapanthus inapertus* offer a perch for a pollinating orange-breasted sunbird; in North American gardens these rich blue flowers attract hummingbirds and butterflies. Kirstenbosch, Cape Town, Republic of South Africa.

LEFT North American hyssops and African kniphofias prove equally attractive to hummingbirds. *Agastache rupestris* and *Kniphofia stricta* with *Gaura lindheimeri,* authors' garden, Fort Collins, Colorado.

Gulf of Mexico, in the foothills of the Sierra Madre, in Turkey, and along the Black Sea. Because of the more favorable geography of Chinese mountain ranges, plants fared better in Asia, which conserved a larger portion of the world's plant riches.

Once this history is understood it makes sense that Asian callery pear (*Pyrus calleryana*), ginkgo (*Ginkgo biloba*), and tree of heaven (*Ailanthus altissima*) now grow as robustly as natives in parts of North America; their fossil leaves and pollen show that just a few million years ago they were. And just as flora exchanged between continents, so did fauna. The vegetation of North America grew successfully for tens of millions of years in company with indigenous American mammals—for much of the time camels, horses, and mastodons rather than animals recognized as native today. These formerly abundant creatures and many others perished soon after the arrival of people, who crossed from Asia sixteen thousand years ago. A little before them came other foreign invaders: buffalo or bison, ironically viewed today as a symbol of native America.

These changes were not always gradual and nature didn't provide plants with warnings and opportunities to escape and adjust. Evidence obtained from ice cores in Greenland shows that a climate similar to today's abruptly shifted to continental glaciation within about fifty years; snow and ice buried mature forests alive. At the same time, southern Florida shifted from a shallow tropic sea filled with now-extinct corals and mollusks to a vast temperate freshwater lake with its own now-vanished flora and fauna, then to the present marshland and near-tropical environment of the Everglades. In a few thousand years more, the unique plants and animals there will in turn perish as the vast marsh silts up to become dry land, with or without the help of lustful developers and aggressive introduced plants like Queensland paperbark (*Melaleuca quinquinervia*) and Brazil pepper (*Schinus terebinthifolius*). Human disruptions to nature can be glaringly rapid but are not necessarily more so than those that occur without our hand.

Both natural history and common sense suggest that in the majority of situations many plants, both native and

This largely native planting easily incorporates an introduced Austrian pine (in background) without disrupting its strongly regional spirit. *Pinus nigra,* *Pinus strobiformis, Forestiera neomexicana, Amelanchier laevis, Krascheninnikovia lanata,* authors' garden in autumn, Fort Collins, Colorado.

ABOVE Camels like these grazing in a Kansas field dotted with *Monarda punctata* are native Americans that evolved on this continent, later migrating to Asia. Conservationists with a background in paleobiology have proposed reintroducing these mammals along with elephants, horses, lions, and others previously native to North America. Known as "rewilding," this controversial plan would return pre–Ice Age, prehuman diversity to the continent; the same rationale supports naturalizing formerly native plants.

ABOVE RIGHT Most native plant species once grew elsewhere. This colossal fossilized stump is all that remains of a giant sequoia (*Sequoia affinis*) that grew near a lake in central Colorado thirty-five million years ago, at the beginning of the Rocky Mountains' uplift. Part of a vanished forest, this tree flourished alongside *Ailanthus*, *Koelreuteria*, and *Zelkova*— genera now known only from Asia. Florissant, Colorado.

exotic, will be acceptable for gardens. Relatively few are likely to present aggressive qualities in nature and these can usually be identified and excluded from the specific regions where they are found to be troublesome.

Whether a plant becomes a problem weed is invariably a highly local issue. For instance, small colonies of Grecian foxglove (*Digitalis lanata*) have naturalized along certain disturbed roadsides near Salt Lake City, Utah, and in a few counties of Kansas, Minnesota, and Wisconsin, yet its attractive spires of tawny bloom do not generally stray from gardens along Colorado's Front Range and in most other parts of the mountain West. Weediness is as much a function of a plant's environment as of the plant itself: problems with so-called invasive plants often arise in disturbed habitats that have been made open to colonization. Most roadsides, agricultural fields, and grazing lands have been considerably degraded; it is the natural function of weedy

plants, both native and introduced, to cover such places, thereby initiating the process of biological recovery. Some geologically young environments like the Mediterranean-climate coast of California, subtropical south Florida, and the volcanic islands of Hawaii are especially susceptible to invading plants. Older, more stable plant communities such as the woodlands and prairies of eastern and central North America have more resilience. Under climax conditions these regions might even be expected to displace or repel most nonnative vegetation.

In practice, however, very little of nature is allowed such a luxury. Most forests and prairies are in various stages of regrowth after human disturbance and the decimation of large mammal faunas; they are likely to be colonized by exotic as well as native species. Whether this should be of concern needs to be judged on a case-by-case basis within the context of people's larger manipulations of the earth.

No plant is inherently invasive, as this quality is environmentally dependent and varies locally. Grecian foxglove—well-behaved as a perennial in gardens along Colorado's Front Range—is considered weedy in parts of Utah and Kansas. *Digitalis lanata, Echinacea paradoxa, Salvia sclarea, Parthenium integrifolium, Picea pungens, Sambucus racemosa* 'Sutherland Gold', authors' garden, Fort Collins, Colorado.

Any plant, even an invading one, ought not to be damned simply because of its origins. Along the Gulf Coast, for instance, Chinese tallow (*Sapium sebiferum*), a tree introduced by Benjamin Franklin with all good intentions, has a well-earned reputation for colonizing damp coastal prairies. Although undeniably weedy, this small tree provides valuable forage and cover for neotropical songbirds on annual northward migrations. The tallow fills in for formerly indigenous southern canebrake (*Arundinaria gigantea*)—long since displaced by agriculture—that once provided for the

Through changing moments, gardens give gardeners reason to pay close attention. Watching carefully builds experience to guide design.

LEFT Fall brings glowing light and color to a dryland border. *Symphyotrichum oblongifolium* 'Dream of Beauty', *Forestiera neomexicana*, *Ericameria nauseosa* var. *hololeuca* 'Santa Fe Silver', *Yucca baccata*, *Tanacetum densum* var. *amani*, *Veronica pectinata*, *Festuca mairei*, *Sesleria heufleriana*, authors' garden, Fort Collins, Colorado.

ABOVE Meadowy companions celebrate summer. *Echinacea angustifolia*, *Achnatherum calamagrostis*, *Oenothera macrocarpa* subsp. *incana*, *Centaurea macrocephala*, authors' garden, Fort Collins, Colorado.

migrating flocks. These Asian invaders have thereby moderated an ecological disaster for avian life in the Americas. With the capacity to yield as much as 635 gallons of biodiesel per acre, Chinese tallow might also reduce the use of petroleum and consequent global climate change.

Plants are not inherently good or bad and they don't actually plan invasions like enemy generals. But when human beings introduce them into a new region and they spread, it's a mistake to glibly absolve ourselves of blame for possible consequences by ascribing this process to "naturalizing." We need to assume responsibility for those we choose and the effects they may have. Introducing weedy plants makes for a poor design and an unmanageable garden as well as potential threats to nature. Filling a garden with plants that need a constant supply of fertilizers, pesticides, or irrigation is equally foolhardy.

Yet creating a garden presupposes that people are entitled to alter their world. At a public garden devoted exclusively to native plants, the director shared her opinions with us, piously presuming the use of lush, leafy palm trees in the sprawling desert landscapes of southern Arizona to be highly inappropriate and insisting that only native mesquites, saguaros, and such ought to be allowed in gardens there. Can people really be expected to inhabit such a torrid climate and live hidden in air-conditioned houses while they forgo the cooling shade of a tall date palm, a tree present in gardens since the dawn of settled life, or even a *Washingtonia* palm, actually native alongside desert springs just a few hundred miles to the west and south? Surely such a purist's approach to native plant gardening conflicts with the basic premise of a garden as an outgrowth of human life. To quote from Lauren's *The Undaunted Garden* (1994), "If an attractive plant has adjusted to the climate of a garden and is not so self-important and antisocial as to preclude it being joined by other plants, why remove it, just because it wasn't a part of the natural landscape at one time?"

And what about the role of gardens as places to preserve indigenous plants endangered in the wild? This is certainly a matter of concern to gardeners and anyone else who loves plants, but it is also a global issue. If anything, concern for endangered flora offers reasons for gardeners to use land in their charge to conserve exotic plants as well as local indigenous species. All plants deserve such attention.

Gardens first came into being through our natural attraction to plants. By carefully watching these green beings in our charge, both in the garden and in the wild, we can gather the details we need to develop our designs. Plants themselves will show how to design a garden if we pay attention.

PARALLEL PLANT SPECIES

Look-alike plants native to Asia and North America have fascinated botanists and gardeners since Linnaeus's time. Split (disjunct) distributions of certain species and at least sixty-five genera appear in many instances in eastern America and eastern Asia; some near-identical relatives of American flora also occur in southern Europe, Turkey, and the Middle East, and a few southwestern and Florida species show strong relationships to cousins in South America. Genetic studies confirm ancestral connections between these plant pairs, suggesting multiple exchanges between continents. For instance, *Arisaema* seems to have entered North America from Asia at least twice, first giving rise to the ancestor of green dragon (*Arisaema dracontium*), then, in a later infusion, the predecessor of Jack-in-the-pulpit (*Arisaema triphyllum*). Both species grow together today in eastern American forests, yet molecular evidence shows they are related to separate Asian relatives. Typical species pairs are conservatively similar, but a few show unique specializations: the Chinese che tree (*Maclura tricuspidata*, syn. *Cudrania tricuspidata*) produces mulberry-like fruits that attract birds and small mammals; its otherwise near-identical American cousin, Osage orange (*Maclura pomifera*), ripens peculiar large green fruits that may have fed now-extinct American mastodons.

Knowledge of intercontinental species pairs can sometimes resolve horticultural challenges: Chinese fringe tree (*Chionanthus retusus*) and Chinese holly (*Ilex cornuta*) thrive on alkaline soils where American fringe tree (*Chionanthus virginicus*) and American holly (*Ilex opaca*) struggle, yet provide similar-looking subjects for gardens. Likewise, disease-resistant Chinese dogwood (*Cornus kousa*) substitutes for indigenous eastern dogwood (*Cornus florida*) where anthracnose limits success. Genera such as mayapple (*Podophyllum* spp.), crabapple (*Malus* spp.), and wild ginger (*Asarum* spp.) are more diverse and pretty in Asia; others such as *Trillium* spp. are better represented and more attractive in North America. Here are a few examples of species pairs.

Close relations from separate continents, the Chinese che and the North American Osage orange constitute a species pair. Such alliances provide evidence for ancient floral connections and help explain why many introduced plants grow as well as natives.

ABOVE LEFT Chinese che (*Maclura tricuspidata*, syn. *Cudrania tricuspidata*)

ABOVE Osage orange (*Maclura pomifera*)

EASTERN NORTH AMERICANS (except where noted)	EASTERN ASIAN RELATIONS (except where noted)
Acer rubrum, red maple	*Acer pycnanthum*, Japanese red maple
Arisaema dracontium, green dragon	*Arisaema candidissimum*, cobra lily
Arisaema triphyllum, Jack-in-the-pulpit	*Arisaema sikokianum*, Japanese cobra lily
Campsis radicans, trumpet creeper	*Campsis grandiflora*, Chinese trumpet creeper
Caulophyllum thalictroides, blue cohosh	*Caulophyllum robustum*, Asian blue cohosh
Cercis canadensis, eastern redbud	*Cercis siliquastrum*, Judas tree (southeastern Europe, Middle East)
Chionanthus virginicus, fringe tree	*Chionanthus retusus*, Chinese fringe tree
Cornus florida, eastern dogwood	*Cornus kousa*, Chinese dogwood
Decumaria barbara, climbing hydrangea	*Decumaria sinensis*, Chinese wood-vamp
Dichondra argentea, silver ponyfoot (southwestern U.S., Mexico)	*Dichondra sericea* (syn. *D.* 'Silver Falls'), Silver Falls ponyfoot (Argentina and Bolivia)
Festuca idahoensis, Idaho fescue (western U.S., Canada)	*Festuca glauca*, blue fescue (Europe)
Habranthus tubispathus var. *texensis*, copper lily (Texas, Louisiana)	*Habranthus tubispathus* var. *variabilis*, pink rain lily (Argentina and Paraguay)
Ilex opaca, American holly	*Ilex cornuta*, Chinese holly
Jeffersonia diphylla, twinleaf	*Jeffersonia dubia*, twinleaf
Liquidambar styraciflua, sweetgum	*Liquidambar orientalis*, oriental sweetgum, Levant storax (Turkey)
Liriodendron tulipifera, tulip poplar	*Liriodendron chinensis*, Chinese tulip poplar
Maclura pomifera, Osage orange (Arkansas, Texas, Oklahoma)	*Maclura tricuspidata*, syn. *Cudrania*, Chinese che
Magnolia acuminata, cucumber tree	*Magnolia denudata*, yulan
Malus coronaria, northern crabapple	*Malus floribunda*, Japanese crabapple
Pachysandra procumbens, Alleghany pachysandra	*Pachysandra terminalis*, evergreen pachysandra
Parthenocissus quinquefolia, Virginia creeper	*Parthenocissus henryana*, silver vein creeper
Platanus wrightii, Arizona sycamore (Arizona, New Mexico)	*Platanus orientalis*, oriental plane tree (Greece, Turkey)
Podophyllum peltatum, mayapple	*Sinopodophyllum hexandrum*, Himalayan mayapple
Prosopis glandulosa, honey mesquite (southwestern U.S.)	*Prosopis alba*, Chilean mesquite (Argentina and Chile)
Styrax platanifolia, sycamore-leaf snowbell (Texas)	*Styrax officinalis*, storax tree (Turkey)
Trillium ovatum, western trillium (Pacific Northwest)	*Trillium kamtschaticum*, Japanese trillium
Vancouveria hexandra, inside-out flower (Pacific Northwest)	*Epimedium grandiflorum*, barrenwort
Viburnum trilobum, American cranberrybush	*Viburnum opulus*, European cranberrybush (Europe)

2

PLANTS WITH PRESENCE
Choosing and creating spaces
for a plant's needs and character

OW DO PLANTS END UP where they do in a garden? Two scenarios present opposite extremes. The designer sits at the drawing board, sketching out a plan on paper and eyeing a particular space. Mind connects with page and a mental image of the site. Visual possibilities begin to spill forth . . . something tall and columnar will look good here, some fuzzy low shapes are called for over here, and definitely something with red foliage there. Now to find plants that fit those descriptions.

Then there's the plant-collecting gardener visiting the nursery, stalking down the aisles and eyeing a particular plant. A narrow 'Sutherland' tree caragana gets pulled from the pack. What's that fuzzy asparagus species over there? Wow, look at the red leaves on that dahlia! While the gardener is unloading the new acquisitions at home the conundrum arises, now to find places for these plants.

Both these approaches have their merits and their pitfalls. The best way to bring plants into a garden combines some of each. A designer's visualization of the site is a way to discover and explore what it offers in terms of plant opportunities, and the collector-gardener's attraction to certain plants and insistence on giving them a home ensures ongoing interaction and personal response. So ideally when a plant is invited into a garden, the person making that decision has been both designer and plant collector in the process. What the extreme scenarios miss entirely is that plant and site are inextricable. They influence each other continually—how the plant grows there, how the site changes by its presence. Neither should be considered before the other; rather, they ought to occur simultaneously. By selecting plants with an understanding of their needs and character, and by placing plants with regard to matching their cultural requirements and intrinsic qualities to a well-understood and well-explored existing site or creating a new site that meets these needs and respects these qualities, one combines the best of both designer and collector approaches.

Truly transcendent gardens are made from a starting point of attraction to and at least a budding familiarity with plants. Having an understanding of a plant refers most obviously to cultural requirements. A plant must have its climatic tolerance, soil predilection, and growth habit accommodated, and its moisture and light demands met.

OPPOSITE Gardenmaking in a natural setting is more challenging than most other design scenarios. Site and plants are inextricable, a truth that applies anywhere. *Penstemon pinifolius* and crack-filling *Gazania linearis*, *Veronica pectinata*, *Thymus pseudolanuginosus*, northern Colorado, Ogden design.

This boulder-strewn hillside hosts an unconventional rock garden. The overall scale of species chosen is larger than that of a typical alpine palette, ensuring that plants are not dwarfed by the size of the stones. This scale also allows for a broader selection of species more tolerant of lower elevation and drought. Plant and site work together, rather than one dominating the other. *Alyssum markgrafii, Allium azureum, Penstemon glaber, Salvia lavandulifolia, Onosma echioides, Achillea* 'Moonshine', California poppies, northern Colorado, Ogden design.

But understanding also involves what the gardenmaker can do to honor the plant's spirit.

Capturing a plant's spirit

All plants have presence; as individuals each offers something special. This relates to the obvious: their physical attributes and what is particularly striking or unique about them, such as size, shape and growth habit, color, texture, scent, flower or foliage, and the like. It also relates to things more subtle and subjective: emotional, often highly personal responses to them, which can be an experience of magnificence, sweetness, sensuality, exuberance, and such, or linked to a particular association or memory. To discover the unique spirit of a plant, ask what makes this particular plant different from other plants, and what attracts you personally to it.

Sometimes this characteristic or set of qualities may seem obvious, but there's still much to be explored. For example, many people will probably concur that if indeed they like lamb's ears, *Stachys byzantina*, it's because they are attracted to their soft countenance. Knowing this isn't enough to translate into ideal garden placement. What makes this plant seem soft? The hair on its foliage feels soft to the touch. And the shimmer of this hair gives the plant an indistinct outline when light washes over it. Also, the gray color mixes and blends so well with other plants. These diverse attributes of softness all call for different approaches to placement. To touch lamb's ears, place them along an edge of a planting where people pass by. To create a shimmering halo, orient the plant to either an eastern or western exposure so that the low light of morning or evening can pass over it. To intensify its softening color effect, repeat and thread it throughout a planting so it can join with many companions. But there may be other reasons for liking the plant. In many of the dry, sunny gardens we are asked to design, we choose lamb's ears as a favorite to mingle among others because it has a larger-textured, more settled form than most drought-tolerant plants, especially silver ones, which tend toward fine textures and sometimes scraggly or spindly shapes. "Rabbit's ears" makes more sense as a name to those of us who know these animals better than sheep, for they also have silken ears, and the softly rounded, low-growing plants remind us of well-behaved rabbits in repose in the garden. As an aside, this plant seems quite resistant to browsing by both rabbits and deer.

Sometimes capturing the spirit of a plant is more highly specific than in the example of lamb's ears. In these cases, not giving thought to what gives a plant its presence may actually result in misuse. Take *Imperata cylindrica* var. *koenigii* 'Red Baron', Japanese blood grass, a plant with rather scruffy-looking leaves and few if any flowers to speak of. Its garden value can be reduced to a single attribute: the striking red color of its foliage, which begins as a combination of green with red tips in spring and intensifies throughout the growing season. Closer inspection of the plant shows that the leaves are quite thin and translucent. When light passes through them from behind, their redness comes alive and glows, in the way of a backlit stained-glass window. Yet when light hits the foliage straight on, or on cloudy days and in shaded spots, the red loses its visual vitality and becomes a dull, muddy hue. What's more, once the color effect loses its captivating power, the plant's coarse texture and often ragged growth habit is revealed. Insensitivity to this plant's spirit is exemplified by a planting along the south side of an east-west path at a prominent botanic garden. A narrow mustache of the grass runs about fifty feet along this path, sited at the base of a berm. Here not one moment occurs throughout the day or the year when the planting can bask in backlighting. When the grass is used as an edge along this well-traveled route, its unfortunate texture and form get top billing rather than the brilliant color drama it performs given the right site.

In the past few years, Japanese blood grass has been banned in several states because of concern about its potential invasiveness in those regions. More dependably well-behaved grasses with similar red foliage are North American native switchgrass selections *Panicum virgatum* 'Shenandoah' and 'Warrior' (though these can also self-sow with abandon in certain sites). While more attractive in form, flower, and foliage texture than Japanese blood

TOP Backlighting plays gently over the felted leaves of lamb's ears growing at the top of a retaining wall where it can be readily touched. *Stachys byzantina* 'Silver Carpet' with *Sesleria glauca*, northern Colorado, Ogden design.

ABOVE Japanese blood grass (*Imperata cylindrica* var. *koenigii* 'Red Baron') warrants a position with dependable backlighting if it is to be planted at all.

Temperate maritime and subtropical climates sustain innumerable plants with strong presence. Combining them to show off their power while still allowing other plants and aspects of the garden their due play takes sensitivity and understanding, similar to seating guests thoughtfully at a table.

ABOVE Aloes (*Aloe maculata* in bloom, *Aloe marlothii*), palms (*Sabal bermudana*, *Trithrinax brasiliensis*), *Yucca linearifolia*, *Phlomis cretica*, cacti, authors' garden, Austin, Texas.

ABOVE RIGHT Cycad (*Macrozamia miquelii*), ginger (*Hedychium gardnerianum*), purple-leafed *Cordyline australis*, *Cuphea* sp., Strybing Arboretum, San Francisco, California, Roger Raiche design.

grass, they also promise a dull future if not allowed to glow. Honoring the special qualities of these red plants means siting the grasses where they receive regular backlighting in a commonly viewed position. The sun's lower angle in mornings or late afternoons is essential. Depending on when you spend the most time in the garden or when you most often look out a particular window or door of the house, choose placement to catch earlier or later lighting.

A plant for the site, a site for the plant

Once plants' intrinsic qualities are discovered and the gardenmaker has a mind jammed full of favorites, it becomes natural not only to find the right place for them on a given site but also to follow the opposite process: approach a particular spot on a site and consider which plants would enhance the space. Much of our home garden in northern Colorado—the entire backyard—faces west to a private view of the foothills. Early on we noticed that afternoon light transforms the space. In the morning, a walk around the back reveals what the day's chores might include—the strong, flat, clinical light from the east exposes overlooked weeds, sagging transplants, and tattered flower stalks gone over, motivating the day's work. By contrast, our favorite late afternoon strolls following the same route, drink rather than weed bucket in hand, feel entirely different. As the light changes and comes from behind, it illuminates colors and highlights textures, meanwhile casting a shimmering haze that diminishes contrast, unifying the space. Knowing this, we now consciously seek out and add plants to this part of the garden that respond especially favorably to back-lighting—those with translucent petals, foliage, or fruits, and with hairy or spiny stems and leaves, fuzzy seeds, fine linearity, and such.

Our home garden in central Texas also affords an area to play with backlighting, most notably in late fall, winter, and early spring, as the back garden has a southern orientation that basks in the low angle of the sun during those times of the year. The plants we choose for rewarding effects are in many ways different from those we've chosen in Colorado. Not only do individual species vary in response to climate, but what's looking good during those seasons when the sun tracks lower in the sky—glittering broadleaf evergreens, translucent paperwhite narcissi, and glowing aloe blossoms—is distinct from what's full on during high season up north. Also, what fits with the garden's character—a subtropical, small urban Texan oasis—makes for a palette distinct from that suggested by the wide-open natural model that inspires our Colorado meadow and steppe garden.

Regional interpretation in plants and design

Such contrasts in the spirit and character of a place and how they affect plant choices highlight the main limitation on giving specifics about anything to do with gardens: obviously the medium—plants—varies from region to region. More and more, regional information is rising to the forefront to assist in plant selection. However, design information lags sorely behind in this regard. Most people who entitle themselves to giving opinions on designing gardens seem to believe there are universal rules, principles, and ideals that need no translation or revision, no matter what the region. We believe this is wrong and one of the biggest shortfalls of garden design today. Certainly there are universal concepts, but these must be explored regionally before anything close to a rule, principle, or ideal can be

discussed. Once again, plants are key. Observing not only the individual species that make up the core of a region's natural and horticultural identity but also how plants in general in a given locality differ from those in other places in the way they grow and look invites discovery that enables the gardenmaker to create spaces that acknowledge and celebrate regionality. This immediately grounds a garden, places it in a locally resonant context, and gives it that elusive sense of place.

Take for instance a very specific example, that of large trees. Most gardens, even the smallest, have some need for at least one or two shade trees. Designers and gardeners often spend a lot of time thinking about this selection, and rightly so as a large tree is a big investment, both up front in terms of cost and effort of installation, and also in terms of time as it will be several years before the tree settles in and begins to create the desired effect. Obviously, a good choice marries the conditions on site with the tree's character and cultural needs, and joins the aesthetic prejudices of the person who will live with the tree with what's possible in terms of plant options. Tree palettes and purposes vary from region to region, as is to be expected. But there's surprising overlap, and the same overused, generic choices and placements show up in the most far-flung places.

Beyond overcoming timidity regarding trying the more unusual tree, there's more to expressing regionality with tree selection. Trees mature differently in different climates. What grows straight and tall in temperate and northern regions grows crooked, gnarly, and picturesque or even picaresque in hotter and/or drier climates. The tradition of the well-grown, straight-trunked nursery tree in its very essence flies in the face of the spirit of southwestern or high mountain trees. Often those same nursery trees, even large specimens, also lack the calm countenance of a tree of some age. We frequently spend many hours combing nurseries for that rogue tree that imparts the same individualistic grace as a windswept pine, an arching live oak, or a low-branching, dwarfed hawthorn in the wild. It makes all the difference to find a tree that gives the right sense of place, and then plant it where it can grow comfortably and show off its special qualities.

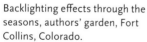
Backlighting effects through the seasons, authors' garden, Fort Collins, Colorado.

OPPOSITE TOP Early spring sun catches *Tulipa vvedenskyi*, *T. sylvestris*, *T. humilis* cv., *Pulsatilla vulgaris* in seed, and *Phlox bifida* 'Betty Blake'.

OPPOSITE BOTTOM, LEFT AND RIGHT Same place in the steppe garden, August and again in October: *Liatris punctata* (prairie gayfeather), *Gutierrezia sarothrae* (broomweed), *Bouteloua gracilis* (blue grama).

ABOVE Translucent *Allium ostrowskianum* and *Phacelia campanularia*, and hairy *Sideritis scardica* make the most of low-angled sunlight.

ABOVE RIGHT Light defines textures of *Allium maximowiczii* 'Alba' and *Koeleria brevis* in the steppe planting.

RIGHT *Stipa pennata*, *Fallugia paradoxa* (Apache plume), and *Tanacetum cinerariifolium* respond to late afternoon light.

Different conditions and climate —often even within the same garden—promote distinct plants with their own characteristic look. The relatively large, profuse, brilliantly hued flowers and sparse leaves of plants suited to dry, sunny, high-elevation climates, and the lush, predominantly green, generous foliar display of temperate woodland plants serve as examples in contrast.

ABOVE *Aubrieta gracilis, Tulipa vvedenskyi*, Rock Alpine Garden, Denver Botanic Gardens.

RIGHT *Athyrium nipponicum* 'Pictum' with hosta and heuchera, Chris Woods garden, Wayne, Pennsylvania.

Gardens comfortable with their climate and conditions have a grace no overworked design or heavily manipulated horticultural pièce de résistance can match.

ABOVE Palms (×*Butiagrus nabonnandii*, *Syagrus romanzoffianum*), gingers (*Costus speciosus* 'Variegatus', *Hedychium* sp.), and bamboos celebrate their subtropical Gulf Coast home with unbridled ebullience. Mercer Arboretum and Botanic Gardens, Humble, Texas.

RIGHT Western North American natives help blend into this arid, distinctively western site. *Fallugia paradoxa, Pinus edulis, Gaillardia aristata*, Arlen Bemer garden, Grand Junction, Colorado.

UNSUNG DECIDUOUS & BROAD-LEAFED EVERGREEN TREES

These attractive trees are not planted as often as they deserve.

Medium-to-large deciduous trees
Cercidiphyllum japonicum, katsura tree
Larix decidua, European larch
Melia azederach 'Jade Snowflake', variegated chinaberry
Paulownia fortunei, white empress tree
Pistachia chinensis, Chinese pistache
Prunus sargentii, Sargent cherry
Pyrus betulifolia, birch-leaf pear
Pyrus ussuriensis, Ussurean pear
Sorbus alnifolia, Korean mountain ash
Syringa pekinensis, Chinese tree lilac
Tetradium daniellii (syn. *Evodia daniellii*), Korean bee tree
Tilia tomentosa, silver linden

Evergreen trees
Arbutus 'Marina' hybrid, madrone
Clethra pringlei, Mexican summersweet
Cordia boissieri, Texas olive
Cornus angustata, evergreen Chinese dogwood
Laurus 'Saratoga' hybrid, bay tree
Phoenix sylvestris, Indian date palm
Quercus germana, Mexican royal oak
Quercus rysophylla, netleaf oak
Sabal uresana, Sonoran blue palmetto

Small deciduous specimen trees
Acer griseum, paperbark maple
Acer pseudosieboldianum, dwarf Korean maple
Acer tataricum 'GarAnn' (sold as Hot Wings), Tatarian maple
Chionanthus retusus, Chinese fringe tree
Cladrastis kentukea 'Perkins Pink', pink-flowered yellowwood
Clethra barbinervis, Japanese summersweet
Cornus alternifolia 'Variegata', pagoda dogwood
Hamamelis virginiana, American witch hazel
Heptacodium miconioides, seven sons tree
Lagerstroemia fauriei 'Fantasy', Japanese crape myrtle
Maackia amurensis, Amur maackia
Magnolia denudata, yulan
Magnolia sieboldii, Oyama magnolia
Magnolia virginiana, sweet bay (evergreen form is subspecies *australis*)
Ostrya virginica, hop hornbeam
Parrotia persica, Persian ironwood
Parkinsonia 'Desert Museum' hybrid, palo verde
Pterostyrax hispida, epaulette tree
Sinojackia rehderiana, jacktree
Stewartia pseudocamellia, Japanese stewartia
Styrax japonica, *S. obassia*, snowbell
Viburnum sieboldii, Siebold viburnum

The well-worn design concept of the garden room illustrates another hazard of applying a principle universally. While the European tradition of enclosing an outdoor space has its roots in walled gardens developed during times in human history when safety was a pressing concern, the same psychology of comfort applies today to creating enclosures. In urban settings, garden rooms function as oases to block noise and unattractive views; in suburbia they afford a chance to create intimacy and privacy for personal expression that is often otherwise lacking. Transposing the garden room to any site or region will not always work, however. The gentle agricultural and often partially wooded wild landscapes of much of Europe, and the similarly small-scale, tree-dominated regions of coastal and eastern North America make a good match. Yet in much of this continent—the Midwest, Plains states, interior West, and the Southwest—a feeling of expansive openness pervades the natural landscape. More often than not, garden rooms feel contrived and claustrophobic in these regions, especially for local people who have grown up far from the sheltering, enclosing spirit of a forest. What's more, the distinctive plant choices of these regions offer much less in the way of good-looking, hardy, dependable hedge-making material than more temperate maritime palettes do, and one is often left with only walls and fences as options for enclosure. Although there are instances where garden

OPPOSITE TOP Texas hill country live oaks grow gnarled and curvaceous, thanks to capricious moisture availability that curtails consistent, straight growth. *Quercus fusiformis*, Enchanted Rock, Llano County, Texas.

OPPOSITE BOTTOM Rocky Mountain aspens, in contrast, make the most of an extremely short season, growing quickly and straight in the strong sunlight at high elevations and with ample water from late spring snowmelt. *Populus tremuloides*, Avon, Colorado.

rooms work well in these regions, consistently embraced as a way to define garden space, certainly not.

The openness intrinsic to the interior of the North American continent is actually defined by plants, or in the case of drier regions, by a lack of them. The ratio of plants to nonplant elements—sky, stone, and soil—is different in the interior, resulting in a peculiar prairie, western, or desert feel. Vast expanses of lower-growing plants consisting of wild and cultivated grasses, herbaceous perennials, and a plethora of agricultural crops spread across the midwestern horizon, making for a visually distinctive, texturally united blanket, dotted periodically by groves of trees, small thickets, or a tree-lined watercourse. Sky fills more than half the view. Roughly west of the ninety-eighth meridian, where less than twenty-five inches of rain falls annually, trees recede altogether except near water or at high elevation, and short grasses and low scrub take over. Much of this half of the continent isn't covered by plants at all: bare earth and rock define the strong outlines and forms characteristic of these western landscapes, and paint this starkly scenic world in brown, tan, buff, red, and ochre.

When gardens reflect these differences in plant stature, texture, and density, and in the overall dominance of green, a sense of place emerges. Here again the universality of design ideals comes into question. The vast swaths of greenery composed of lawns, shade trees, and shrub plantings traditionally used to create repose need to be questioned in these regions, not only culturally but also aesthetically. Serenity can be interpreted as panels of tawny grasses interwoven with perennials, or water-thrifty plants more silver and blue than green in color, combined with stone or gravel. Beds and borders usually expected to be filled to the gills with lush, leafy plants can in turn make use of wider spacing with rocks or grasses or architectural succulent and fiber plants interspersed amid the floral melee, whether in a formal pattern or naturalistically. Here and there gardeners and designers are experimenting along these lines, but the majority still adhere to design tenets created in and for other regions.

Regional design interpretation deserves consideration also in relation to the oft-touted ideal of continuous bloom.

It was a breath of fresh air for us to hear a client, unlike most, say that she actually did not want flowers all season, that she longed for the tranquility of greens and tans and textures. Most parts of the world experience times of floral extravagance punctuated by partial quiescence or complete dormancy. In cold regions this follows the calendar seasons; in warm climates it is in rhythm with the rains. Following this in the garden with plants that respond as do those in the surrounding natural landscape would be a much more intelligent design ideal than continual bloom. Not only is it environmentally more feasible—requiring less water, fertilizer, and rotation of plants—but it also gives a sense of connection with the rhythm of nature and provides anticipation and the excitement of special floral events.

The ebb and flow of floral versus textural emphasis makes for a dynamic garden, one that mirrors the surge in popularity of perennials and plants with foliar interest over flowering annuals during the last three decades. People like gardens that look different throughout the year, and they like plants that look good out of bloom. German plantsman Karl Foerster was perhaps the first person in modern times to champion such plants and spent the first half of the twentieth century selecting species with these attributes, including many heretofore horticulturally unknown North American natives. A few presently prominent designers, especially Dutch Piet Oudolf and the German-American team of Wolfgang Oehme and James Van Sweden, have been deeply influenced by Foerster's and Germany's naturalistic legacy. They have made perennials with extended seasons of interest and good-looking dried forms a hallmark of their styles. Our own design work takes place in generally more punishing climates than central and northern Europe, the East Coast, or even the Midwest. Where we work and garden, flowers are often fleeting and many herbaceous perennials look tawdry for much of the year. As a starting point in our design process, we give overall plant texture priority over floral choices. We see flowers as the much-anticipated and expected dessert that we provide with panache, but not as the main course.

Still, for most people flowers remain the most cherished happenings in the garden. Finding plants that present them

Spaces feel different across the globe, and gardens do well to reflect this with sensitivity and resonance.

ABOVE Many of England's most compelling gardens make use of partial or complete enclosure by lovely masonry. Such gardens fit well into the small-scale agrarian patterns of the English countryside. Kiftsgate Court Gardens, Gloucestershire, England.

LEFT In the interior West of North America, enclosure often feels contrived or stifling, and risks obliterating distant views and/or sky, two of the West's most distinctive attributes. A sandstone firepit and seating area amid an orchard and an open meadow of thermopsis and daffodils feel natural and generous in the Rockies. Authors' garden, Fort Collins, Colorado.

LEFT Prickly pear, Mexican feather grass, red yucca, and fernbush mimic the lively textural counterpoints characteristic of western and southwestern dryland plant communities. *Opuntia macrorhiza, Nassella tenuissima, Hesperaloe parviflora, Chamaebatiaria millefolium*, Water-Smart Garden, Denver Botanic Gardens, Ogden design.

ABOVE Looking at plant associations in the wild spurs creativity and aids in the selection of adapted plants. Grasses, *Yucca constricta*, and prickly pear (*Opuntia lindheimeri*) grow on parched, infertile granitic soil in the Texas hill country, creating a picturesque plant community. Inks Lake State Park, Burnet County, Texas.

at different times of the year, marking floral time, is something most gardeners will continue to try to achieve. Some climates have a season of floral explosion—high-elevation and far northern gardens show this off, where perennials bloom for several months on end in a brilliance of color display matched only by its opposite, the depths of gray, brown, and white that the other side of the year endures. Warm and hot climates have floral sputterings over most of the year, accentuated by rain. Trying to have flowers all year while forcing enthusiasm about so-called winter interest in the North, or trying to have a summer-long "florgasm" in the South amount to a futile battle against these climates and an insensitivity to plants adapted to them, but that is exactly what most gardeners in those regions long for and attempt.

It all comes back to plants as the starting point for design. More than any other element in a garden, plants determine the ultimate outcome and continue to affect and change it over time. If an outdoor space is to be a *garden*, not merely an extension of an indoor space or a landscape installation, both choosing plants and selecting the best places for them on the site have a more powerful effect than opting for any particular style, color scheme, or artifact. Those latter dimensions should be developed in tandem with plant selection or subordinate to it, not prior to choosing plants as is frequently the case.

Reviving the mundane

Perhaps the most dramatic examples of honoring a plant's spirit by choosing or creating spaces for that plant's needs and character involve reviving the mundane. Common plants appear with stultifying regularity in certain regions, so unimaginatively placed that people revile them or

RIGHT TOP Gardens that remain beautiful during times when they are devoid of flowers speak volumes about both respect of natural cycles and the ability of the designer. Here a verdant East Coast garden takes a floral breather during the sultry heat of late July. *Yucca recurvifolia*, *Miscanthus sinensis* 'Variegatus', Wave Hill, Bronx, New York, Marco Polo Stufano design.

RIGHT BOTTOM In the extreme seasons of high-latitude Alaska, summer is the gardening end-all and be-all, offering almost continual sunlight, dependable moisture, and gentle temperatures that coax gargantuan vigor and brilliant flower color from average garden subjects. Delphiniums, *Cephalaria gigantea*, *Centaurea macrocephala*, Palmer, Alaska, Jim Fox design.

worse yet, don't even notice them anymore. Sometimes plants become associated with unfortunate locations and thoughtless ugliness. Take trampled, litter-strewn median strip junipers. Here once again, site and plant are inextricable, but in these cases in an unintended, bad collusion. The plants are then made scapegoats for their poor usage and deemed ugly, boring, or clichéd. Yet these plants have as much to offer as any.

As plantspeople, we are always lured by the latest selection or newly discovered species. But often these are not an improvement over the tried-and-true, rather just something interesting and different. For example, Lauren falls prey to many a newly introduced dwarf conifer and spends a lot of time and effort trying to find places in our gardens where the plants can thrive and shine. Yet we both are equally pleased with our many junipers, some of which are unusual but just as many utterly ordinary and also seen, albeit in much less interesting surroundings, at the gas station half a mile down the road. We admire their textures, their subtle color variations, and their four-season ability to tie together a hodgepodge of rare and often unpredictably persnickety perennials and subshrubs in our rockery and dryland mixed plantings. They also blend well with grasses, sedges, and small naturalized bulbs in the wilder, less carefully tended parts of our garden.

Plant lovers look at plants with as unprejudiced an eye as possible, finding the best qualities in both old and new and enjoying them all. Surely there must be something special about the prosaic ones for them to have become so commonly chosen. It might be ease of production and adaptability that helped push them into overpopularity, but in most cases there is something about the essence of the plant that has broad appeal.

Each region has its overused plants. Some cases, such as the hulking overgrown conifer on the front lawn, traverse many state lines and even longitudes and latitudes. Individual species may change, but the look is the same. Take for example the screaming powder blue of most common selections of Colorado spruce, *Picea pungens*. No doubt that striking color is what catches the eye. But as a giant landscape specimen, the tree dominates home and garden, and in some regions quickly becomes inelegant and ratty. Why not choose a smaller blue selection, such as ten- to fifteen-foot 'Sester Dwarf', and combine it with a few of the greener cultivars, or with other similarly shaped green species of spruces or firs? Its remarkable color gets center stage, yet the plant is set in scale with the site, and in context with plants that enhance it and are enhanced by it. If climate takes its toll on this denizen of cool, dry mountain air, perhaps a more heat- and drought-tolerant blue conifer is in order. Depending on the region, alternatives might include alligator juniper (*Juniperus deppeana*), *Podocarpus elongatus* 'Monmal' (sold as Icee Blue), blue Atlas cedar (*Cedrus atlantica* f. *glauca*), or blue selections of Arizona cypress (*Cupressus arizonica*) or silver fir (*Abies concolor*).

Similarly, Norway spruce, Austrian pine, and southern magnolia are often placed alone and with such prominence that their dark, somber silhouettes cast a morose air over the entire space. Again, perhaps a smaller selection is called for—a 'Gowdy' oriental spruce (*Picea orientalis* 'Gowdy'), a Bosnian pine (*Pinus heldreichii* var. *leucodermis*), or a 'Mary Nell' holly (*Ilex latifolia* hybrid) might be good substitutes where size is an issue. If space does allow, these common but handsome evergreens deserve companions to play off their stalwart forms and dark hues. Deciduous trees with pale or colorful bark or those with a froth of precocious spring flowers, such as birches, serviceberries, alders, magnolias, ornamental pears, plums, apricots, peaches and cherries, small-sized willows, and some dogwoods all make sprightly music against the deep bass notes the evergreens provide.

Sometimes it's part of the actual spirit of a plant that can make for clichéd misuse. In warm climates, palms and palmlike plants with their powerful sculptural qualities often suffer this fate. Take for example cycads, of which the hardy sago palm, *Cycas revoluta*, is still the most commonplace (though with the rapid spread of recently introduced Asian cycad scale, other more resistant cycads may replace it in popularity). These ancient evergreens entice people with their deep green foliage, exotic palmlike form, and ferny

JUNIPERS TO LOVE

In North America, junipers are among the most ubiquitous landscape plants. With this popularity comes unfortunate disdain. By contrast, gardenmakers in other parts of the world do not fall prey to such prejudice, and honor these evergreen trees, shrubs, and ground covers for the versatile, colorful, textural, adaptable plants that they are. Here are a few of the best.

Trees

Juniperus chinensis 'Ames' (tight, dark green teardrop shape, humidity-tolerant)

J. chinensis 'Spartan' (narrow, rich green, heat- and humidity-tolerant)

J. deppeana 'McFetters' (turquoise blue, extremely heat- and drought-tolerant)

J. scopulorum 'Medora' (fresh blue-green color, holds together in snow)

J. scopulorum 'Pathfinder' (natural gray-green color, holds together in snow)

J. virginiana 'Canaertii' (picturesque irregular form, heat- and humidity-tolerant)

J. virginiana 'Taylor' (tight, narrow, dark green profile, very drought-tolerant)

Shrubs

J. communis 'Berkshire' (gunmetal blue, gracefully loose, drought-tolerant)

J. horizontalis 'Limeglow' (striking chartreuse color, turns copper in winter, shade-tolerant)

J. ×media 'Blue Vase' (compact, silvery blue, nice blue fruits, very heat- and humidity-tolerant)

J. ×media 'Holbert' (feathery pale blue, good fruits, drought-tolerant)

J. ×media 'Sea Green' (same as 'Mint Julep') (fresh green, feathery profile, heat- and humidity-tolerant)

J. squamata 'Blue Star' (elegant texture and tiered form, good for small spaces, shade-tolerant)

J. virginiana 'Grey Owl' (silver-gray, feathery, lots of pretty fruit)

Ground covers and dwarf forms

J. chinensis 'Echiniformis' (sometimes listed as a *J. communis* selection) (slow-growing, dwarf, prickly green mound, heat- and humidity-tolerant, excellent rock garden plant)

J. communis 'AmiDak' (sold as Blueberry Delight) (alkaline- and shade-tolerant, good fruits)

J. conferta 'Emerald Sea' (blue-green, graceful feathery texture, heat- and humidity-tolerant)

J. horizontalis 'Holden Arboretum' (slow, tight, gunmetal blue, excellent in small gardens)

J. horizontalis 'Monber' (sold as Icee Blue) (the palest blue, very feathery)

J. horizontalis 'Prince of Wales' (compact, dense spreader, rich green)

J. procumbens 'Nana' (picturesque cascading habit, fresh pale green)

J. sabina 'Monna' (sold as Calgary Carpet) (keeps bright green color all winter, feathery)

J. scopulorum 'Blue Creeper' (very drought-tolerant, feathery blue)

TOP Mountain juniper (*Juniperus communis* var. *saxatilis*) and *Juniperus sabina* 'Monna', sold as Calgary Carpet, skirt the sprightly blue seasonal flourish of *Muscari armeniacum* 'Saffier' while offering a much-needed evergreen backdrop to this long-blooming, nonseeding bulb. Authors' garden, Fort Collins, Colorado.

ABOVE Following a long, dry summer, cool blue 'Grey Owl' juniper sets off sugar pink aster and tawny grass. *Juniperus virginiana* 'Grey Owl', *Symphyotrichum oblongifolium* 'Dream of Beauty', *Festuca mairei*, authors' garden, Fort Collins, Colorado.

LEFT For high-contrast plants such as firs and spruces, planting more than one and/or in multiple sizes can help them blend into the garden and surrounding landscape. *Abies concolor* with sumac, barberry, and variegated red stem dogwood, Red Butte Botanical Garden, Salt Lake City, Utah.

ABOVE Mixing conifers—especially eye-catching dwarf specimens—into a context of other plants averts the common pitfall of an inert collection of oddities. *Abies procera* 'Glauca Prostrata' nestles among other conifers, ferns, campanulas, and sedges. The Garden House, Devon, England, Keith Wiley design.

SELECT CONIFERS DESERVING MORE GARDEN USE

Many gardens would benefit from the inclusion of some of these handsome conifers. (Junipers, listed elsewhere, are not included here, nor are true miniatures best suited for rock gardens.)

Tall trees

(exceeding twenty feet after ten years)
Abies concolor, silver fir
Abies firma, Momi fir
Abies numidica, Algerian fir
Abies pinsapo, Spanish fir
Calocedrus decurrens, incense cedar
Picea likiangensis 'Purpurea', purple-cone spruce
Picea orientalis, oriental spruce
Pinus ayacahuite, Mexican white pine
Pinus bungeana, lacebark pine
Pinus koraiensis, Korean white pine
Pinus montezumae, Montezuma pine
Pinus pinea, Italian stone pine
Pinus wallichiana, Himalayan white pine
Podocarpus elongatus 'Monmal' (sold as Icee Blue), Breede River yellowwood
Sequoiadendron giganteum, giant sequoia
Taxodium mucronatum 'Pendulum', weeping Montezuma cypress
Tsuga canadensis 'Albospica', white-tipped eastern hemlock
Xanthocyparis nootkatensis 'Pendula', weeping Alaska cypress

Midsize trees

(under twenty feet after ten years, some eventually that big)
Abies koreana, Korean fir
Cephalotaxus fortunei, Chinese plum yew
Nageia nagi, syn. *Podocarpus nagi*
Picea pungens 'Gentry's Gem', Colorado spruce
Pinus aristata, bristlecone pine
Pinus densiflora 'Umbraculifera', Tanyosho pine
Pinus leucodermis 'Iseli Fastigiate', Bosnian pine
Pinus mugo 'Tannenbaum', mugo pine
Pinus thunbergii 'Oculis-Draconis', dragon's eye Japanese black pine
Platycladus orientalis 'Rosedale', oriental arborvitae
Sciadopitys verticillata, umbrella pine
Taxus globosa subsp. *floridana*, Florida yew
Torreya spp., nutmeg yew
Tsuga canadensis 'Forest Fountain', eastern hemlock

Midsize shrubs

(under ten feet after ten years)
Abies koreana 'Horstmann's Silberlocke', compact Korean fir
Abies lasiocarpa var. *arizonica* 'Compacta', corkbark fir
Cedrus deodara 'Feeling Blue', prostrate deodar cedar
Chamaecyparis pisifera 'Curly Tops', Sawara cypress

Pinus strobus 'Macopin', compact eastern white pine
Pinus sylvestris 'Glauca Nana', compact Scots pine
Pinus thunbergii 'Thunderhead', compact Japanese black pine

Small shrubs

(under six feet after ten years)
Picea abies 'Witch's Brood', dwarf Norway spruce
Picea glauca 'Cecilia', dwarf white spruce
Picea omorika 'Pimoko', dwarf Serbian spruce
Picea pungens 'Hillside', 'Mrs. Cesarini', 'Procumbens', dwarf Colorado spruce
Pinus densiflora 'Globosa', dwarf Japanese red pine
Pinus mugo 'Valley Cushion', dwarf mugo pine
Pinus nigra 'Helga', dwarf Austrian pine
Pinus pumila 'Blue Dwarf', dwarf Siberian pine
Pinus strobus 'Pygmaea', dwarf eastern white pine
Pinus sylvestris 'Albyn Prostrata', prostrate Scots pine
Podocarpus macrophyllus 'Pringles', dwarf Japanese yew
Tsuga canadensis 'Bennett', dwarf eastern hemlock

texture, as well as their tough, no-care constitution. The sago palm looks so special and unusual that it often winds up placed ornament- or statue-style at the sides of a doorway or in the middle of a lawn. This certainly shows off its architectural character, but the plant loses its power to evoke a lush scene from another time and place when sited without a context of other plants. Instead, a suitable place might be beneath a tree that casts some shade to create a primeval understory feeling yet not so dense as to preclude growing most plants. Planted in small groupings of differing sizes and allowed to pup rather than subjected to typical shearing and trunking up, the cycad can then distinguish itself as an elegant player in a garden scene rather than as a gawky trophy or lonely specimen. When allowed to consort with other plants of a variety of forms and textures, such as low-growing grasslike sedges or liriope, wispy asparagus, and rounded peacock gingers (*Kaempferia* spp.), a rich tapestry results without the sago losing any of its sculptural beauty.

If the site and its buildings suggest formality, the unique year-round shape of the sago can be highlighted by planting a number of them on a linear axis—either along a path or against part of a structure—and intermingling pale bulbs such as white Naples onion (*Allium neapolitanum*) or yellow or white tazetta narcissi. These play off the cycad seasonally, their translucent, ephemeral petals and lax, casual habits a counterpoint to the dark, almost waxen, reflective foliage and stiff "scratchy fern" form of the sago. Adding more plants in context with the sago does not diminish its spirit but makes it more powerful and striking. Though with entirely different effects—one formal and the other naturalistic—both schemes enhance cycad, companions, and site simultaneously. Captivated by the plants, people are then drawn to the space for yet more involvement; a landscape is well on its way to becoming a garden.

TOP LEFT Adding more of certain plant players gives power to a seasonal event and avoids the suburban solitary specimen syndrome. Grouping them loosely prevents the stiff "parsley-around-the-turkey" look of clichéd foundation plantings. If crabapples and lilacs flourish, why not plant several of each together? Arnold Arboretum, Jamaica Plain, Massachusetts.

LEFT Sensual curves convert this boxwood planting into a rollicking vision with musical qualities. Its playful irreverence belies the regular shearing and careful hand necessary. *Buxus sempervirens*, Bury Court, Surrey, England, Piet Oudolf design.

Sometimes just a slight change in the way a plant is used makes all the difference in the world. Boxwood (*Buxus* spp.) falls into this category. This hardworking plant responds so well to shearing that one rarely sees it in its natural form. It has become more architecture than plant. When allowed to go unclipped, boxwood has a form that is sensual and curvaceous, like a plump unshorn ewe. A wonderful way to marry its useful architectural qualities with its innate spirit is to make boxwood hedges that roll, bulge, and undulate rather than pulling out the old string line and bowing to the familiar rectilinear master.

Reviving the mundane means having a fresh look at a common plant, and then considering its context, coming up with new combinations of plants it might grow with, and deciding how it might best be placed in and associate with site and space. It is a starting point for the process of plant-driven design, for if you can make a plant once considered boring seem suddenly engaging by the way you invite it into a garden, most certainly you can do the same for plants not saddled with the burden of being unjustly labeled horticulturally passé.

BELOW LEFT Plants native to the Sonoran desert region mingle in a melee of texture and ephemeral spring bloom. *Penstemon parryi, Baileya multiradiata, Dioon* sp., *Stenocereus thurberi, Parkinsonia florida*, Arizona-Sonora Desert Museum, Tucson, Arizona.

BELOW The spirit of a plant respected and displayed can make a simple design sublime. Gently weeping Japanese maple brushes the side of bluestone steps, with bamboo threading through and a fall-clad golden rain tree as a background beacon. Brookside Gardens, Wheaton, Maryland.

POWER PLANTS Plants with strong presence

People usually either love or hate these plants; indifference is rare, as their powerful forms are hard to ignore.

Trees with bold forms and distinctive foliage

Aleurites fordii, tung oil tree
Catalpa spp., Indian bean
Cedrus spp., cedar
Cupressus sempervirens 'Stricta', Italian cypress
Fagus spp., beech
Ficus carica, fig
Firmiana simplex, Chinese parasol tree
Magnolia grandiflora, bull bay, southern magnolia
Picea spp., spruce
Pinus pinea, Italian stone pine
Populus deltoides, plains cottonwood
Quercus macrocarpa, bur oak
Quercus virginiana, southern live oak
Salix babylonica, weeping willow
Taxodium distichum, bald cypress

Large-growing palms, hardiest species

Brahea armata, Mexican blue palm
Brahea edulis, Guadalupe palm
Butia (most species), jelly palm
Jubaea chilensis, Chilean wine palm
Livistona chinensis, Chinese fan palm
Phoenix canariensis, Canary Island date palm
Phoenix dactylifera, date palm
Phoenix hispanica, Elche date palm
Phoenix sylvestris, sugar date palm
Phoenix theophrasti, Cretan date palm

Sabal bermudana (syn. *S. blackburniana*, *S.* sp. 'Riverside'), Bermuda palmetto
Sabal mexicana, Mexican palmetto
Sabal palmetto, cabbage palmetto
Sabal uresana, Mexican blue palmetto
Trachycarpus (most species), windmill palm
Washingtonia filifera, California fan palm

Shrubby palms, hardiest species

Brahea moorei, powder palm
Chamaedorea microspadix, hardy bamboo palm
Chamaedorea radicalis, hardy parlor palm
Chamaerops humilis, Mediterranean fan palm
Guihaia argyrata, Asian needle palm
Nannorrhops ritchieana, Mazari palm
Rhapidophyllum hystrix, needle palm
Sabal minor, dwarf palmetto
Serenoa repens, saw palmetto
Trithrinax campestris, Argentine silver palm

Cacti, succulents, yuccalike plants

Agave spp., century plant
Aloe spp.
Carnegiea gigantea, saguaro
Cereus hildmannianus subsp. *uruguayanus* (syn. *Cereus peruvianus*), candelabra cactus
Cordyline australis, New Zealand cabbage tree
Dasylirion spp., sotol
Dracaena draco, dragon tree
Echinocactus spp.
Ferocactus spp., barrel cactus

Neobuxbaumia polylopha, torch cactus
Nolina spp., beargrass
Opuntia cacanapa 'Ellisiana', spineless prickly pear
Opuntia englemanii, Engleman prickly pear
Opuntia ficus-indica, Indian fig
Trichocereus terscheckii, cardon del valle
Xanthorrhoea spp., grass tree
Yucca spp.

Other plants with striking foliage and form

Alocasia spp., elephant's ear
Alpinia spp., shell ginger
Bambusa spp., clumping bamboo
Colocasia spp., taro
Cortaderia selloana, pampas grass
Cycas spp., sago palm, cycad
Dioon spp., chamal
Ensete ventricosum, Abyssinian banana
Farfugium japonicum 'Giganteum', giant groundsel
Gunnera manicata, giant gunnera
Macrozamia spp., Australian cycad
Musa spp., banana
Petasites japonicus, butterbur
Phormium spp., New Zealand flax
Phyllostachys spp., running bamboo
Saccharum arundinaceum, hardy sugar cane
Saccharum ravennae, hardy pampas grass
Xanthosoma spp., elephant's ear

VERY SILVER PLANTS

This list includes plants with especially whitened foliage and omits those more gray or blue in hue.

Trees, shrubs, and subshrubs more than a foot tall

Abies concolor 'Candicans', silver fir

Acacia baileyana, Cootamundra wattle

Artemisia 'Huntington', 'Lambrook Silver', silver wormwood

Atriplex corrugata, *A. gardneri*, saltbush

Bismarckia nobilis, Bismarck palm

Brachyglottis greyi (syn. *Senecio greyi*) 'Sunshine', daisy bush

Buddleia marrubiifolia, *B. nivea*, butterfly bush

Chamaerops humilis var. *cerifera*, silver Mediterranean fan palm

Convolvulus cneorum, silver bush morning glory

Eleagnus 'Coral Silver', 'Quicksilver', 'Silverscape', silverberry

Eremophila latrobei, emu bush

Ericameria nauseosa (syn. *Chrysothamnus nauseosus*) var. *albicaulis*, silver rabbitbrush, chamisa

Eucalyptus cinerea, *E. cordata*, *E. gunnii*, silver gum

Euryops acraeus, *E. pectinatus*, silver daisy bush

Hippophae rhamnoides, sea buckthorn

Lavandula ×*allardii*

Lavandula dentata var. *candicans*, silver French lavender

Lavandula lanata, woolly lavender

Lavandula pinnata, fernleaf lavender

Lavandula 'Silver Frost'

Leucadendron argenteum, silver tree

Leucophyllum candidum, dwarf ceniza

Leucophyllum frutescens 'Alba', white-flowered ceniza

Leucophyllum minus, ceniza

Leucophyllum zygophyllum, boxleaf ceniza

Leucophyta brownii (*Calocephalus brownii*), cushion bush

Maireana sedifolia, pearl bluebush

Nannorrhops ritchieana, Mazari palm

Pyrus salicifolia cultivars, silver willowleaf pear

Salix helvetica, dwarf silver willow

Salvia pachyphylla, desert sage

Senna artemisioides (syn. *Cassia artemisioides*), feathery senna

Senna phyllodinea, silverleaf senna

Serenoa repens, silver saw palmetto

Seriphidium filifolium (syn. *Artemisia filifolia*), threadleaf sage, sand sage

Shepherdia rotundifolia, roundleaf buffaloberry

Teucrium fruticans 'Azureum', shrubby silver germander

Viguiera lanata, woolly-leaf sunflower

Yucca elephantipes 'Silver Star'

Low subshrubs, herbaceous perennials, and ground covers

Achillea ageratifolia, *A.* ×*kelleri*, dwarf silver yarrow

Ajuga reptans 'Silver Carpet', silver bugleweed

Anaphalis spp., pearly everlasting

Antennaria parvifolia 'McClintock', dwarf pussytoes

Anthemis marschalliana, alpine marguerite

Artemisia caucasica

Artemisia ludoviciana 'Silver King', 'Valerie Finnis', silver prairie sage

Artemisia pycnocephala 'David's Choice'

Artemisia schmidtiana 'Silver Mound'

Artemisia stelleriana, beach wormwood

Artemisia versicolor, seafoam sage

Astelia nervosa var. *chathamica*, silver spear

Athyrium 'Ghost', silver painted fern

Baileya multiradiata, desert marigold

Brunnera macrophylla 'Jack Frost', 'Looking Glass', Siberian forget-me-not

Celmisia spp., silver daisy

Centaurea cineraria, old-fashioned dusty miller

Cerastium candidissimum, alpine snow-in-summer

Cerastium tomentosum, snow-in-summer

Cotula hispida

Cyclamen cultivars

Dalea bicolor var. *argyraea*, silver dalea

Dalea greggii, trailing indigo bush

Dichondra sericea 'Silver Falls' (often erroneously listed as *D. argentea*), silver ponyfoot

Eriogonum niveum, *E. ovalifolium* (and others), buckwheat

Gazania rigens 'Bicton Orange'

Geranium argenteum

Helichrysum angustifolium, curry plant

Helichrysum argyrophyllum

Helichrysum milfordiae

Helichrysum petiolare, licorice plant

Helichrysum splendidum

Helichrysum thianschanicum 'Icicles'

Helichrysum virgineum

Heuchera 'Silver Scrolls', alumroot

Hieracium lanatum, woolly hawkweed

Lamium maculatum 'White Nancy'

Lotus berthelotii, silver lotus vine

Lychnis coronaria, rose campion

Oenothera fremontii 'Shimmer', narrow-leaf evening primrose

Oenothera macrocarpa subsp. *incana* 'Comanche Campfire', evening primrose

Penstemon californicus

Penstemon linarioides var. *coloradoensis*

Plecostachys serpyllifolia

Plectranthus argentatus

Potentilla argyrophylla

Potentilla calabra

Potentilla cinerea

Psilostrophe spp., paper flower

Pulmonaria 'Majeste', 'Samourai', 'Silver Ribbons', and other cultivars, lungwort

VERY SILVER PLANTS, continued

Raoulia australis, vegetable sheep
Salvia apiana, bee sage
Salvia argentea, silver sage
Salvia chamaedryoides, germander sage
Salvia chionophylla, snowleaf sage
Salvia cyanescens
Salvia daghestanica, dwarf silverleaf sage
Salvia discolor, Andean silverleaf sage
Salvia dorrii, blue ball sage
Salvia 'Newe Yaar' (syn. *S. fruticosa* hybrid)
Santolina chamaecyparissus 'Nana', dwarf santolina
Scabiosa graminifolia, silver pincushion flower
Senecio cineraria 'Cirrhus', dusty miller
Senecio vira-vira
Sideritis clandestina
Sideritis scardica
Sideritis taurica
Sphaeromeria capitata
Stachys byzantina 'Silver Carpet', lamb's ears
Stachys inflata
Stemodia tomentosa, trailing ceniza

Tanacetum densum var. *amani*, partridge feather
Tanacetum ptarmiciflorum 'Silver Feather'
Tanacetum praeteritium
Teucrium cossonii
Teucrium polium
Verbascum bombyciferum, woolly mullein
Veronica bombycina
Veronica incana, silver speedwell
Veronica thymoides subsp. *pseudocinerea*
Zauschneria californica 'Wayne's Silver', hummingbird trumpet, California fuchsia

Cacti and succulents

Astrophytum myriostigma, bishop's cap cactus
Cephalocereus senilis, old man cactus
Cleistocactus straussii, Bolivian torch cactus
Cotyledon orbiculata, pig's ears
Crassula arborescens, silver dollar plant
Dudleya spp.
Dyckia fosteriana (select cultivars)
Dyckia marnier-lapostollei

Dyckia velascana 'La Rioja'
Echeveria elegans, *E. pulvinata* 'Frosty', hen and chicks
Echinocereus dasyacanthus, rainbow cactus
Echinocereus delaetii, old man hedgehog cactus
Echinocereus niveus, snowy hedgehog cactus
Echinocereus reichenbachii var. *albispinus*, white lace cactus
Graptopetalum paraguayense, ghost plant
Kalanchoe pumila
Mammillaria geminispina, *M. parkinsonii*, *M. perbellus*, nipple cactus
Opuntia erinacea, grizzly bear cactus
Opuntia tunicata, creeping cholla
Opuntia whipplei, cholla
Oreocereus trollii, Bolivian old man cactus
Parodia haselbergii, scarlet ball cactus
Puya coerulea
Puya venusta
Sedum spathulifolium 'Cape Blanco'
Sempervivum arachnoideum, spiderweb houseleek

SELECT PLANTS WITH REDDISH FOLIAGE

This list includes good garden plants with red, burgundy, bronze, purple, or blackish foliage.

Woody plants

Acer palmatum (select cultivars), Japanese maple
Acer platanoides (select cultivars), Norway maple
Acer pseudoplatanus (select cultivars), sycamore maple
Albizzia julibrissin 'Summer Chocolate', bronze-leaf mimosa
Berberis thunbergii (select cultivars), Japanese barberry

Betula pendula (select cultivars), European silver birch
Cercidiphyllum japonicum 'Red Fox', redleaf katsura tree
Cercis canadensis 'Forest Pansy', eastern redbud
Coprosma (select species and cultivars)
Corokia ×*virgata* (select cultivars)
Corylus (select cultivars), filbert
Cotinus coggygria (select cultivars), smokebush
Dodonaea viscosa 'Purpurea', hop bush
Euphorbia cotinifolia
Fagus sylvatica (select cultivars), European beech

Gleditsia triacanthos 'Ruby Lace', honey locust
Hebe (select species and cultivars)
Hypericum androsaemum 'Albury Purple', purple-leaf St. John's wort
Hypericum fortuneanum 'Purple Fountain'
Loropetalum chinense (select cultivars), Chinese witch hazel
Physocarpus opulifolius (select cultivars), ninebark
Prunus cerasifera
Prunus ×*cistena*, purple-leaf plum
Sambucus nigra (select cultivars), European elder
Weigela florida (select cultivars)

Vitis vinifera 'Purpurea', purple-leaf grape

Herbaceous perennials, biennials, and annuals

Acalypha spp.

Actaea racemosa (syn. *Cimicifuga racemosa*) (select cultivars), black snakeroot

Actaea simplex (syn. *Cimicifuga simplex*), Atropurpurea Group snakeroot

Ajuga pyramidalis 'Metallica Crispa', *A. reptans* 'Bronze Beauty', 'Atropurpurea', bugleweed

Anthriscus sylvestris 'Ravenswing'

Astilbe ×arendsii (select cultivars)

Beta vulgaris 'Bull's Blood', beet

Carex buchananii, C. comans, C. petriei, C. testacea, brown sedge

Clematis recta (select cultivars)

Coleus ×hybridus (select cultivars)

Eupatorium rugosum 'Chocolate'

Euphorbia amygdaloides 'Purpurea', red-leaf spurge

Euphorbia epithymoides 'Bonfire', red-leaf cushion spurge

Foeniculum vulgare 'Purpureum', bronze fennel

Gaura lindheimeri 'Crimson Butterflies'

Geranium pratense 'Midnight Reiter'

Geranium sessiliflorum 'Nigricans'

Heuchera hybrids (many cultivars)

Hibiscus acetosella 'Red Shield'

Hylotelephium telephium subsp. *maximum* 'Atropurpureum'

Imperata cylindrica var. *koenigii* 'Red Baron', Japanese blood grass

Iresine lindenii

Lactuca sativa (select cultivars), lettuce

Ligularia dentata (select cultivars)

Lobelia (some hybrids)

Lychnis ×arkwrightii

Lysimachia ciliata 'Rubra', purple loosestrife

Ocimum basilicum (select cultivars), basil

Ophiopogon planiscapus, black mondo grass

Panicum virgatum 'Shenandoah', 'Warrior', red switch grass

Pennisetum setaceum 'Cupreum', purple fountain grass

Penstemon digitalis 'Husker Red'

Perilla frutescens, beefsteak plant

Phedimus spurius (syn. *Sedum spurium*) (select cultivars)

Primula vulgaris (some cultivars), English primrose

Ranunculus ficaria 'Brazen Hussy'

Rheum palmatum (select cultivars), ornamental rhubarb

Rodgersia 'Chocolate Wings'

Saccharum officinale 'Pele's Smoke', purple sugarcane

Saxifraga stolonifera 'Maroon Beauty'

Sempervivum spp., hen and chicks

Setcreasea pallida (syn. *Tradescantia pallida*), purple heart

Tiarella hybrids (select cultivars), foamflower

Trifolium repens 'Atropurpureum', redleaf clover

Uncinia uncinata var. *rubra*, red sedge

Viola labradorica, violet

Bulbs, corms, and tubers

Caladium (select cultivars)

Canna (select cultivars)

Canna warsczewiczii

Crinum procerum 'Queen Emma'

Crinum hybrid 'Sangria'

Curcuma rubescens

Curcuma sp. 'Scarlet Fever'

Dahlia (select cultivars)

Eucomis comosa 'Oakhurst', 'Sparkling Burgundy', pineapple lily

Oxalis purpurea 'Garnet' (and others)

Oxalis regnellii 'Triangularis', purple false shamrock

Specimen plants

Aechmea 'Burgundy'

Aeonium arboreum 'Zwartkop'

Cordyline australis (select cultivars), Australian cabbage tree

Echinocereus rigidissimus var. *rubrispinus*, rainbow cactus

Ensete ventricosum 'Maurelii'

Phormium tenax (select cultivars), New Zealand flax

3

PLANTS AS HEROES
Garden challenges and opportunities

T'S A BRIGHT FALL MORNING and the view out our south-facing bedroom window takes in translucent, feathered broom fern (*Asparagus virgatus*) rambling alongside a reflective yet dark, shrubby needle palm (*Rhapidophyllum hystrix*). These fill a bed shaded by a massive live oak, one of the original native inhabitants of our Austin garden. The lush textures set off a sunlit informal lawn of tousled, emerald green sedge (*Carex retroflexa*) overlooked by varied architectural plants. Suckering aloes; globular, shrubby, and columnar cacti; Mediterranean cypress; treelike *Yucca linearifolia;* wild olive; and cycads frame the scene, with warmth-loving, xeric perennials, bulbs, and subshrubs like phlomis, leucophyllum, teucrium, and salvia interspersed. All these receive quite casual care, yet on this mild autumn morning their combined effect is magnetic, drawing our attention through the window. It was a brutally hot summer with even less rain than usual and unrelenting heat, the kind that defeats plants, but after years of trial on the thin, chalky soils of Austin, with a host of garden denizens replaced or exiled, nearly all the species seen from our window appear to be thriving.

Beauty in any garden begins with vibrantly healthy plants. A sense of well-being emanates from clean foliage and abundant flowers to confirm that nature is our benign partner. When plants seem happy we feel the same. For this simple reason a garden always deserves site-specific plantings that respect local climate, soil, and exposures. It is of course possible to grow many plants by supplying their every need—artificial soil, perpetual irrigation, ritually repeated applications of fertilizers, pesticides, and tonics—but imposing a poorly attuned planting inevitably overwhelms the spirit of a place rather than melding with it. This actually detaches us from nature, the opposite of what a garden ought to do.

Perhaps a few favored spots on earth offer a temperate climate, rich soil, and a gentle aspect that combine benevolently so almost any plant prospers. Our own fates, like those of many gardeners, have more often placed us in situations that seem determined to thwart efforts at planting. Yet the key word here is *seem*, for what at first appears to present difficulty can be turned to advantage. Like meter and rhyme in a poem, these horticultural hurdles set up the rules to play by; gardens wouldn't be nearly so interesting—or their beauty so moving—without them.

OPPOSITE Beneath the dry shade of a live oak draped in Spanish moss, feathery broom fern, dark green needle palm, and other hardy dwarf palms offer verdant textures year-round, needing little attention. *Asparagus virgatus, Rhapidophyllum hystrix, Brahea moorei, Chamaedorea radicalis, Daphniphyllum humile, Olea sylvestris*, authors' garden, Austin, Texas.

Plant and site

The spirit of a particular place—its *genius loci*—grows naturally from geology, aspect, and climate, and their certain and indelible imprints on the growth of plants. Each place offers opportunities as well as pitfalls. By exploring and nurturing fortunate marriages between plants and sites, gardeners develop compositions both radiant with natural beauty and expressive of the unique vitality of a region.

Scott once began a planting on a newly developed suburban lot in central Texas where a long easement lay along a south-facing perimeter; this accommodated underground utilities the developer had buried beneath convenient fill obtained from highway demolition. The result was a low berm ten feet wide by two hundred feet long comprised of limy road base, chunks of broken asphalt, and rough gravel. This "soil" held a bit of moisture during winter, but generally dried out in summer, wicking dampness away through

Winners in the local survival lottery, this mix of succulents, shrubby perennials, bulbs, and sedge prospers on thin, chalky soil in a hot climate that shifts between humid and arid. *Aloe maculata* (blooming) and other aloes, *Yucca linearifolia, Opuntia ficus-indica, Neobuxbaumia polylopha, Teucrium fruticans* 'Azureum', *Foeniculum vulgare, Puya dyckioides, Carex retroflexa,* authors' garden, Austin, Texas.

the lime rubble; it solidified into a bricklike mass in July and August. What would grow on that?

As it turned out, rosemary grew exceptionally well on the berm, for this plant comes naturally from rocky lime-rich soils around the Mediterranean Sea, a region in which rain falls mostly in winter. With the success of this species as a clue, Scott tested other plants from the same region and found them to be adaptable; for instance, beautiful autumn-flowering *Crocus goulimyi* of southern Greece flourished on the berm, actually benefiting from the dry summer conditions. This same species struggled to survive in parts of

the garden with "better" soil that held more moisture. A prairie plant native to dry, limy ridges nearby, xeric gay-feather (*Liatris mucronata*) also thrived on the berm, where the mostly arid conditions helped delay its lavender blooms until cool autumn weather prevailed, allowing for a longer season of flowering.

Other heroic drought-loving westerners such as penstemon, agave, and yucca soon were thriving on this "poor" soil as well, and the rubbly, lime-filled berm eventually became one of the most fascinating parts of the garden, showcasing a variety of plants adapted to and benefiting from its peculiar conditions. A surprise discovery was that several shrub roses performed better in the berm soil than on deeper clay-loam found elsewhere in the garden: the lean conditions apparently helped slow growth, making bushier, more attractive shrubs with more flowers and tougher, less succulent shoots that resisted diseases. Like indigenous

ABOVE LEFT Many plants have specific soil preferences or adaptations. Eastern columbine favors limy soils, sometimes even growing in crevices of limestone boulders. *Aquilegia canadensis*, central Texas

ABOVE Each site presents challenges yet well-chosen plants prevail. Self-sufficient agastache, evening primrose, New Mexican olive, grasses, and dwarf conifers romance this western garden, thriving in the face of summer drought and alkaline soil. Authors' garden, Fort Collins, Colorado.

guides of a former era who directed cavalry regiments through seemingly hostile, unfamiliar territory, a few well-attuned plants can create the practical means—through observation of their varied adaptations and cycles—to educate gardeners on rhythms and idiosyncrasies of a site.

A plant-driven site assessment

One of the early steps in a garden's design is to look at the horticultural potential of the place. "What might happily grow here?" is the question to be raised, with the desired answer a listing of plants with diverse forms, textures, and hues over the seasons. The selection begins with true regional champions that offer unrivaled performance under local conditions. Plants known to grow adequately—yet not at their very best locally—may be included but ought to rank lower on the list. Just as important are plants to exclude for unbearably long or unacceptable down times, unrealistic management requirements, or aesthetic qualities and associations opposed to the overall spirit of the site and design.

Planting possibilities need to be explored simultaneously with other requirements of the garden. In this way plants inform and resolve goals of the design; at the same time they are ensured fair treatment and consideration for their individual needs and potential. Pathways, patios, lawns, shaded or sheltered areas, and other modifications are often desired to accommodate people. Spatial relationships, flow, and views near and far need to be considered at the outset as well: should a particular scene be screened, framed, enclosed, or widened by clearing away existing vegetation? Will plantings define a sense of separation from views beyond, or will they echo and connect with them by repeating similar forms, colors, and textures? Any garden presents several possible answers to these questions; none are inherently wrong as long as they take into account the needs and characters of plants.

Climate

When considering plants the first parameter many gardeners try to define is climate, and popular resources offer ways to assign plant adaptabilities by region. These convenient systems give only approximate information, however, and reflect unavoidable biases; they often become less accurate the farther they extend from their place of origin. The well-known National Arboretum/USDA hardiness zones create what is in essence a death map: they define areas where freezing weather is sufficient to kill various plant species by mapping a single parameter, winter cold. As a result these maps include Washington DC, Dallas, and Seattle in the same zone—8a, defined as having average minimum winter temperatures of 15 to 10 degrees F. Yet anyone who visits gardens in these three cities can see that each has a distinct environment conducive to different plants and plant growth. This is not surprising given other variables such as ambient temperature, annual number of sunny days, humidity, rain and snowfall, and evaporation rate. When these conditions are considered, even the supposedly universal assessment of cold-hardiness becomes unreliable. For example, the vigorous hybrid crape myrtle 'Natchez'—a cross with Japanese *Lagerstroemia fauriei* developed and evaluated at the National Arboretum in Beltsville, Maryland—is more cold-tolerant than common crape myrtle (*Lagerstroemia indica*) along the temperate eastern seaboard but proves less hardy to cold in north Texas. Perhaps the extra autumn heat prevalent in the southern plains fails to harden stems, or dryness during winter desiccates the tender, exfoliating bark of this small tree. Whatever the cause, subtle differences in climate make a 'Natchez' growing in Dallas more likely to freeze than a common crape myrtle, just the opposite of results seen near Washington DC. Lack of hot, sunny weather, save for a few weeks in August, makes any crape myrtle a poor choice for Seattle gardens unless it can be located near a sun-baked wall or paving. The American Horticultural Society heat zone map might be called upon in this instance to help rate climates warm enough for crape myrtles, but this arbitrary horticultural tool suffers from an even narrower perspective than the USDA map—it expresses only the number of days annually above 86 degrees F, making it of limited practical value. Another snag for both hardiness and heat mapping is that portions of North America, especially the continental

interior, experience periodic extremes drastically contra-dicting climate norms; these can shift regional tempera-tures well beyond the neatly divided zones of the maps.

Smaller-scale growing zones like those originally de-fined by the University of California at Davis for cultivating wine grapes and later modified for gardeners and popular-ized in the well-known *Sunset Western Garden Book* offer more precise assessments of climate-plant relations, but this detailed information is not equally available or accu-rate for the whole continent. Attempts have been made to extend the *Sunset* zones to the east, but these have not yet received wide acceptance. Even in California, where they

At best, USDA climate zones describe limited aspects of plant adaptability; these decidedly different plantings both occur in USDA zone 8.

ABOVE LEFT Fennel, columnar cactus, bulbine, silver germander, aloe, and lipstick tulip in central Texas. *Foeniculum vulgare, Neobuxbaumia polylopha, Bulbine frutescens, Teucrium*

fruticans 'Azureum', *Aloe* hybrid, and *Tulipa clusiana*, authors' garden, Austin, Texas.

ABOVE Large-leafed hydrangea and giant Himalayan lily in the woods of the Pacific Northwest. *Cardiocrinum giganteum, Hydran-gea macrophylla,* Heronswood Nursery, Kingston, Washington, Dan Hinkley design.

KÖPPEN ZONES

The climate classifications known as Köppen zones were conceived around 1900 by a Russian-born German meteorologist and botanist, Wladimir Köppen, who used plant communities to help establish climatic boundaries. Individual plant varieties often occur in more than one climate region, and for garden purposes many species are actually most valued outside their indigenous range. Exotic plant varieties introduced into regions with closely matched climate may be expected to thrive; in some instances they may locally naturalize or invade.

Montane

This climate dominates uplands of middle and high latitudes such as the snow-capped mountain ranges of the American West. Cool, damp springs are followed by mild summers, frequently moist at higher elevations; much annual precipitation arrives as winter snow. Native vegetation includes coniferous forest, aspen groves, and damp meadows.

Maritime

Maritime climates develop near cool oceans at high latitudes; oceanic waters near these regions raise humidity and keep temperatures mild. In North America they can be found in the Pacific Northwest and along the immediate coastline of the northeast United States and adjacent Canada. Moist, cool or cold winters are followed by mild, moist summers; cloudy weather prevails much of the year and springs are long and cool. Traditional British horticulture thrives in a maritime climate and well-loved woodland plants like rhododendrons, deciduous magnolias, and conifers prosper; flowers of many types are long-lasting. Consistently cool, damp conditions favor development of acid soils; natural vegetation is dominated by coniferous forest.

Modified continental

The interior Northeast and regions adjacent to the eastern Great Lakes and Appalachians show a modified continental climate. The relatively nearby Atlantic Ocean and immediately adjacent lakes and mountains increase the number of cloudy days, partly tempering more extreme weather of the North American interior, but this region is both hotter and colder than maritime climates. Moisture is generally available year-round and periodic snows can be expected in winter. Deciduous forest is the common native vegetation and brilliant fall colors are characteristic.

Continental

This is the climate of the Great Plains and the midwestern prairies and it is typical of the windswept interior of continents. Winters are generally cold, sometimes dry; summers are hot and punctuated by thunderstorms, yet subject to periodic droughts. Midgrass and tallgrass prairies commonly merge and mingle in this region, with bur oak savannahs developing along watercourses and adjacent woodlands.

Steppe

Steppe climates recall the dry, open grasslands of central Asia. They experience relatively moist winters followed by fast, capricious springs and hot, mostly arid summers. Steppes appear in elevated, cold-winter areas; in North America they are found on the high plains, foothills, and valleys of the Intermountain West. Shortgrass prairie, pinyon-juniper scrub, and sagebrush provide the typical vegetation in this windy, semiarid region, also known as the cold or high desert.

Mediterranean

Mediterranean climates develop at middle latitudes east of upwelling oceanic waters; in North America they dominate California, Baja California, and the interior of the coastal Northwest. These climates are warm cousins of steppes, with mild, fairly moist winters followed by mild or hot, essentially dry summers. Typical vegetation in North America includes chaparral, evergreen oak savannah, and cool-season grassland. A winter growing season followed by summer dormancy is typical for most plants.

Desert

Desert climates develop at latitudes just above the tropics where ocean currents or north-south trending mountains block regular rainfall. The dry climates of the southwestern United States and northern Mexico are typical. Cool or mild winters are followed by intensely hot summers; evaporation rates generally exceed rainfall. Nevertheless, winter rains may be adequate to support spring displays of wildflowers and erratic thunderstorms can revive plants for brief periods of growth and bloom with a summer monsoon. Vegetation includes thorny shrubs, annuals, bulbs, cacti, and other succulents.

Savannah or matorral

Savannah climates occur in transition areas between deserts and humid subtropical zones. In North America these are found in south-central Texas, northeastern Mexico, and semiarid portions of western Mexico. Winters can be mild or cool and vary from moist to moderately dry; summers are hot and subhumid, with both drought and periodic thunderstorms at times. Vegetation superficially resembles Mediterranean regions and includes oak savannah, mesquite-acacia thickets, and semiarid shrub (matorral).

Subtropical

These sultry climates occur at the same latitudes as deserts but develop in areas near warm ocean waters with humid, unstable air masses bringing frequent rains. In North America this climate is typical of the lower South. Winters are mild and vary from somewhat dry to moist; summers are warm to hot with abundant thunderstorms; humidity remains high at all seasons. Typical vegetation includes mixed woodland, palmetto thicket, and cypress swamp.

Tropical

Fully tropical climates develop in regions at less than 30 degrees of latitude on either side of the equator, wherever warm, frost-free conditions combine with a year-round supply of moisture. Although some areas receive evenly distributed precipitation, rainfall may arrive during a distinct wet season or monsoon. Winters and summers are warm to hot and humidity remains high. In North America tropical climates dominate south Florida and southern Mexico. Vegetation includes evergreen and seasonally deciduous forests and palm groves.

OPPOSITE LEFT A montane meadow with little red elephant and American bistort. *Pedicularis groenlandica, Polygonum bistortoides*, South Park, Colorado.

OPPOSITE RIGHT Maritime woodland with gnarled tree trunks and moss. Devon, England.

BELOW LEFT Steppe, with *Stipa ichu*. Catamarca, Argentina.

BELOW Subtropical woodland with dwarf palmetto. *Sabal minor*, Ottine, Texas.

are best defined, these growing zones may neglect important details or lack sufficient precision. No system is fully reliable; gardeners need to seek out local hardiness ratings, heat tolerances, and other aspects of adaptability to gain a full understanding of their planting possibilities.

Although the subject is vast, gardeners have much to gain by learning all they can about the relationship between plants and climate. One way is by broadly grouping plant-climate adaptations into a few characteristic associations known as Köppen zones. Familiarity with these naturally occurring communities can help organize a garden to address varied plant needs.

When assessing plant adaptability, there is no good substitute for firsthand experience, yet novice gardeners and newcomers to a region need to start somewhere. Visiting a good local nursery can provide some foundation for exploring plant possibilities and certainly will introduce the varieties most readily available, but information gathered there ought to be measured against observations in actual gardens. Walks in public parks, down tree-lined streets of older neighborhoods, or through half-neglected cemetery grounds often reveal a cast of hardy plants capable of long-term success. Getting a sense of these mature plantings also prevents potential mistakes by indicating which species might get out of hand or become unattractive as they age; with luck, plant placement and combinations worth duplicating await discovery. Even if not actually seen in local gardens, plants known to hail from similar regions to those found thriving offer good candidates for garden experimentation, as was the case with the limy rubble-filled berm.

Knowing a bit about a plant's native environment, preferred soils and exposures, natural companions, and such is invaluable for designing a garden. When possible, locally native species ought to be observed in habitat firsthand. Information on the indigenous haunts of exotic plants may be discovered in wildflower guides and floras that cover their native regions and through the Internet. A simple picture of a plant growing in the wild conveys a sense of its potential character and may inspire its best placement.

No matter how experienced a designer becomes, he or she ought to explore within the garden itself; the most exciting designs often come about because their experimenting creators willingly kill and discard plants—even healthy ones—in the process of developing a garden.

Exposure and microclimate

Varied temperatures over the seasons both at night and during the day factor into how well a plant's metabolism runs and how vigorously a plant grows in a particular garden. Most hardy species require cool winter rests in order to prepare for growth in the spring and subsequent flowering; likewise, plants attuned to seasonally dry tropical climates may need several weeks of hot weather, mimicking the dormant period of their homelands, before initiating growth and bloom. Beyond air temperature, the intensity of wind, sunlight, and the ambient heat stored and radiated by soil, rocks, and nearby buildings all exert potent climatic effects.

Most gardens offer exposures and positions capable of supporting multiple palettes of plants. Trees, paving, architecture, and terrain modify climates in small-scale but powerful ways. Exploiting these differences adds diversity and interest to plantings; taking advantage of them is a goal for any plant-driven design.

In Colorado our house's southern foundation backs long garden beds that receive full sunlight during winter and summer; the house deflects the worst gusts of prevailing cold winter winds from the northwest. Although this area is too hot for many plants in summer, the extra warmth and sunshine create a unique microclimate suited to cacti, hardy species of agave and yucca, and several selections of desert willow (*Chilopsis linearis*) that prefer more heat than northern Colorado typically provides. Because frosts arrive late here and freezes are not long-lasting, we are also able to coax a marginally hardy Mount Lemmon daisy (*Tagetes lemmonii* 'Compacta') native to southern Arizona to grow and offer its golden end-of the-season blooms along the sunny, sheltered house wall.

In contrast, the north side of our house remains in shade

PLANT METABOLISM AND CLIMATE

As living organisms that breathe, grow, and make food through photosynthesis, plants have evolved several strategies to deal with climate. Essential metabolic tasks require plants to take in water and carbon dioxide, using these materials along with the energy of sunlight to make food in the form of starches and sugars while exhaling oxygen as a by-product. To this end most plants use a chemical pathway known as C3 (for carbon 3) that works best at moderate temperatures between 50 and 70 degrees F. C3 plants grow prodigiously in mild, temperate climates but may lose efficiency as temperatures—especially nighttime temperatures—rise. Some species stop growing altogether in hot weather; others need supplemental watering and added fertilizer to keep going.

Some plants such as warm-season grasses exploit a different chemical path, C4, that functions better at higher temperatures and requires less moisture; this adapts C4 plants to warm, dry climates. Succulents usually rely on CAM (Crassulacean acid metabolism, named after the succulent family *Crassulaceae*), a pathway that combines the C3 and C4 reactions, dividing them in time so that carbon dioxide can be absorbed at night for use in photosynthesis the following day. This reduces water loss and works best in climates where humidity remains low—CAM plants grow heartily in the strong sunlight and thin air of high elevations where nights are cool and days are warm; they sometimes have difficulty respiring during warm, humid nights at or near sea level.

Many succulents prefer climates with cool nighttime temperatures that assist evening respiration, known as Crassulacean acid metabolism.

ABOVE Fully hardy to cold, red-leaved houseleek and blue-gray Afghan stonecrop nestle in a rock wall. These high-elevation succulents struggle where summers are hot and humid. *Sempervivum* cv., *Hylotelephium pachyclados* (syn. *Sedum pachyclados*), Tower Gardens, Spokane, Washington.

ABOVE RIGHT Drought-resistant Canary Island natives *Aeonium balsamifera* and *A. canariense*, and *Aloe arborescens* from coastal South Africa thrive in a mild Mediterranean climate. Strybing Arboretum, San Francisco, California.

Microclimates in the same garden offer widely different habitats for plants.

ABOVE Avoiding northern Colorado's early frosts and winter blasts, marginally hardy blue sage, century plant, pig's ear, and late-blooming Mount Lemmon daisy prosper along the authors' sheltered south foundation. *Salvia farinacea* 'Texas Violet', *Agave havardiana*, *Cotyledon orbiculata*, *Tagetes lemmonii* 'Compacta', Fort Collins, Colorado.

ABOVE RIGHT On the opposite side of the house, shade from a north-facing wall holds moisture and provides a congenial home for evergreen yew, Christmas rose, lungwort, and cowslip, as well as spring vetchling and Molly the witch peony. *Taxus ×media, Helleborus niger, Pulmonaria saccharata, Primula veris, Lathyrus vernus, Paeonia mlokosewitschii, Juniperus horizontalis* 'Limeglow'.

much of the winter. This benefits evergreens in the Colorado climate, where subfreezing temperatures, low humidity, and strong sunlight often combine to desiccate foliage. Although subject to more intense cold and wind than other parts of the garden, the north foundation retains moisture during summer; its cooler, damper, shadier environment accommodates hardy evergreen plants like daphnes, hellebores, select epimediums, hemlocks, and yews that would have trouble enduring in hotter, sunnier positions. Here early spring blooms of deciduous magnolias are less likely to be awakened by the false encouragement of short-lived warm spells, so they stand a better chance of blooming after hard frosts have passed for the season. In our north garden a large gray-green Colorado spruce and sizable silver corkbark fir have been placed to help block winter gusts and to offer a backdrop for pale spring flowers.

Eastern exposures are often favorable positions in a garden, for they warm early with morning sun, making them less frosty, and receive shelter from the afternoon sun, moderating heat. Roses and flowering perennials such as geraniums or daylilies, whose blooming seasons might be cut short by hot weather elsewhere in the garden, continue in blossom for weeks with the benevolent afternoon shade of an east-facing wall or fence.

Whereas eastern exposures temper climate, western aspects exaggerate extremes, heightening the fierce, often reflected glare of afternoon sun while still exposing plants to winter gusts from the northwest. These hot and cold conditions together seem to heighten fall colors, as testified to annually by coppery displays of a dwarf Korean maple (*Acer pseudosieboldianum*) and Spanish oak (*Quercus buckleyi*) near our west foundation. West-facing exposures are often ideal places to add deciduous shade trees or, as we chose for our Colorado garden, a vine-covered arbor to help moderate the intensity of the late-day sun.

Air and temperature

Without wind to mix it together, chilled air behaves like a liquid, becoming dense and sinking so that it flows into low-lying areas, collecting there. Clear, still nights allow heat to escape from the atmosphere, and radiation cooling becomes common under such conditions. Where a garden sits locally, whether near the top or at the base of sloping terrain, can determine just how cold it gets, often making the difference between a hard freeze or none whatsoever. Our Colorado garden, just a mile or so from the foothills, receives cool air draining down from the mountains. In summer this helps moderate temperatures, keeping us milder than nearby scorched plains; in winter our garden can be a few degrees colder than adjacent downtown Fort Collins. The topographically lower valley of the Cache la Poudre River, just down the road, becomes colder still,

The moisture regime of gardens, whether wet or dry, favors specific types of plants.

TOP With abundant blooms and thick mats of downy foliage, this shade-loving fleabane suggests lushness. Its lusty growth belies adaptation to dry, root-filled soil found at the base of trees. *Erigeron pulchellus*, Chanticleer, Wayne, Pennsylvania.

ABOVE Camas lilies and ostrich ferns prosper in damp, even swampy conditions; here they fill low, heavy, wet soil along a small stream. *Camassia leichtlinii* 'Blue Danube', *Matteuccia struthiopteris*, Chanticleer, Wayne, Pennsylvania.

fortuitously draining the frostiest air away from our garden. Differences such as these can be dramatic at times and are often perceptible over small distances, even within the same garden.

In a similar way, tree canopies help retain heat like a large blanket. On cold nights in our Texas garden the benevolent spreading branches of evergreen live oaks help protect winter flowers like cyclamen growing beneath them, warding off the worst effects of a freeze. The patchy patterns of frost pockets and thermal belts that result from the interplay of terrain, foliage, and atmosphere create distinct microclimates suited to varied plants, so that each garden offers unique opportunities.

Rooting out

As important as temperature variables may be in assessing local plant adaptability, a second site characteristic, soil, is equally critical. The chemistry and texture of the substrate into which plants extend their roots often determine just what varieties will be most suited to a garden, for the soil's chemistry plays directly into the life of plants and has done so since green things first spread from rivers and the sea onto land.

Primitive plants—lichens and fairy-sword lipferns—begin the slow process of building soil from raw granite. *Acarospora* spp. and *Cheilanthes lindheimeri*, Llano County, Texas.

A primitive stage in the relationship between plants and soil can be seen in colorful lichens that colonize dead logs and rugged boulders. These low-growing encrustations are not plants per se but actually a collaboration between fungus and a green partner, usually algae or cyanobacteria. The fungal partner surrounds the green cells, absorbing and providing water while extracting minerals from bare rock, soil, or wood; the green partner photosynthesizes, manufacturing food that is then partly absorbed by the fungus. A not-too-different partnership exists between many higher plants, including most familiar trees and shrubs, and mycorrhizae, threadlike fungal partners that envelop plant roots and extend into the soil. These mycorrhizae provide a conduit for green plants to obtain raw minerals and nutrients, vastly increasing the effective root area for plants. Complex relationships such as these exist with many species and play into the way certain plants adapt to particular soils.

The distinctive appearance of wild vegetation in the countryside often reflects local geology as well as climate. Some plant families have an affinity for particular soil types or a capacity to grow on a given substrate; their presence in a native landscape provides a subliminal clue to the chemistry of the earth beneath. Members of the olive family, for instance, occur on limy soils around the world: privet (*Ligustrum* spp.), lilac (*Syringa* spp.), jasmine (*Jasminum* spp.), ash (*Fraxinus* spp.), olive (*Olea* spp.), and sweet olive (*Osmanthus* spp.) are characteristic of calcareous (lime-rich) or alkaline soils in nature and are equally at home on them in gardens. In North America native stands of beech (*Fagus grandifolia*), columbine (*Aquilegia canadensis*), smokebush (*Cotinus obovatus*), and fendlerbush (*Fendlera* spp.) often imply similar underlying soils. Along the same lines, members of the heath family such as azaleas, rhododendrons, and mountain laurels (*Kalmia* spp.) prefer acid soils and reveal this condition when seen in the wild. Camellias, gardenias, and pieris do the same for gardens. Large-leafed hydrangeas (*Hydrangea macrophylla*) succeed on either acid or mildly alkaline soils but respond to the chemistry of the earth like litmus paper: their dome-shaped flowers open pink or ruddy when grown on limy soil and expand with intense blue hues on acid ground.

A soil's texture, whether fine (clay), coarse (sand), or somewhere in between (loam), also affects plant adaptability, as these qualities interact with chemistry and climate. The small pore spaces and layered mineral structures typical of clay allow it to absorb and hold nutrients as well as water; clay soils remain cooler and moister in the summer than light-textured soils and are generally considered mineral rich. Nevertheless, some elements may become chemically bonded in ways not readily accessible to plants and especially tight soils can be anaerobic, lacking the oxygen plants need to absorb and metabolize minerals. Sandy soils are generally full of air but relatively inert chemically; they offer rapid drainage but hold little moisture or food. Loam soils, if you are lucky enough to garden in them, hold air, water, and nutrients equally well.

During winter the texture of a soil can influence plant hardiness, as sandy earth often remains warmer than clay. Subtropical bulbs and tuberous plants like cannas, amaryllises, and gingers withstand many degrees of frost if planted in sand, as do many Mediterranean subshrubs; these same plants often succumb to winter rot in clays that lie cold and damp. Sandy ground also seems to improve hardening to cold; where they are marginally frost-hardy, oleander, rosemary, California fan palm (*Washingtonia filifera*), and pindo palm (*Butia capitata*) succeed in gardens with light, sandy soils yet freeze nearby in heavy clay. This effect probably relates to the greater warmth and dryness of sand but may also reflect improved hardening in the fast-draining soil and greater availability of minerals such as potassium, important for plant hardiness yet easily tied up in clays.

Plants adapted to life in naturally drought-prone soils often show distinctive character with small, slender, or thickened, hardened foliage; this helps pines, post oaks (*Quercus stellata*), blackjack oaks (*Quercus marilandica*), St. Johns worts (*Hypericum* spp.), blue stars (*Amsonia* spp.), and hollies (*Ilex* spp.) survive droughts common on fast-draining sandy soils in eastern America. An Afrikaner

nickname for plants common to poor, sandy soils in South Africa—*fynbos*, literally "fine bush"—aptly describes the typical reedy or heathlike character of native vegetation in that similarly drought-prone region. Frequently equipped with gray, felted foliage, several shrubby members of the mint family show adaptation to humus-poor soils and dry situations: in nature species of *Salvia*, *Lavandula*, *Agastache*, *Perovskia*, *Phlomis*, and *Stachys* are often denizens of rocky embankments and other harsh habitats; they generally indicate a droughty, mineral soil beneath.

By contrast, plants of moist earth, including many tall grasses and perennials like compass plants (*Silphium* spp.), coneflowers (*Rudbeckia* spp.), Joe Pye weeds (*Eutrochium* spp.), and goldenrods (*Solidago* spp.) often present an abundance of coarse foliage. Trees growing in deep, moist soil rise straight and tall, contrasting with those in thin, dry ground, which become crooked and craggy. In adapting to soil and climate, plants change form; thereby they help interpret the mood of a place, something they may bring with them into gardens. In other instances plants assume a new aspect when cultivated away from their native haunts: the windswept cypresses of California's Monterey peninsula, *Cupressus macrocarpa*, say as much about their seaside habitats as their inheritance; planted elsewhere these trees assume upright forms like a common juniper, losing their romantic horizontal character.

Where an individual plant comes from genetically—its provenance—often proves critical for garden adaptability. Red maples (*Acer rubrum*), known to many as denizens of damp birch- and spruce-filled woods in Canada and the frosty Northeast, also range through the mixed temperate forests of eastern America south to the subtropical Gulf Coast and all the way down through Florida to the near-tropical Everglades, sharing habitat with palms and bromeliads. The varied populations within this vast range have radically different climate adaptations; these and other similarly wide-ranging species need to be selected for gardens accordingly, not simply by botanical name. Eastern redbuds, for instance, are small flowering trees native mostly to the south that can be damaged by subzero temperatures, yet

Found on nutrient-deprived sandy soils, grasslike restios (Restionaceae), feathery heaths (*Erica* spp.), and exotically whorled, shrubby *Protea* and *Leucodendron* spp. create the distinctive texture of South African *fynbos*.

LEFT Acid yellows and pinks predominate in *fynbos* flowers. Fernkloof Reserve, Western Cape, Republic of South Africa.

ABOVE Tiny, pinkish heath blossoms and tawny seedheads of restios glow in backlighting on the Great Swartberg. Western Cape, Republic of South Africa.

Opulently broad foliage typifies plants of rich, moist soil and steady, temperate climate.

ABOVE Giant butterbur and ferns fill waterlogged soil near the edge of a pond. *Petasites japonicus*, Longwood Gardens, Kennett Square, Pennsylvania.

LEFT Fresh green North American native *Darmera peltata* (syn. *Peltiphyllum peltatum*) contrasts with the bronze tone of Asian *Rodgersia podophylla* 'Rotlaub'. Royal Horticultural Society Garden at Wisley, Surrey, England.

a few ultra-hardy populations from the Midwest include thoroughly adaptable trees for northern gardens. Soil preferences also vary within a species; butterfly weed (*Asclepias tuberosa*), commonly associated with sandy ground, occurs locally on clay in parts of the Midwest. Spicebush (*Lindera benzoin*) and witch hazel (*Hamamelis virginiana*), typical of acid woods in eastern North America, thrive on limestone soils in a few central Texas counties. Although visually similar, these discrete populations inherit different adaptabilities for gardens.

The alternative to matching a garden's plants to its soils and exposures—heedlessly installing plantings with little understanding of local conditions—seems like an obvious error. Nevertheless, it remains a common approach among both horticulturists and landscape designers. For some, the ideal of "making things grow" is hard to relinquish, an attitude fed by a cherished presumption that the

Damp spring snow creates a moment of beauty, coating early blossoms of an eastern redbud. This widespread North American species has a range of hardiness; northern ecotypes shake off late spring snows with indifference, while a southern clone may suffer damage. *Cercis canadensis*, northern Colorado.

"right" soil mix, protective structure, irrigation system, or chemical additive can be called upon to resolve any garden challenge. Soil tests often recommended and performed by state agricultural extension services underscore this production-oriented philosophy: they generally provide reports based on an assumed crop, usually vegetables or lawn grass, or perhaps hungry annual flowers. As a result, they recommend adding amendments, nitrogen fertilizers, and perhaps sulfur or lime to "correct deficiencies." A report that instead listed plants adapted to these so-called deficiencies—also known as local soil conditions—would be of greater value to many gardeners.

BIG- AND BOLD-LEAVED PLANTS

Most plants listed here prefer average soil moisture; a few relish consistently moist, even boggy conditions. A large number of plants native to the tropics offer bold foliage but are not included here, as few succeed outside frost-free climates. Also, bold-leaved plants requiring dry conditions such as agaves, mulleins, and *Salvia argentea* have been left off; many are included in "Power plants."

Acanthus mollis, *A.* 'Summer Beauty', bear's breech
Aesculus spp., buckeye, horse chestnut
Aleurites fordii, tung oil tree
Alocasia spp., elephant's ear
Alpinia zerumbet, shell ginger
Anemone tomentosa, *A. hupehensis*, *A.* ×*hybrida*, Japanese anemone
Angelica pachycarpa, Portuguese angelica
Aralia spp., Hercules club
Aristolochia durior, pipe vine
Asimina triloba, pawpaw
Aspidistra elatior, cast iron plant
Astilboides tabularis
Begonia grandis, hardy begonia
Bocconia frutescens, tree poppy
Brunnera macrophylla, Siberian forget-me-not
Bupthalmum speciosum (syn. *Telekia speciosa*)

Cacalia spp.
Caladium spp.
Canna spp.
Catalpa spp., Indian bean
Chorisia speciosa, floss silk tree
Clerodendron spp., glory bower
Colocasia spp., elephant's ear
Crambe spp., sea kale
Crinum spp.
Curcuma spp., hidden ginger
Cussonia paniculata, cabbage tree
Darmera peltata (syn. *Peltiphyllum peltatum*), umbrella leaf
Deinanthe caerulea
Diphylleia spp.
Ensete spp., hardy banana
Eriobotrya japonica, loquat
Farfugium japonicum 'Giganteum', giant groundsel
Fatsia japonica, Japanese aralia
Filipendula kamtschatica
Firmiana simplex, Chinese parasol tree
Glaucidium palmatum
Gunnera manicata
Hedychium spp., butterfly ginger
Hosta spp.
Hydrangea spp. (many)
Inula helenium
Inula magnifica
Kirengeshoma spp.
Ligularia spp.
Lysichiton spp., skunk cabbage
Macleaya spp., plume poppy

Magnolia acuminata, cucumber tree
Magnolia ashei
Magnolia delavayi
Magnolia grandiflora
Magnolia macrophylla
Magnolia officinalis
Manihot esculenta, tapioca
Melianthus major, honeybush
Musa spp., banana
Nelumbo spp., lotus
Nymphaea spp., water lily
Oplopanax horridus, devil's club
Paeonia spp., peony
Paulownia spp., empress tree
Petasites spp., butterbur
Philodendron bipinnatifidum (syn. *P. selloum*), split-leaf philodendron
Podophyllum spp., mayapple
Rheum spp., ornamental rhubarb
Ricinus communis, castor bean
Rodgersia spp.
Rudbeckia maxima, giant coneflower
Rohdea japonica, Manchu lily
Sabal minor, dwarf palmetto
Sanguinaria canadensis, blood root
Silphium perfoliatum, compass plant
Symphytum spp., comfrey
Tetrapanax papyrifer, rice paper plant
Trachystemon orientalis
Veratrum spp.
Xanthosoma spp., elephant's ear
Zingiber spp., pinecone ginger

PLANTS THAT ENJOY LIMY SOILS

These plants come from areas of the world with limy soils such as southern Europe, the Mediterranean basin, Mexico, and southern China. They do well in alkaline soils or those underlain with limestone or chalk. Most will thrive in neutral to moderately acidic conditions as well. Many desert plants not included in this list also prosper in alkaline soils.

Acantholimon spp., spikethrift
Acanthus spp., bear's breech
Acer grandidentatum, bigtooth maple
Acer griseum, paperbark maple
Acer semenovii, Turkestan maple
Acer tataricum, Tatarian maple
Adiantum capillus-veneris, Venus' maidenhair fern
Aethionema spp., stonecress
Anemone spp. (many), windflower
Anthemis spp., marguerite
Aquilegia canadensis, eastern columbine
Athyrium nipponicum 'Pictum', Japanese painted fern
Bauhinia lunareoides, Anacacho orchid tree
Buddleia spp. (many), butterfly bush
Buxus spp., boxwood
Ceratostigma willmottianum, Miss Willmott's plumbago
Cercis canadensis v. *texensis*, Texas redbud
Chamaerops humilis, Mediterranean fan palm
Chionanthus retusus, Chinese fringe tree
Cistus spp., rockrose
Clematis spp.
Cotinus spp., smoke tree
Cotoneaster buxifolius, grayleaf cotoneaster
Cotoneaster lacteus 'Parneyi'
Crocus goulimyi, Greek crocus

Cyclamen spp.
Cyrtomium falcatum, holly fern (often erroneously listed as acid-loving)
Cytisus battandieri, pineapple broom
Daphne spp. (many)
Dianthus spp. (many), pinks
Eremurus spp., foxtail lily
Festuca glauca, blue fescue
Fraxinus cuspidata, flowering ash
Fraxinus ornus, manna ash
Genista lydia, hardy dwarf broom
Gladiolus byzantinus, Byzantine gladiolus
Gypsophila spp., baby's breath
Hedera spp., ivy
Helleborus spp., hellebore
Hermodactylus tuberosa, widow iris
Heuchera americana, alum root
Iris bearded types, *I.* ×*hollandica*, *I. unguicularis*, *I. spuria*
Jasminum spp. (many), jasmine
Leucophyllum spp., ceniza
Lilium candidum, *L. formosanum*, *L. henryi*, *L. regale*, lily
Linum narbonense, *L. lewisii*, *L. perenne*, blue flax
Lupinus texensis, Texas bluebonnet
Melampodium leucanthemum, blackfoot daisy
Nannorrhops ritchieana, Mazari palm
Oenothera macrocarpa, Missouri evening primrose
Olea europaea, olive
Oncostemma peruviana (syn. *Scilla peruviana*), Cuban lily
Origanum spp., marjoram and oregano
Ornithogalum arabicum, star of Bethlehem
Osmanthus spp., tea olive
Otatea acuminata, Mexican weeping bamboo
Paeonia spp. (many), peony

Parrotia persica, Persian ironwood
Penstemon spp. (many)
Perovskia atriplifolia, Russian sage
Philadelphus spp., mock orange
Phillyrea angustifolia
Phlomis spp., Jerusalem sage
Pinus montezumae, Montezuma pine
Pinus pinea, Italian stone pine
Prunus sargentii, Sargent cherry
Punica granatum, pomegranate
Quercus buckleyi, Spanish oak
Quercus fusiformis, escarpment live oak
Quercus ilex, holm oak
Quercus muhlenbergii, chinquapin oak
Quercus polymorpha, Monterrey oak
Rhapidophyllum hystrix, needle palm
Rosmarinus officinalis, rosemary
Salvia spp. (many), sage
Sisyrinchium sp. 'Suwannee', blue-eyed grass
Sophora secundiflora, Texas mountain laurel
Sparteum junceum, Spanish broom
Sternbergia lutea, autumn daffodil
Syringa spp., lilac
Taxodium mucronatum, Montezuma cypress
Tecoma stans var. *angustata*, yellow bells
Tetraneuris scaposa (syn. *Hymenoxis scaposa*)
Teucrium fruticans 'Azureum', silver germander
Thelypteris kunthii, southern shield fern
Trachycarpus fortunei, windmill palm
Tulipa bakeri, *T. batalinii*, *T. clusiana*, *T. humilis*, species tulips
Ungnadia speciosa, Mexican buckeye
Veronica spp. (many), speedwell
Viburnum spp. (many)
Vitex agnus-castus, chaste tree

PLANTS THAT THRIVE IN ACID SOILS

These plants—from areas of the world with heavily leached, low-pH, often humus-rich soils over nutrient-poor rock such as sandstone—thrive in acidic conditions. They are not as adaptable to a wide range of soils as are the lime-lovers.

Acer spp. (many, including *Acer palmatum*), maple
Agarista spp.
Andromeda polifolia, bog rosemary
Anigozanthus spp., kangaroo paw
Arctostaphylos uva-ursi, bearberry
Calluna vulgaris, heather
Calopogon tuberosus, grass pink orchid
Calycanthus floridus, sweetshrub
Calypso bulbosa, lady slipper
Camellia spp.
Cassiope spp.
Celmisia spp., silver daisy
Chimaphila spp., pipsissewa
Chamaecyparis spp., false cypress
Chamaedaphne spp.
Clethra alnifolia, sweet pepper bush, summersweet
Cliftonia monophylla, pink-flowered titi
Clinopodium spp., Georgia savory
Comptonia peregrina, sweet fern
Conradina spp., Florida rosemary
Cornus canadensis, bunchberry
Cyananthus lobatus
Cyrilla racemiflora, titi
Cytisus scoparius, Scots broom
Daboecia spp.
Darlingtonia californica, pitcher plant
Deinanthe caerulea
Dierama spp. (many), African harebell

Diosma, breath of heaven
Elliottia racemosa
Empetrum spp.
Enkianthus spp.
Epigaea repens, trailing arbutus
Epimedium spp. (many)
Erica spp. (except *E. carnea*), heath
Eucryphia glutinosa
Fothergilla gardenii, dwarf fothergilla
Galax aphylla, galax
Gardenia augusta
Gaultheria (syn. *Pernettya*) spp., wintergreen
Grevillea spp.
Halesia spp., silverbell
Hamamelis spp. (many)
Houstonia caerulea (syn. *Hedyotis caerulea*), bluets
Hudsonia spp.
Hypericum spp. (many, especially *Hypericum frondosum*)
Ilex spp. (many), holly, winterberry, inkberry
Illicium spp., star anise
Itea spp., sweetspire
Ixora spp.
Jasione spp.
Juniperus communis, mountain juniper
Kalmia spp., mountain laurel, sheep laurel
Kirengeshoma spp.
Ledum groenlandicum
Leiophyllum buxifolium
Leptotaenia purpurea
Leucothoe spp., fetterbush
Lilium spp. (many, especially *L. auratum*, *L. speciosum*)

Linnaea borealis, twin flower
Lithodora diffusa 'Grace Ward'
Loiseleuria procumbens
Luma apiculata
Lyonia spp., fetterbush
Magnolia virginiana, sweet bay
Mitchella repens, partridgeberry
mosses (many genera and species)
Myrica cerifera, Southern wax myrtle
Myrica pensylvanica, bayberry
Narcissus bulbocodium (syn. *Bulbocodium vernum*), hoop peticoat
Osmunda spp., royal fern, common fern
Ourisia spp.
Phyllodoce spp.
Pieris spp., andromeda
Pinus spp. (many, especially *P. parvifolia*, *P. strobus*)
Polypodium spp., polypody fern
Pteridium aquilinum, common brackenfern
Pyrola spp.
Quercus palustris, pin oak
restios (*Chondropetalum*, *Thamnochortus*, *Elegia*), cape reeds
Rhododendron spp. (including azaleas)
Sarracenia spp., pitcher plant
Serenoa repens, saw palmetto
Shortia galacifolia
Skimmia japonica
Stewartia spp.
Styrax japonica, Japanese snowbell
Tanakaea spp.
Vaccinium spp., blueberry, huckleberry
Xanthorrhiza simplicissima, yellowroot
Zenobia pulverulenta, zenobia

Drought and extremes

Editorial cartoonist Lou Erickson once quipped that "gardening requires lots of water—most of it in the form of perspiration." Beyond this, wherever annual rainfall is less than thirty inches gardeners usually want to ensure some additional source of water, even if plantings are composed of species adapted to dry conditions. Severe droughts visit all regions periodically, challenging the survival of plants, even natives. Watering rewards gardeners almost instantly, extending planting possibilities and prolonging blooming seasons. Even under moist conditions new plants invariably demand irrigation until rooted out and established, sometimes for as long as a year or more for large tree specimens, evergreens, or slow-growing plants. In most instances a simple hose and sprinkler will do the job, or soaker hoses or an aboveground drip system can be laid out. During dry spells the gardener can position these as needed to supplement rainfall and can move them to stations around a garden to provide coverage. Especially thirsty subjects such as lawns may require more abundant water, but gardens that receive an inch of moisture every two weeks or so, either from rainfall or hose, will sustain most established plants if these are appropriately matched to the site.

Garden owners often lack time to supervise such interventions and therefore elect to install permanent in-ground systems to supply water. These irrigate gardens quickly and efficiently, and can be broken into zones to partly address the differing water needs of varied plantings. In most instances they rely on programmable time clocks to repeat waterings on a fixed schedule, although some systems employ moisture sensors as an alternative. This seems like an ideal solution for watering a garden, and if thoughtfully managed it can be. Yet for varied reasons these systems often prove to be a false promise.

In our experience, interesting, diverse gardens rarely come into being if they rely entirely on automated irrigation. The supposed permanence of an in-ground system is at odds with the dynamic spirit of a garden, for plants grow and change shape, blocking sprinklers and emitters, and gardeners rethink and redirect plantings, changing beds

and compositions, thereby altering water needs. Planting new bulbs, shrubs, or perennials becomes a strategic nightmare when irrigation pipes break with every shovel set in the ground. Worse, the seductive automation of the time clock disconnects gardeners from an interventionist role; without consciously directing irrigation, gardeners lose their sense of participation and responsibility for plants and their connection to the rhythms of the climate. Irrigating by the calendar rather than by observed need wastes precious water and ignores the varied capacities and demands of plants. Some plants—cool-season bulbs like crocuses, tulips, and certain daffodils, for instance—often perish in gardens with sprinkler systems simply because they are not allowed to dry sufficiently during summer dormancy; this is especially problematic for gardens in warm regions where rot-inducing fungi are most active. If water or underlying soil and rock include dissolved minerals, repeated irrigation can raise pH and salt levels by bringing these to the surface, causing humus to break down and disappear prematurely, and even poisoning plants. At best, rather than enabling diverse plantings, an automated supply of water alters garden conditions to favor one group of plants at the expense of another.

Plant heroes really do exist for almost any garden challenge, whether water regime, soil, climate, or exposure, yet adapted varieties too are mortal and cannot be expected to assure success. Unforeseen changes and outright disasters occur in gardens, as in life. A windstorm may take out several trees that provide shade for other plants growing beneath them, ruining an entire planting; an unseasonable freeze can catch long-established shrubs when not fully hardened, killing them outright, even though they have given years of faithful service; unexpected rains may flood beds for weeks, drowning roots and stimulating bacteria and fungi so that perennials collapse in soggy, rotted masses. Nature, our partner in creating gardens, is both fickle and uncompromising.

Lauren created a garden in the northern Colorado foothills, consciously emphasizing a diverse array of adapted plants, many of them natives. The majority grew well on the

In a cow pasture, heirloom daffodils surviving from a long-departed garden flourish in natural cycles of wet and dry. Like many cool-season bulbs, this double-flowered variety—known colloquially as butter and eggs—commonly perishes in nearby gardens supplied with automated irrigation. *Narcissus ×incomparabilis* 'Sulphur Phoenix', northeastern Texas.

site without any added irrigation, but three years after the initial planting an extended drought set in and over time this eventually caused the well for the house to fail. Water for human and animal consumption had to be hauled in; plants for the most part were left to fend for themselves. As spring arrived and the earth thawed, the soil in the garden moved hastily from barely moist to utterly dry as the protracted heat of summer set in. Over several seasons of ongoing rain deficit even native penstemons, eriogonums, and other "drought-resistant" species failed. This was an unforeseen challenge.

The garden certainly needed new plant heroes that would survive and look good under its drier regime; just as important, the plantings had to strike a compromise between this parched world and the gardenmaker's visual ideals. A flower-filled garden just was not going to be possible at this point. Yet a number of species had survived and even thrived under these trying conditions; a lively textural composition was developing on its own, albeit more brown than green at times. More clumps of glistening dryland grasses like Mexican feather grass (*Nassella tenuissima*), European *Stipa pennata*, and Mount Atlas fescue (*Festuca mairei*) were recruited to show off their lithe, flowing silhouettes against masonry walls, lichen-covered boulders, and paving stones, along with the reedy stems of blue jointfir (*Ephedra equisetina*). Ruggedly xeric shrubs provided texture: mountain desert sage (*Salvia pachyphylla*), with silvery foliage and long-lasting purplish bracts around small

Relying primarily on texture rather than floral color, a garden continues in beauty through protracted drought.

ABOVE Boulders rest among succulents, grasses, and xeric subshrubs to sustain this garden's appeal. California poppies and hummingbird trumpet add a few notes of color, as does the shining blond head of son Russell. *Zauschneria garrettii, Yucca baccata, Ballota pseudodictamnus, Caryopteris ×clandonensis, Artemisia versicolor, Fallugia paradoxa, Nassella tenuissima*; in pots *Echinocactus grusonii, Yucca thompsoniana*, authors' garden, northern Colorado.

RIGHT Amos the cat stalks through sere *Stipa capillata, Verbascum bombyciferum, Salvia officinalis* 'Minima', *Atriplex canescens, Fallugia paradoxa*, and coppery *Agastache rupestris*. Authors' garden, northern Colorado.

blue flowers; manzanita (*Arctostaphylos* spp.), with sprawling red stems bearing elliptical olive evergreen leaves; and Apache plume (*Fallugia paradoxa*), with willowy form and frothy seed heads to catch the afternoon light. Plants that added interest as they entered premature drought-induced dormancy were also key to this design; annuals and biennials like woolly mullein (*Verbascum bombyciferum*) and *Nigella damascena*—called love-in-a-mist in its flowering phase but known as devil-in-a-bush when its inflated horn-bearing seedpods ripen—gave as much through attractive form as they dried and died in midsummer as through their showy but fast-fading blooms earlier in the year. In this new vision for the garden, beauty continued through drought, redefined almost entirely in textural terms.

After three years, as quickly as it had begun, the drought ended and again native penstemons and eriogonums were able to grow and flower in the garden; it was time for new plant champions to make the best of new opportunities.

Slope

Another challenge plants help tackle is slope. While relatively shallow inclines offer few problems and can even be managed as lawns—as long as they receive adequate moisture—steep grades are inherently difficult to maintain and deserve special treatment. Irrigating any significant slope poses problems unless it is terraced so that water pools and percolates; stabilizing a steep rise often demands hard materials—stone, brick, concrete, or wire-enclosed gabions—as well as green plants.

Aesthetically, grade changes are among the most influential features in a garden; they have the power to establish flow and definition between spaces and offer some of the best opportunities to show off plants at or above eye level. People usually perceive flat or nearly flat garden spaces as an outdoor room of sorts or a place to be, even if only casually defined with turf, low ground cover, and surrounding plantings. On the other hand, one may invest in paving, walls, grand stairways, and other obvious architectural improvements, yet a sloping area still feels like a transitional space—a place to move through or pass by. In

response to these inherent moods of land and the practicalities of garden management, designs on sloping ground tend to evolve into alternations between relatively level destinations and inclined transitions, with particular plants occupying slopes and helping define and emphasize their character.

Plants with rosette forms look especially at home on slopes and these regularly colonize such places in nature. Hostas, heucheras, and Christmas ferns, for instance, naturally inhabit moist, shaded embankments in the wild; in gardens they can do the same, displaying bold whorls of foliage against sloping ground or, if an embankment has been partly stabilized with boulders, nested between stones to give leafy, naturalistic cover. If closely planted these perennials create a lush, layered effect, almost like shingles on a roof.

On a nearly vertical, rocky but shaded north-facing ledge in Austin, Scott created a planting using a gallery of rosette-forming plants native to the mountains of northeastern Mexico. Shining green specimens of nearly thornless *Agave mitis* (syn. *Agave celsii*) grow interspersed among drought-tolerant ladder brake ferns (*Pteris vittata*), dwarf cycads (*Dioon angustifolium*), and sheets of trailing succulents—Palmer's stonecrop (*Sedum palmeri*) and velvet creeper (*Tradescantia sillamontana*)—all of which occur on similar dry, shaded cliffs in the wild. The bold forms of the agave, cycad, and fern rosettes help measure and show off the small escarpment, making it feel larger and more impressive, while the pendant stems of sedum and velvet creeper sheet over the rocks to provide a green veneer, heightening the sense of verticality. An added bonus for this hard-to-irrigate site is that these inhabitants get by on little water.

Plants with arching leaves, hanging flowers, or weeping stems and branches make ideal treatments for slopes, recalling the grace of wild vegetation. Gently curving shoots of Solomon's seal (*Polygonatum* spp.) sprout at intervals from creeping rootstocks; likewise, glossy green, arched leaves of crested Japanese iris (*Iris japonica*) rise in discretely spaced fans from wiry, fast-spreading roots. Such colonial

plants bring lush greenery to shady hillsides, creating processions of parallel, seemingly moving forms that cascade downslope. Vertical walls or ledges offer choice perspectives for experiencing pendant blooms of vining wisterias, hanging clusters of ripening grapes, or the down-turned, urn-shaped flowers of 'Rooguchi', a blue-toned hybrid of *Clematis integrifolia*. Less severe inclines show off nodding blossoms of flowering maple (*Abutilon* spp.) and Lenten rose (*Helleborus* ×*hybridus*), delicate, down-facing sprays of barrenwort (*Epimedium* spp.), dangling racemes of Chinese indigo (*Indigofera incarnata*), or the ground-level flowering cones of shampoo ginger (*Zingiber zerumbet*) that might otherwise remain hidden under overly exuberant foliage. Sprawling shrubs—jasmines, forsythia, winter honeysuckles (*Lonicera fragrantissima* and *L.* ×*standishii*), bush clovers (*Lespedeza* spp.), and many cotoneaster species—that may seem coarse or unruly on level ground come into their

Like bright green shuttlecocks, repeated rosettes of ostrich fern reveal their striking form on a shaded slope. Matteuccia struthiopteris, Chanticleer, Wayne, Pennsylvania.

own on slopes, where their bowed stems suggest movement in response to the falling terrain. Positioned at or near the crest of a ledge, plants with trailing habits such as prostrate rosemary, low-spreading junipers, weeping selections of spruce and pine, coral blow (*Russelia* spp.), beargrass (*Nolina* spp.), and many *Puya* species drape branches or leaves downward, emphasizing and instantly aging even a modest cliff.

Plants that seek rocky, sloping habitats in nature, such as many cushion-forming alpines and succulents, can give even shallow inclines the feel of a wild mountainside if convincingly placed in a garden. Their subliminal associations with craggy hillsides and mountaintops suggest a

ROSETTE-FORMING PLANTS

The following plants provide symmetrical rosettes of foliage that lend striking form to plantings, especially when viewed on slopes or from above.

Aeonium spp.
Agave spp., century plant
Aloe spp.
Beschorneria spp.
bromeliads (many; hardier types include *Dyckia* spp. and *Puya* spp.)

Carex spp. (some), sedge
cycads
Cyrtomium falcatum, holly fern
Dasylirion spp., sotol
Dryopteris filix-mas, male fern
Echeveria spp., hen and chicks
Eryngium venustum (and others)
Graptopetalum spp., ghost plant
Heuchera spp., coral bells
Hosta spp.

Manfreda spp.
Matteuccia struthiopteris, ostrich fern
Polystichum acrostichoides, Christmas fern
Polystichum setiferum, soft shield fern
Rohdea japonica, Manchu lily
Sempervivum spp., houseleek
Tupistra spp.
Verbascum spp., mullein
Yucca spp.

LEFT The succulent rosettes of agaves often colonize semi-arid cliffsides in nature. *Agave inaequidens* subsp. *barrancensis*, Durango, Mexico.

ABOVE Luxuriating on a rocky, shaded ledge, bright green agaves mix with ladder brake ferns and velvet creeper. *Agave mitis* (syn. *Agave celsii*), *Pteris vittata*, *Tradescantia sillamontana*, Austin, Texas, Ogden design.

precipice when very little change in terrain is actually present. A simple composition using creeping mats of moss phlox (*Phlox subulata*) mingled among half-buried boulders alone may create the feel of a sunny mountain slope. On a reduced scale, just a trough filled with sedums and houseleeks (*Sempervivum* spp.) among jagged stones can transport a viewer to miniature Alps.

Strongly vertical trees and upright-growing plants enhance perspective, giving the eye a way to measure rise and fall of terrain. In our Colorado garden a shallow slope planted with dwarf conifers and cushion-forming rock plants among sandstone boulders instantly became more prominent with the addition of several sapling oaks, apples, and flowering plums nearby. The slender trunks of the young trees provide linear sentinels that repeat up- and downslope next to the rock garden; this creates visual definition for an otherwise hardly noticeable change in elevation. When we first moved in, undifferentiated lawn covered this portion of the garden and the vast sea of turf made the natural slope nearly invisible.

Distinctive plant forms complement slopes and walls.

ABOVE An assortment of dwarf and cushionlike perennials gives a small garden stairway the feel of a floral carpet. *Dianthus ×allwoodii*, *Aethionema schistosum*, *Sideritis scardica*, *Festuca glauca*, *Oenothera caespitosa*, dwarf bearded iris, *Nepeta mussinii*, *Scutellaria supina*, northern Colorado, Ogden design.

ABOVE RIGHT Dangling, fragrant blossoms of Chinese wisteria soften a limestone wall. *Wisteria sinensis*, Austin, Texas.

PLANTS WITH WEEPING OR PENDULOUS HABIT

This is not a complete listing but a good representation of plant species available for weeping or pendulous effects in the garden.

Abies alba (several selections), white fir

Acacia pendula, shoestring acacia

Acer palmatum (many selections), Japanese maple

Aesculus glabra 'Klein's Weeping'

Albizia julibrissin 'Pendula', mimosa

Alnus incana 'Pendula', alder

Betula nigra 'Summer Cascade', river birch

Betula pendula 'Dalecarlica', 'Tristis', 'Youngii', 'Crimson Frost', European birch

Buddleia alternifolia, silverleaf butterfly bush

Caragana arborescens 'Lorbergii', 'Walker'

Carpinus betulus 'Pendula', hornbeam

Cedrus atlantica 'Glauca Pendula', blue Atlas cedar

Cedrus deodara (several selections), deodar cedar

Cedrus libani 'Pendula', cedar of Lebanon

Celtis sinensis 'Green Cascade', Chinese hackberry

Cercidiphyllum japonicum 'Pendula', katsura tree

Cercis canadensis 'Covey', 'Lavender Twist', eastern redbud

Cercis canadensis var. *texensis* 'Traveller', Texas redbud

Chamaecyparis lawsoniana (several selections)

Cotoneaster apiculatus (several selections)

Cotoneaster lacteus 'Parneyi', red clusterberry

Cupressus arizonica 'Raywood's Weeping', Arizona cypress

Fagus sylvatica 'Pendula', European beech

Forestiera angustifolia 'Weeping', desert olive

Ilex myrtifolia 'Woodlander's Weeping'

Ilex vomitoria 'Folsom Weeping', yaupon

Jasminum floridum, Italian jasmine

Jasminum mesneyi, primrose jasmine

Jasminum nudiflorum, winter jasmine

Juniperus communis 'Oblonga Pendula', mountain juniper

Juniperus flaccida, Mexican drooping juniper

Juniperus rigida, Korean weeping juniper

Juniperus scopulorum 'Tolleson's Weeping', Rocky Mountain juniper

Juniperus virginiana 'Pendula', eastern red cedar

Laburnum alpinum 'Pendulum', golden chain tree

Larix decidua 'Pendula', European larch

Larix kaempferi 'Diana', Japanese larch

Malus 'Louisa', 'Molten Lava', 'Red Jade', 'Royal Fountain', 'White Cascade' (and other selections), crabapple

Morus alba 'Chaparral', 'Pendula', fruitless mulberry

Muhlenbergia dumosa, bamboo muhly grass

Nolina lindheimeriana, devil's shoestring

Nolina texana, beargrass

Parrotia persica 'Pendula', Persian ironwood

Picea abies 'Frohburg', 'Inversa', 'Pendula', Norway spruce

Picea breweriana

Picea glauca 'Pendula', white spruce

Picea omorika 'Pendula', Serbian spruce

Picea orientalis 'Pendula', oriental spruce

Picea pungens 'Glauca Pendula', 'Procumbens', Colorado spruce

Pinus densiflora 'Pendula', Japanese red pine

Pinus flexilis 'Glauca Pendula', limber pine

Pinus pinceana, weeping pinyon

Pinus strobus 'Pendula', eastern white pine

Pinus sylvestris 'Albyn Prostrata', 'Hillside Creeper', Scots pine

Prunus subhirtella 'Pendula' (and others), Higan cherry

Prunus yedoensis 'Perpendens', Yoshino cherry

Pseudotsuga menziesii 'Glauca Pendula', 'Graceful Grace', douglas fir

Pyrus salicifolia 'Pendula', willowleaf pear

Rhus trilobata 'Autumn Amber', three-leaf sumac

Robinia pseudoacacia 'Monophylla Pendula', black locust

Rosa banksiae, Lady Banks' rose

Rosmarinus officinalis (many weeping forms), rosemary

Salix alba 'Tristis', golden weeping willow

Salix babylonica, weeping willow

Salix caprea 'Kilmarnock', pussy willow

Salix ×*elegantissima*

Salix ×'Prairie Cascade'

Salix purpurea 'Pendula', arctic blue willow

Salix repens 'Boyd's Pendulous'

Sequoiadendron giganteum 'Pendulum', giant sequoia

Sophora japonica 'Pendula', scholar tree

Sorbus aucuparia 'Pendula', European mountain ash

Styrax japonica 'Carillon', 'Pendula', Japanese snowbell

Taxodium distichum 'Cascade Falls, 'Pendens' (and others), bald cypress

Thuja occidentalis 'Pendula', arborvitae

Tsuga canadensis 'Pendula', 'Sargentii' (and others), eastern hemlock

Ulmus alata 'Lace Parasol', winged elm

Ulmus glabra 'Camperdownii', Camperdown elm

Xanthocyparis nootkatensis (syn. *Chamaecyparis nootkatensis*) 'Pendula', Alaska false cypress

Flowering pear trees arch in search of sunlight, bringing a responsive, lively sense of nature to a city street. *Pyrus calleryana*, Boston, Massachusetts.

Overbuilt spaces

Perhaps the most common garden challenges are those that spring from architecture and its unanticipated consequences: narrow, poorly drained, or arid spaces between paving and buildings; places near roads and drives where an expanse of concrete creates a harsh, unfriendly environment; positions near extravagantly large structures that visually overwhelm landscapes. Plants are needed to redeem these man-made spaces, to stand up to the rigors of life in a mostly artificial environment, to soften the effects of architecture on the outdoors. Somehow green heroes need to establish a garden spirit within an overbuilt setting, returning a balance of power to nature.

Such challenging sites commonly come about because no one bothered to consider the needs of a garden when buildings and paving were planned and installed. Sometimes this oversight happens even in professionally planned landscapes; when it does, it may call for both architectural and horticultural responses. Lauren was once asked to design a romantic wedding garden within an area where gazebos, paving, walls, and water features had already been installed according to a landscape architect's master plan. These sweeping, mostly architectural schemes sometimes paint with a broad brush and may omit important details for plants; in this case the master plan left just a few narrow strips of soil for the new "garden." Adrift in a sea of walkways, patios, and decorative architecture, the plantings—to be composed mostly of flowering perennials—needed to be fairly tall to be noticed, something the small size of the beds would not accommodate. Under the circumstances it actually made sense to place several fanciful colored columns within the skimpy planting areas to fortify perspective and give depth to the garden. A bold mix of species with warm, bright colors and striking textures rather than a demure, clichéd "romantic" palette of fluffy pastel plants plays off these columns to further empower the garden. This creates a composition vibrant enough to stand up to and engage its overbuilt surroundings.

Sometimes unfriendly garden spaces are inherited from a previous function; this situation may also warrant an architectural assist for plants. For instance, a concrete slab foundation left from a former building covered the soil of a walled area at Wave Hill, a public garden in the Bronx. A series of troughs were added to create homes for a collection of miniature plants there. Leaving the concrete saved considerable expense and also retained a personal, roomlike atmosphere in the space. By focusing attention on an intimate scale, this design succeeds in bringing a garden experience to an otherwise harsh, wholly urbanized setting.

ABOVE Fanciful colored columns and bright-tinted flowers give a needed lift to stingily narrow borders in an overpaved public garden space. *Echinacea purpurea, Kniphofia* 'Alcazar', *Consolida regalis, Alcea rosea* 'Nigra', roses, Romantic Garden at Denver Botanic Gardens, Ogden design; column design by Little and Lewis.

LEFT Reclaiming the site of a former building as a garden, a collection of troughs filled with fascinating plant miniatures obscures the old concrete foundation. Wave Hill, Bronx, New York, Marco Polo Stufano design.

Tall plants with skinny profiles—
fastigiate in horticultural par-
lance—remediate overbuilt
spaces and add perspective
to narrow beds and borders.

ABOVE With Mediterranean flair,
a triad of Italian cypress joins
suckering agaves and masses
of self-seeding mullein to bring
architectural power to a sunny
slip of a bed sandwiched between
buildings and sidewalk. *Cupressus
sempervirens* 'Glauca', *Agave
asperrima*, *Verbascum thapsus*,
Ficus pumila, Hotel San José, Austin, Texas, Big Red Sun design.

ABOVE RIGHT A perimeter
planting takes on vertical potency
with tall, slender trees and
elegantly upright foxtail lilies.
Quercus robur 'Fastigiata', *Pinus
sylvestris* 'Fastigiata', *Juniperus
chinensis* 'Spartan', *Eremurus
robustus* hybrids, *Helictotrichon
sempervirens*, *Festuca mairei*,
Sesleria autumnalis, *Salvia
argentea*, *Oenothera fremontii*
'Shimmer', *Hemerocallis* 'Golden
Chimes', authors' garden,
Fort Collins, Colorado.

In cities, and with the popularity of new urbanist styles
now in suburbia as well, homes are placed close together,
creating a landscape dominated by buildings. The small
planting areas that remain call for bold vegetation that can
stand up to the dimensions of the architecture. Such limited spaces deserve especially rewarding plants and those
that can be experienced and appreciated at close range.

Tall, narrow (fastigiate) trees give a lift to overbuilt situations, and their powerful forms can be slipped into
restricted spaces, helping equal the strong lines of buildings. To balance with architecture, however, these formal-
looking plants need to be used in informal groupings.

COLUMNAR, FASTIGIATE, AND NARROWLY UPRIGHT PLANTS

The following list, while a good representation of plants available, is by no means complete. The species and genera included give an indication of which plants have the genetic tendency to produce narrow forms.

Acer platanoides (several selections), Norway maple

Acer pseudoplatanus (several selections), sycamore maple

Acer rubrum 'Scarlet Sentinel' (and others), red maple

Acer saccharum (several selections), sugar maple

Berberis thunbergii 'Helmond Pillar', 'Pow Wow', barberry

Betula pendula 'Fastigiata', upright European birch

Betula platyphylla 'Dakota Pinnacle', Japanese white birch

Buxus sempervirens 'Graham Blandy', 'Green Tower', 'National', boxwood

Caragana arborescens 'Sutherland'

Carpinus betulus 'Columnaris' (syn. 'Fastigiata'), 'Frans Fontaine', hornbeam

Cedrus atlantica 'Fastigiata', Atlas cedar

Chamaecyparis lawsoniana 'Columnaris' (and others), Lawson cypress

Chamaecyparis thyoides 'Andeleyensis'

Crataegus monogyna 'Stricta', hawthorn

Crataegus phaenopyrum 'Fastigiata', Washington hawthorn

Cryptomeria japonica (several selections)

Cupressus guadalupensis 'Greenlee's Blue Rocket', Guadalupe cypress

Cupressus sempervirens 'Stricta', Italian cypress

Fagus sylvatica 'Fastigiata', European beech

Ginkgo biloba 'Princeton Sentry'

Gleditsia triacanthos 'Columnaris', honey locust

Ilex crenata 'Jersey Pinnacle', 'Sentinel', 'Sky Pencil', Japanese holly

Ilex decidua 'Sentry', possumhaw holly

Ilex vomitoria 'Will Fleming', yaupon

Juniperus chinensis 'Spartan' (and others)

Juniperus communis 'Compressa', 'Hibernica' (and others), mountain juniper

Juniperus scopulorum 'Medora', 'Skyrocket', 'Woodward'

Juniperus virginiana 'Taylor' (and others), eastern red cedar

Koelreuteria paniculata 'Fastigiata', golden rain tree

Laburnum ×watereri 'Sunspire' (syn. 'Columnaris'), golden chain tree

Malus 'Velvet Pillar' (and others), crabapple

Metasequoia glyptostroboides 'Sheridan Spire', dawn redwood

Osmanthus heterophyllus 'Fastigiata', holly osmanthus

Parrotia persica 'Vanessa', Persian ironwood

Picea abies 'Cupressina', Norway spruce

Picea orientalis 'Gowdy', oriental spruce

Picea pungens 'Blue Totem', 'Iseli Fastigiate', Colorado spruce

Pinus cembra 'Chalet', Swiss stone pine

Pinus leucodermis 'Iseli Fastigiate', Bosnian pine

Pinus nigra 'Arnold Sentinel', Austrian pine

Pinus strobus 'Fastigiata', eastern white pine

Pinus sylvestris 'Fastigiata', 'Sentinel', Scots pine

Platycladus orientalis 'Sunshine', oriental arborvitae

Populus canescens 'Tower', silver poplar

Populus deltoides 'Tower', plains cottonwood

Populus nigra 'Italica', Lombardy poplar

Populus tremula 'Erecta', Swedish columnar aspen

Prunus sargentii 'Columnaris', Sargent cherry

Prunus serrulata 'Amanogawa', Japanese cherry

Pyrus calleryana 'Chanticleer', Callery pear

Quercus palustris 'Pringreen' (sold as Green Pillar), pin oak

Quercus robur 'Fastigiata', English oak

Rhamnus frangula 'Ron Williams' (sold as Fine Line), buckthorn

Sophora japonica 'Fastigiata', 'Princeton Upright', scholar tree

Sorbus aucuparia 'Fastigiata', European mountain ash

Sorbus thuringiaca 'Fastigiata', mountain ash

Taxodium ascendens 'Prairie Sentinel', pond cypress

Taxodium distichum 'Peve Minaret', bald cypress

Taxus baccata 'Bean Pole', 'Black Rod' (and many others), yew

Taxus ×media 'Hicksii', yew

Thuja occidentalis 'DeGroot's Spire' (and others), arborvitae

Tilia cordata 'Swedish Upright', littleleaf linden

Tsuga canadensis 'Kingsville', eastern hemlock

Xanthocyparis nootkatensis (syn. *Chamaecyparis nootkatensis*) 'Green Arrow', Alaska false cypress

Planting a line of matched cypresses, upright equally spaced palms, or columnar Swedish aspens simply extends and reiterates the linear effects of a building; adding a triad of cypresses in varied heights, a cluster of palms with gently arching trunks—some tall and some just sprouting—or a grove of the same columnar aspens staggered and spaced irregularly provides a counterpoint to the architecture that is equally strong in design yet imbued with the random spirit of nature.

Overbuilt spaces also invite gardeners to plant feathery bamboos. These tall, evergreen grasses effectively screen views for gardens even when restricted to quite narrow beds; their lush, lacy foliage helps temper the cacophony of the concrete jungle, creating rustling sounds as antidotes to the noise of city life. Ornamental stems (culms) and translucent leaves of bamboos can be readily exchanged for shabby views when planted to grow directly in front

of windows. Running bamboos whose culms rise vertically at intervals from the rootstock provide the most certain screens, remaining full to the ground; their perpetually questing roots are best restrained with underground barriers—metal roof flashing or a heavy vinyl liner succeeds for this purpose if installed to cant a few degrees away from the bamboo. Clumped bamboos are more easily managed in gardens and also create elegant plantings for narrow beds, but these types most often make better specimens than hedges or screens. They generally develop fountainlike arching silhouettes that bear most of their feathery foliage on the upper portions of the culms; the bases of these stems are often naked, providing less of a screen yet accentuating their polished surfaces.

Massive plantings of cacti and other succulents at the Getty Museum in Los Angeles are characterized by some critics as artificial, resembling whole fields transplanted

The upright stance and graceful carriage of bamboo makes it ideal for planting by a courtyard wall. Classical Chinese Garden, Portland, Oregon.

BAMBOOS

These bamboos are some of the most versatile available to North American gardeners.

Tropical clumping bamboos

(adapted to USDA zones 10–11)

Bambusa chungii, tropical blue bamboo

Bambusa lako, Timor black bamboo

Bambusa vulgaris 'Vittata', painted bamboo

Gigantochloa atroviolacea, tropical black bamboo

Himalayacalamus hookerianus, blue bamboo

Otatea glauca, Mayan silver bamboo

Semi-hardy clumping bamboos

(adaptable to USDA zones 8–11)

Bambusa beecheyana, beechey bamboo

Bambusa dolichomerithalla 'Green Stripe'

Bambusa multiplex (many selections), hedge bamboo

Bambusa oldhamii, giant timber bamboo

Bambusa textilis, weaver's bamboo, Wong Chuk bamboo

Bambusa textilis var. *gracilis*, graceful textile bamboo

Bambusa tuldoides, punting pole bamboo

Bambusa tuldoides 'Ventricosa', Buddha's belly bamboo

Otatea acuminata, Mexican weeping bamboo

Temperate clumping bamboos

These bamboos originate in the mountains of China, Burma, the Himalayas, and South Africa; new to American gardens, most can be expected to thrive in USDA zones 7–9. The hardy *Fargesia* species (noted individually) also succeed in USDA zone 6 and protected areas of zone 5 (minimum winter temperatures of −20 degrees F), but not all perform well in high summer heat.

Borinda angustissima

Borinda boliana

Borinda utilis

Fargesia denudata (USDA zone 5)

Fargesia dracocephala (USDA zone 5), dragon's head bamboo

Fargesia murielae (USDA zone 5), umbrella bamboo

Fargesia nitida (USDA zone 5), fountain bamboo

Fargesia robusta (USDA zone 6)

Fargesia sp. 'Rufa' (USDA zone 5)

Thamnocalamus tesselatus, bergbamboes

Running bamboos for screening

(adaptable to USDA zones 7–9 unless otherwise noted)

Chimonobambusa tumidissinoda (syn. *Qiongzhuea tumidissinoda*), Chinese walking stick

Hibanobambusa tranquillans 'Shiroshima'

Indocalamus tesselatus (syn. *Sasa tesselata*), large-leafed bamboo

Phyllostachys angusta, stone bamboo

Phyllostachys aurea 'Holochrysa', golden bamboo

Phyllostachys aurea 'Koi', green groove golden bamboo

Phyllostachys aureosulcata, yellow groove bamboo

Phyllostachys bambusoides, hardy timber bamboo

Phyllostachys bambusoides 'Castillon'

Phyllostachys bissetii (USDA zones 6–9), Bisset's bamboo

Phyllostachys decora (syn. *P. mannii*), beautiful bamboo

Phyllostachys dulcis, sweetshoot bamboo

Phyllostachys nigra, black bamboo

Phyllostachys nigra 'Henon'

Phyllostachys viridis 'Robert Young'

Phyllostachys vivax (USDA zones 6–9)

Pleioblastus linearis

Pseudosasa japonica, arrow bamboo

Sasa palmata (USDA zones 6–9)

Sasa veitchii, kuma zasa bamboo

Semiarundinaria fastuosa, Japanese palm tree bamboo, temple bamboo, Narihira bamboo

Shibataea kumasaca, kumasaca bamboo

Yushania anceps 'Pitt White' (not adapted to high summer heat and humidity)

from a cactus nursery. While this is a valid analogy for the vast beds, the succulents occupy wings and terraces that jut out to views of the Los Angeles basin. The strong forms and large numbers of columnar and barrel-shaped cacti, tree-like aloes, and spiky agaves are complementary to the modern travertine lines of the immense museum building and also in keeping with the distant views of the city, itself an equally artificial jumble of arresting shapes. Plants with sculptural qualities such as these often feel at home against masonry or in urban settings, recalling the walled garden traditions of Persia and the Mediterranean. Casting bold shadows, these spare plants create modernist compositions responsive to building-dominated landscapes; they almost seem to be architecture themselves. Nevertheless, in a heavily built environment their most potent effects spring from random placement and multiple sizes, for this suggests process and nature at work as well as people.

For truly large houses or buildings in wholly urban settings, the bigger their tree companions the better. Monumental species like sycamores, elms, and Canary Island date palms have long been favorites for softening the canyon effects of city streets. Such robust plantings help balance masses of architecture but are not always possible

or desirable in narrow quarters. Surprisingly, choosing fairly insubstantial plants with diaphanous foliage also works well, for these provide textural contrast, dissolving the overbearing effects of a building. Fine-textured trees like honeylocusts, mesquites, California pepper trees, and baldcypresses—long favored by architects who appreciate these plants' see-through qualities near their prized products, the buildings—offer airy counterpoints to overbuilt landscapes, casting feathered shadows that break up the otherwise imposing façades. These garden-friendly trees also allow sunlight to filter through their canopies, preserving planting possibilities where space and opportunity are limited.

Vines, espaliers, and trees or shrubs planted flush help cloak barren walls and create a sense of age and process; they immediately make a new building seem less raw. At the same time wall plantings modify their environment, providing cooling shade for masonry surfaces that absorb and reflect hot sun. This can be critical for creating livable outdoor spaces near buildings; unless shaded, they might remain too hot during warm months to become inviting gardens. Walls offer places to showcase plants; climbing roses, clematis, pyracantha, and unlimited varieties

LEFT With sculptural qualities equal to nearby travertine façades and distant city views, boldly grouped yet casually interfingered cacti and other succulents make winning companions to their modern architectural surroundings. *Cereus hildmannianus* var. *uruguayanus*, *Echinocactus grusonii*, *Agave americana* 'Marginata', *Senecio mandraliscae* (syn. *Kleinia mandraliscae*), J. Paul Getty Center, Los Angeles,

California, Olin Partnership design.

ABOVE Historically popular for its massive size, fast growth, and handsomely flaked bark, a London plane tree enlivens inert buildings and street in wintry Manhattan. Especially tolerant of city life, this hybrid sycamore is a cross between a North American and an Asian species. *Platanus ×acerifolia*, New York.

TREES AND SHRUBS WITH STRIKING BARK

Acacia karoo, whitethorn acacia

Acacia willardiana, birchbark acacia

Acer davidii, stripebark maple

Acer griseum, paperbark maple

Acer pensylvanicum, moosewood

Acer tegmentosum, Manchurian stripebark maple

Arbutus spp. (many), madrone

Betula spp. (many), birch

Caesalpinia paraguayensis

Carpinus caroliniana, ironwood

Chionanthus retusus, Chinese fringe tree

Chorisia insignis, white floss silk tree

Chorisia speciosa, floss silk tree

Clethra barbinervis, Japanese summersweet

Cornus alba, *C. sericea*, *C. stolonifera*, red-stem dogwood

Cupressus arizonica var. *glabra*, smooth Arizona cypress

Cytisus spp. (many), broom

Diospyros texana, Texas persimmon

Eucalyptus spp. (many), gum

Firmiana simplex, Chinese parasol tree

Genista spp. (many), broom

Heptacodium miconioides, seven sons tree

Jasminum nudiflorum, winter jasmine

Juniperus deppeana, alligator juniper

Kerria japonica

Lagerstroemia fauriei, Japanese crape myrtle

Lagerstroemia indica, crape myrtle

Myrsianthes fragrans, Simpson stopper

Myrtus communis, myrtle

Parkinsonia spp. (many), palo verde

Parrotia persica, Persian ironwood

Pinus bungeana, lacebark pine

Pinus densiflora, Japanese red pine

Pinus echinata, shortleaf pine

Pinus pinea, Italian stone pine

Platanus spp., sycamore

Poncirus trifoliata, trifoliate orange

Populus tremuloides, quaking aspen

Prunus maackii, *P. sargentii*, *P. serrula*, cherry

Pseudocydonia sinensis, Chinese quince

Salix spp. (many), willow

Sophora japonica, scholar tree

Spartium junceum, Spanish broom

Stewartia koreana, Korean stewartia

Stewartia monadelpha

Stewartia pseudocamellia, Japanese stewartia

Stewartia sinensis, Chinese stewartia

Syringa pekinensis, Chinese tree lilac

Syringa reticulata, Japanese tree lilac

Ulmus parvifolia, Chinese elm

Zelkova serrata

of flowering and fruiting vines as well as pliant shrubs or trees can be trained on wires or trellises to partially cover surfaces. The reflected heat and warmth of the walls, and sometimes the training itself, encourages bloom and fruit production for many species. Twiggy plants like evergreen mountain mahogany (*Cercocarpus ledifolius* var. *intricatus*), weeping yaupon (*Ilex vomitoria* 'Folsom Weeping'), and Harry Lauder's walking stick (*Corylus avellana* 'Contorta') make the most of spare walls; their intricate branching is often lost in leafier landscapes. Likewise the fat, furry buds of deciduous magnolias and the spidery winter blooms of witch hazels are never more telling than when backed by

masonry. Narrow beds near buildings and walls are places to show off slender or small upright-growing trees with ornamental bark: where adapted, Japanese crape myrtle (*Lagerstroemia fauriei*), rainbow gum (*Eucalyptus deglupta*), white-barked acacia (*Acacia willardiana*), hybrid western birch (*Betula* 'Rocky Mountain Splendor'), and paperbark maple (*Acer griseum*) make fine choices.

To soften effects of an oversized stone house on a sloping site in Austin, Scott combined several of these planting strategies. Perched adjacent to a plunging street, the villa-style building had been romantically aged by distressing doors, lintels, balusters, and gates; the garden adopted

Colorful walls invite dramatic planting.

OPPOSITE LEFT Ribbony multicolored bark of rainbow gum and variegated leaves of dracaena play off a brightly colored wall. *Eucalyptus deglupta, Dracaena reflexa* 'Song of India', Naples Botanical Garden, Florida.

OPPOSITE RIGHT Coolly sculptural gray-green cacti contrast with the saturated warmth of a red wall. *Opuntia ficus-indica, Cereus hildmannianus* var. *uruguayanus* 'Spiral', *Tecoma* 'Orange Jubilee', *Macfadyena unguis-cati, Lantana montevidensis*, Tucson, Arizona.

Even in close quarters, a few plants can be found to soften walls and create gardens.

ABOVE A brick wall and much of a patio disappear behind a luxuriant floral cloak of Japanese climbing hydrangea. *Schizophragma hydrangeoides*, Ed Rasmussen garden, Fort Calhoun, Nebraska.

ABOVE RIGHT Flowing tussocks of Japanese forest grass, swirling ivies, and a potful of mother-in-law's tongue bring foliar sophistication to a barren urn and skimpy courtyard bed. *Hakonechloa macra* 'Aureola', *Hedera helix* 'Buttercup', *Sansevieria trifasciata*, Chanticleer, Wayne, Pennsylvania.

a similar slightly disheveled theme, as if it had been partly abandoned and allowed to overgrow an old estate compound. A massive stone parking court created ten-foot walls along the street with little room for planting; in response, a series of terraces and a rubbly dry-stack stone wall were devised and added to front the court. These retain rough earth and random plantings of crape myrtles, pomegranates, fragrant roses, jasmines, shrubby palms, sprawling cotoneasters, and varied plants with arching habits. Vines like *Parthenocissus* sp. 'Hacienda Creeper', Lady Banks' rose, and orange crossvine (*Bignonia capreolata* 'Tangerine Beauty') clamber over balustrades and up walls, while feathery-leafed Montezuma cypresses flank a large wooden gate, softening the garden's exterior stone walls. A key plant for the design—a massive Mexican sycamore—grows next to the street even though some of its roots had to be shoe-horned into a narrow space partly over concrete. This fast-growing, adaptable tree accepts disturbed soils and thrives in this position where other species would have failed; it gives shade to the vast, stone-surfaced parking court and, as important, introduces height, mass, and perspective to further shrink and age the house.

Herbivores

Drought, steep slopes, and the trials of urban living seem like small challenges when compared to persistent threats from resident herbivores. Deer, elk, moose, and their smaller but no less destructive co-conspirators rabbits, voles, and gophers can make creating a garden especially frustrating. Many remedies on the market purport to deter these creatures if applied as periodic sprays, but such repetitive, short-lived solutions are as unsustainable and burdensome to gardenmakers as committing to plantings of acid-loving plants over chalk. Fencing (or for burrowing pests, buried caging) is more likely to deter these mammals over the long term but can be expensive to install over large areas and challenging to integrate aesthetically, and may be prohibited in some communities. For large gardens New Zealand–style livestock fencing is one of the least obtrusive options and is also relatively economical. Cats are effective in patrolling many smaller interlopers.

The easiest response is to choose plants that allow a garden to coexist with these herbivores. Contrary to popular belief, most of these animals are browsers rather than grazers. Unlike domestic horses, cattle, sheep, and goats, who relish both grasses and forbs, native wildlife customarily leaves grassy plants alone. This permits a vast array of heroic and beautiful grasses to populate deer- and rabbit-plagued gardens, as well as many champion herbaceous genera whose foliage includes alkaloids or other substances distasteful and/or toxic to these browsing creatures. Choices of trees and shrubs are more limited, but here, too, a number of rarely browsed species exist for almost any climate. In the absence of a fence, the challenge to creating gardens with resident deer or other herbivores is not in finding attractive, resistant plants—there are many; rather it is in letting go of desires for certain cherished varieties—roses, tulips, and rhododendrons come to mind—that the creatures find irresistible.

It would be useful here to include a list of resistant plants for designing gardens in deer country; we initially planned to provide one, but after consulting other deer-afflicted gardeners and comparing our own widely varying experiences with repeated deer damage we thought better of this idea. A given plant's resistance to browsing animals can be a highly local phenomenon, for it depends on the changing tastes of local deer species and also on chemical attributes that vary with soil and climate. Under conditions of drought or overpopulation, starving animals will eat almost anything. Likewise, at interfaces between encroaching suburbs and wilderness where it has become common for residents to set out feed corn, natural diets have been distorted and deer may nibble on plants they ordinarily avoid. Newly planted, well-fed and -watered plants fresh from the nursery are almost always enticing, no matter which species. Helpful regional lists of deer-resistant plants can be had from university extension services and numerous sites on the Internet, but all will need on-site testing and some reinterpretation; even the most accurate listings represent only relative—not absolute—freedom from damage.

Dogs

In recent years a rash of books has sought to portray a mythical peaceable kingdom that includes dogs, gardeners, and plants living happily together. Although these carnivores

Wildlife loses its charm quickly when garden plants are on the menu. The choices are either to exclude deer, rabbits, and other threats, if possible, or give up on growing certain cherished plants. Rabbit with a garden mouthful, Santa Fe, New Mexico.

do not actually eat plants for food, not all of them can be trusted in a garden. Some dogs, usually small breeds, well-trained individuals, or those of a mellow temperament, present few problems. Others, particularly neglected and bored members of herding and working breeds, adopt the habit of chewing plants for entertainment; sometimes they prefer to dig them up by the roots. If several are kept together in a yard—we use this term because it will not really be a garden if it is filled with dogs—they often develop pack behavior, establishing regularly patrolled routes that become promptly evident in paths worn through beds and lawns, and torn and broken limbs marking trails through shrubbery. Plant-rich gardens can't easily develop alongside such rambunctious animals; excluding them from areas with intensive, vulnerable plantings is usually the best course.

Some gardenmakers are blessed with mild-mannered canines who seem to respect gardens, but more than one dog—the beginning of a restless pack— often spells trouble. Daphne Shackleton's well-behaved dogs Rebel and Tyrant in her garden, Lakeview House, Mullagh, Ireland.

Engineering with plants

A final heroic role for plants draws on their mostly untapped potential for addressing varied engineering needs. In addition to their aesthetic value for gardens, they offer biological alternatives to help hold stream banks and lake edges, clean and disperse runoff from streets and buildings, and remove chemicals and biological poisons from soil through their growth processes. Well-chosen plants not only dress up slopes for a garden; they also stabilize them, providing alternatives to expensive and harsh concrete or block walls. Overpriced engineered bulkheads along streams and rivers could easily be foregone if strong-rooted baldcypress trees were planted at intervals along shores instead; these remarkable trees send out woody, protruding roots ("cypress knees") that grow into a living bulwark, protecting edges of lakes and rivers. Other plants have become popular choices for so-called green roofs that moderate urban temperatures and reduce runoff. If left standing, native prairie grasses like little bluestem (*Schizachyrium scoparium*) suspend as much as an inch of rainfall along their leaves in tiny droplets; these later evaporate instead of running off to create floods downstream. Meadows of these plants would greatly reduce urban runoff—and the need for expensive engineering to deal with it—if allowed to grow alongside road verges and other public properties. Actively growing marsh and water plants also filter and cleanse septic fields and waterways by encouraging aerobic bacteria on their roots; these absorb and break down toxic materials, converting them into nutrients helpful for plant growth. All these heroic capacities, as well as the most obvious, the simple but profound ability of plants to offer cooling shade, contribute to the life of both gardens and people.

Plants offer engineering services as well as beauty. These baldcypress roots create buttressed bulwarks of long-lasting wood that naturally stabilize stream edges against flooding—something usually accomplished more expensively, less attractively, and no more effectively with concrete. The living roots, leaves, and stems also help purify air and water. *Taxodium* sp. aff. *mucronatum*, Guadalupe River, Comal County, Texas.

MATCHING CLIMATES AND PLANTS Three cases

Homeoclimatic assessment refers to the process of finding potentially adaptable plants from similar climates for use in a specific garden. First look at what thrives, then find out where it comes from, and last, find more plants to grow from those regions. By compiling such lists, one can find all kinds of plants that will grow well together in a particular place. As examples for this exercise, we have chosen three disparate regions we know intimately. Each of the following lists includes a sampling of clichéd plants (which have become clichéd for a reason—their superb performance) as well as some lesser-known species and genera that have shown great adaptability in the region. Omitted from the lists for semi-arid Colorado and Texas are otherwise well-adapted plants in need of regular irrigation (for example, European lady's mantle, native spruce and baldcypress, and several thirsty South African genera).

MID-ATLANTIC COASTAL

New York City and Philadelphia metro areas

Temperate China, Japan, and Korea

Anemone hupehensis and hybrids, Japanese anemone
Ceratostigma plumbaginoides, leadwort
Cornus kousa, kousa dogwood
Corylopsis spp., winter hazel
Hakonechloa macra, Japanese forest grass
Hamamelis mollis and hybrids, witch hazel
Hosta spp.
Hydrangea spp.
Magnolia spp.
Miscanthus sinensis, maiden grass
Prunus serrula, P. serrulata, P. subhirtella, P. ×yedoensis, flowering cherry

Rhododendron spp., rhododendron and azalea
Stewartia spp.
Viburnum dilatatum, linden viburnum
Viburnum plicatum var. *tomentosum*, doublefile viburnum
Viburnum rhytidophyllum, leatherleaf viburnum
Viburnum setigerum, tea viburnum
Viburnum sieboldii
Wisteria floribunda, Japanese wisteria
Wisteria sinensis, Chinese wisteria

European mountains

(moderate elevations of Pyrenees, Alps, Balkans, Caucasus)
Ajuga reptans, carpet bugle
Asarum europaeum, European ginger
Buxus sempervirens, boxwood
Colchicum spp.
Daphne spp.
Galanthus nivalis, snowdrop
Hedera spp., ivy
Helleborus spp., hellebore
Hyacinthoides hispanica, Spanish bluebells
Narcissus spp., daffodil
Picea abies, Norway spruce
Picea omorika, Siberian spruce
Picea orientalis, oriental spruce

Woodlands of the United States

(eastern and midwestern)
Aesculus parviflora, bottlebrush buckeye
Cercis canadensis, eastern redbud
Chionanthus virginicus, fringe tree
Cornus florida, flowering dogwood
Fothergilla spp.
Halesia spp., silverbell
Phlox divaricata, blue woodland phlox
Tiarella spp., foamflower
Trillium spp., wake robin

Grasslands of the United States

(eastern and midwestern)
Amsonia spp., bluestar
Baptisia spp., false indigo
Echinacea spp., coneflower
Panicum virgatum, switch grass
Parthenium integrifolium, wild quinine
Rudbeckia spp., black-eyed Susan
Solidago spp., goldenrod
Sporobolus heterolepis, prairie dropseed
Symphyotrichum spp., aster

COLORADO FRONT RANGE

Fort Collins, Boulder, Colorado Springs, and Denver metro areas

Mountains of Europe, North Africa, and Asia Minor

Acantholimon spp., spikethrift
Acer tataricum, Tatarian maple
Crocus spp.
Dianthus spp., pink
Festuca spp., fescue
Iris germanica, I. pallida, bearded iris
Muscari spp., grape hyacinth
Papaver atlanticum, Spanish poppy
Papaver orientale, oriental poppy
Pinus leucodermis, Bosnian pine
Pinus mugo, mugo pine
Puschkinia spp.
Scilla (syn. *Chionodoxa*) spp.
Sedum sediforme, big blue spruce sedum
Sempervivum tectorum, houseleek, hen and chicks
Syringa vulgaris, common lilac
Veronica spp., speedwell
Viola corsica, Corsican pansy

Central Asia

Acer semenovii, Turkestan maple
Allium karataviense, Turkestan allium
Caragana spp., Siberian peashrub
Corylus colurna, Turkish filbert

MATCHING CLIMATES AND PLANTS, continued

Central Asia, continued
Crataegus ambigua, Russian hawthorn
Eremurus spp., foxtail lily
Iris lactea, milky iris
Ixiolirion tataricum
Ornithogalum magnum
Perovskia spp., Russian sage
Salvia daghestanica
Tulipa spp.

Eastern Asia
(Japan, Korea, coastal Siberia, and China)
Berberis koreana, B. thunbergii, barberry
Caryopteris spp., blue mist spirea
Heptacodium miconioides, seven sons tree
Kolkwitzia amabilis, beautybush
Malus spp., crabapple
Paeonia spp., peony
Pinus bungeana, lacebark pine
Syringa pekingensis, tree lilac
Viburnum carlesii, Korean spicebush

Interior West, high-elevation Southwest, and Great Plains, United States
Agastache spp., anise hyssop
Callirhoe involucrata, prairie winecup
Eriogonum spp., buckwheat
Fallugia paradoxa, Apache plume
Helianthus maximiliani, Maximilian's sunflower
Juniperus scopulorum, Rocky Mountain juniper
Oenothera spp., evening primrose
Penstemon spp., beardtongue
Pinus aristata, bristlecone pine

Pinus edulis, pinyon pine
Pinus flexilis, limber pine
Pinus ponderosa, ponderosa pine
Pinus strobiformis, western white pine
Ribes aureum, golden currant
Yucca spp.

SOUTH-CENTRAL TEXAS
Austin and San Antonio metro areas

Mediterranean basin and western Asia
(Irano-Turanian region)
Chamaerops humilis, Mediterranean fan palm
Ficus carica, fig
Iris unguicularis, Algerian iris
Narcissus tazetta
Phlomis spp., Jerusalem sage
Punica granatum, pomegranate
Rosmarinus officinalis, rosemary
Vitex agnus-castus, chaste tree

South China, Southeast Asia, Ryukyu Islands of Japan
Aspidistra spp., cast iron plant
Ceratostigma willmottianum, Miss Willmott's plumbago
Cotoneaster buxifolius, grayleaf cotoneaster
Eriobotrya japonica, loquat
Lagerstroemia indica, crape myrtle
Lycoris radiata, red spider lily
Ophiopogon spp., mondo grass
Photinia serrulata, Chinese photinia
Rosa banksiae, Lady Banks' rose

Northern Argentina and southern Brazil
Cortaderia selloana, pampas grass
Dichondra sericea, silver ponyfoot
Habranthus spp., rain lily
Nierembergia gracilis, cup flower
Oxalis crassipes, O. regnellii, shamrock
Puya spp.
Rhodophiala bifida, oxblood lily

Eastern Cape, South Africa
Aloe maculata
Asparagus spp.
Bulbine frutescens
Crinum spp.
Dietes spp., fortnight lily
Freesia laxa, painted petals
Gladiolus dalenii, parrot glad
Moraea polystachya
Myrsine africana, African boxwood

Texas and northeastern Mexico
Agave spp., century plant
Dasylirion spp., sotol
Dioon edule, cycad
Lantana spp.
Leucophyllum spp., ceniza
Quercus spp., oak
Russelia coccinea, coral blow
Sabal mexicana, Mexican cabbage palm
Sophora secundiflora, Texas mountain laurel
Tradescantia sillamontana, velvet creeper
Zephyranthes spp., rain lily

FERTILITY AND PH

In addition to hydrogen, oxygen, and carbon in the form of carbon dioxide absorbed from air and water, plants take in elements from the soil to build cells and the all-important chlorophyll molecules used in photosynthesis. Scientists who analyzed plants in the nineteenth century discovered nitrogen (important for vigor and greenery), phosphorus (known to aid flowering and fruiting), potassium (associated with root growth), calcium, and magnesium in their tissues. Later research also found small quantities of iron, manganese, boron, copper, zinc, molybdenum, chlorine, nickel, sulfur, and silicon. Of these nutrients, nitrogen, phosphorus, and potassium are the ones needed in greatest abundance and therefore included in most "complete fertilizers"; the others are generally known as micronutrients since these are needed in smaller quantities. All are naturally taken up by plants from soil, but because of variations in local minerals and absorption capacities of the plants themselves as well as their fungal partners, various elements are more or less available. This is most obvious in one of the common differences among plants: whether they prefer limy soils or abhor them.

The variable at play in this instance is pH, a measure of the concentration of hydrogen ions that expresses whether a soil is acid or alkaline. On a scale where 7 is neutral, a lower pH like 6.5 is considered mildly acid and a higher pH like 8.2 is regarded as alkaline. As soils become more alkaline some elements bind chemically, making them difficult for certain plants to absorb; these species, said to be acid-loving, including woodland shrubs such as azaleas and rhododendrons, may be unable to take in elements like iron, zinc, or magnesium needed to build chlorophyll, perhaps as a result of losing their mycorrhizal partners under alkaline conditions. Whatever the underlying metabolic cause, the visual result is sickly yellowing leaves with characteristic green veins (chlorosis); unless corrected chemically, this deficiency will eventually result in death. In highly acid soils different restrictions apply and so-called lime-loving plants struggle to obtain nitrogen, calcium, and other minerals they require,

inhibiting their growth. Neutral or slightly acid soils accommodate a wide variety of species, but some plants demand strongly acid (sour) conditions; others are invariably at their best only on alkaline (sweet) soils.

Gardeners sometimes manipulate soil chemistry by adding powdered sulfur, Epsom salts, or aluminum sulfate to increase acidity, or by applying ground dolomitic limestone to make a sour soil turn sweet or neutral. This chemical conversion succeeds for a time in modest flower boxes or small vegetable plots but must be renewed with added treatments as the natural chemistries of native rocks and subsoils (and often irrigation water) reassert themselves. For large-growing shrubs or trees whose roots reach down into underlying soil it is not feasible to alter pH significantly. No plant can truly be at home in a garden if its needs are at odds with the indigenous soil.

Soil itself is a complicated mixture of minerals derived from underlying rocks, sediment, organic debris, and associated bacteria, fungi, and other creatures that live within it. To a considerable extent the parent rock or substrate determines which minerals are in greatest supply. Granite, sandstone, schist, and gneiss often decay to develop strongly acid soils; volcanic basalt and sediments transported by rivers, glaciers, or wind often yield mineral-rich, neutral to slightly acid soils; limy or alkaline rocks like marble, limestone, serpentine, and some shales yield high-pH soils. Under arid conditions any soil may become alkaline as a result of an accumulated layer of evaporated lime (caliche) or salt near the surface.

The presence of humus—a spongy, partly decayed mass of vegetable matter—modifies this chemistry, making a wider range of nutrients available to plants. This material accumulates readily under cool, humid conditions, as can be seen by the thick layer of organic debris common in northern forests. In warm, moist climates decay is rapid and humus persists for only a few weeks, requiring continuous renewal; under alkaline or arid conditions it may hardly form at all. Fallen leaves, rotted vegetation, and animal manures are the

FERTILITY AND PH, continued

natural sources of humus, providing the basis for soil fertility; for this reason such organic materials (composts) have traditionally been applied by gardeners as fertilizer. Although the actual level of nutrient in this material is small compared with commonly applied chemical fertilizers, humus in the soil acts as a powerful catalyst to make nutrients available in a form readily absorbed by plants. (We often employ alfalfa pellets for this purpose in our garden as these are easily spread and inexpensive—commonly sold as animal feed—and have been shown to have enzymes beneficial to soils.) Even more important, perhaps, is the role of humus as a chemical binder: the living, organic slime of this natural material helps tie loose, otherwise sterile particles of sandy soils together, increasing their capacity to hold water and nutrients; in tight clay soils it likewise binds together minute particles into larger crumbs, making soil friable and helping it breathe. Thereby humus increases the capacity to deliver nutrients to plants and moderates the restrictive chemical effects of pH.

Supplying plants with a shallow layer of mulch over their roots, either through partly rotted leaves, compost, pine straw, or other organic debris (best for plants from moist or woodland habitats), or crushed stone, grit, or gravel (ideal for naturally drought-resistant species and those native to rocky or mineral soils), can help conserve moisture and humus. A mulch reduces evaporation and also moderates summer temperatures around plant roots; this slows breakdown of organic materials, helps preserve soil texture, and reduces runoff. Mulched soils more efficiently absorb and store rains when they arrive, often alleviating much of the need for irrigation. Uncomposted bark or wood chips usually should be avoided; when applied as mulch these carbon-rich materials tend to rob nitrogen from soil as they decay, inhibiting growth; and wood from certain species actually has been shown to harm some plants. From an aesthetic standpoint, few types of mulch are as appealing to look at as a dense planting with leafy cover, which offers the best mulch of all.

PLANTS FOR DRY SHADE

These plants would for the most part prefer good, moist woodland soil, but in our experience they stalwartly tolerate dry shaded conditions and poor soil without losing much vigor or visual appeal.

Trees, shrubs, woody ground covers, and vines
Ageratina havanensis (syn. *Eupatorium havanense*), shrubby boneset
Arctostaphylos spp. (many), manzanita, kinninnick
Aucuba japonica
Callicarpa americana, beautyberry
Camellia spp. (many)
Chimonanthus spp., wintersweet

Clematis armandii
Clethra pringlei, Mexican summersweet
Comptonia peregrina, sweetfern
Danae racemosa, poet's laurel
Epigaea repens, trailing arbutus
×*Fatshedera lizei*
Fatsia japonica, Japanese aralia
Ficus pumila, F. vaccinoides, creeping fig
Hedera spp., ivy
Hibiscus calyphyllus, Pondoland mallow
Hypericum spp. (many), St. John's wort
Jamesia americana, waxflower
Juniperus communis, mountain juniper
Juniperus squamata
Justicia spicigera, Mexican honeysuckle
Laurus nobilis, bay

Lonicera prolifera 'Kintzley's Ghost', ghost vine
Loropetalum chinense, Chinese witch hazel
Mahonia spp. (many), grape holly
Malvaviscus arboreus var. *drummondii*, Turk's cap
Microbiota decussata, Siberian arborvitae
Myrtus communis, myrtle
Nandina domestica
Neviusia alabamensis, snow wreath
Pachystima canbyi, mountain lover
Phillyraea angustifolia
Pittosporum tobira
Prunus laurocerasus, P. lusitanica, Portuguese cherry laurel
Ribes aureum, golden currant

Ribes ×*gordonianum*

Ribes odoratum, clove currant

Rubus calycinoides, creeping raspberry

Rubus deliciosus, boulder raspberry

Rubus ×*tridel* 'Benenden', hybrid boulder raspberry

Ruscus aculeatus

Russelia coccinea, coral blow

Sarcococca spp., sweetbox

Ungnadia speciosa, Mexican buckeye

Viburnum obovatum

Viburnum ×*pragense*

Viburnum rhytidophylloides

Viburnum rhytidophyllum, leatherleaf viburnum

Viburnum suspensum

Viburnum tinus, laurustinus

Vinca spp.

Nonwoody perennials, ferns, bulbs, tubers, corms

Acanthus spp., bear's breech

Allium neapolitanum, Naples onion

Antennaria spp., pussytoes

Arum spp.

Asarum arifolium, evergreen wild ginger

Asparagus spp.

Aspidistra spp., cast iron plant

Bergenia spp., pigsqueak

Bletilla spp., ground orchid

Brunnera macrophylla, Siberian forget-me-not

Carex spp. (many), sedge

Chasmanthium latifolium, wild oats

Cheilanthes alabamensis, Alabama lip fern

Cheilanthes fendleri, Fendler's lip fern

Cheilanthes tomentosa, woolly lip fern

Chlorophytum saundersiae (syn. *Anthericum saundersiae*), weeping anthericum

Chrysogonum virginianum var. *australe*, green and gold

Clivia miniata

Conoclinium (formerly included in *Eupatorium*) spp. (many), mistflower

Convallaria majalis, lily-of-the-valley

Cyclamen spp.

Cyrtomium falcatum, holly fern

Dicliptera suberecta, velvet honeysuckle

Dietes spp., fortnight lily

Digitalis lutea, straw foxglove

Dracunculus vulgaris, dragon flower

Epimedium spp. (many), barrenwort

Erigeron pulchellus, robin's plantain

Eryngium venustum, Mexican sea holly

Euphorbia amygdaloides var. *robbiae*, daphne spurge

Galium odoratum, sweet woodruff

Helleborus foetidus, green hellebore

Helleborus ×*nigercors*

Helleborus ×*sternii*

Heuchera spp., coral bells

Hippeastrum ×*johnsonii*, *H.* 'San Antonio Rose', hardy amaryllis

Hyacinthoides hispanica, Spanish bluebells

Iris foetidissima

Iris 'Nada'

Iris tectorum, Japanese roof iris

Iris unguicularis, Algerian iris

Justicia brandegeana, shrimp plant

Luzula nivea, *L. sylvatica*, wood rush

Lycoris spp., spider lily

Ophiopogon spp., mondo grass

Origanum spp., ornamental oregano

Oxalis crassipes, wood sorrel

Oxalis regnellii, false shamrock

Pellaea atropurpurea, purple cliff brake

Pteris multifida, spider brake fern

Pteris vittata, ladder brake fern

Pulmonaria cevennensis, longleaf lungwort

Rehmannia angulosa, false foxglove

Reineckia carnea

Rohdea japonica, Manchu lily

Salvia coccinea, tropical sage

Salvia darcyi, red mountain sage

Salvia forsskaohlii

Salvia madrensis, Sierra Madre sage

Salvia mexicana, Mexican sage

Salvia regla, royal sage

Salvia roemeriana, cedar sage

Salvia sclarea, clary sage

Saxifraga stolonifera, strawberry geranium

Senecio obovatus, golden groundsel

Solidago caesia, wreath goldenrod

Solidago sphacelata

Spigelia marilandica, Indian pink

Stylophorum lasiandrum, Asian celandine poppy

Symphyotrichum cordifolium (syn. *Aster cordifolius*), blue wood aster

Symphytum grandiflorum, comfrey

Teucrium scorodonia 'Crispum', curly wood sage

Trachystemon orientalis

Tradescantia sillamontana, velvet creeper

Viola spp. (many)

Woodsia obtusa, blunt-lobed woodsia

Zephyranthes sp. 'Labuffarosa', pink rain lily

Palms, fiber plants, succulents

Aechmea recurvata, hardy bromeliad

Agave attenuata, *A. bracteosa*, *A. mitis* (syn. *A. celsii*), century plant

Beschorneria spp.

Billbergia nutans and hybrids

Chamaedorea radicalis, hardy parlor palm

cycads (most)

Dasylirion berlandieri, Mexican blue sotol

Dyckia spp.

Graptopetalum paraguayense, ghost plant

Guihaia argyrata, Asian needle palm

Manfreda undulata

Nolina sp. 'La Siberica', giant Mexican beargrass

Rhapidophyllum hystrix, needle palm

Sansevieria spp., mother-in-law's tongue

Sedum confusum, *S. nevii*, *S. palmeri*, stonecrop

Sempervivum tectorum, houseleek, hen and chicks

Yucca cernua

Yucca elephantipes

Yucca pallida, pale yucca

Yucca rupicola, twist-leaf yucca

4

PATTERNS, PLACEMENT, AND PROCESS
How plants make gardens into Edens

A FEW WINTERS AGO, a foot and a half of snow fell overnight while we were staying in Manhattan. With aboveground transportation at a standstill and subways a crowded jumble, we had to punt on our prior plans, opting for a bundled-up crosstown walk instead. The snow's whiteness intensified distinctions among the myriad tones of muted grays, browns, and blacks of this statuesque city, and the flakes' layers of softness rounded all urban angles and edges. Our movement was clumsy and hampered by the unshoveled sidewalks; the streets lay strangely quiet, and what sounds broke through the white silence were muffled. This transformation of New York City by snow left us in an altered state of bedazzlement and with a sense of smallness and belonging that mirrors the cohesion so many of us feel when we reconnect with the world beyond the one thought to be under human control.

Call of the wild

Several millennia have passed since the human race began large-scale modification of its environment, yet within our hearts, bones, and collective memory we still respond in a most primal manner to the natural world, whether a snowstorm, a sunrise, or the sound of wind through trees. In modern times many people of industrialized nations have come to question our so-called progress and to realize that with all the gains have come many losses. Much of the romantic period in music, art, and literature was based on a recognition of this loss and on a sense that beneath intellect and technology there still beats a heart that is untameable and untrainable, that yearns for the simpler basics of existence that were carried out at one with nature. Along parallel lines, the United States developed a national park system at the turn of the nineteenth century; more recently on a smaller scale but with potentially a much wider-ranging effect, a policy of land acquisition and/or protection has become the norm in many communities across this country. Strong interest in native plants and habitat restoration over the past few decades derives in part from this longing for the natural, for what once was, and is in direct response to the inertness and cacophony so common in man-made spaces and landscapes. It is no accident that the primordial pull toward wildness is strengthening just as these places that embody that spirit are dwindling.

In the evolution of gardens this yearning and change in orientation are both strikingly evident. The early gardens of the Islamic world and medieval Europe walled out nature and kept plants under obvious control by clipping, shearing, potting, and planting them into strict geometrical

OPPOSITE In autumn, patterns made by the contrast of deciduous and evergreen trees are all the more striking. Red Butte Botanical Garden, Salt Lake City, Utah.

layouts, giving a sense of safety, order, and serenity in contrast to the perceived ugliness, chaos, and often real danger that lay beyond. The idealized Garden of Eden was not wild and unconstrained but tame and benevolent. European gardens slowly diverged as people felt more in control of their surroundings. Mediterranean cultures kept to more architectural, less naturalistic styles while northern European cultures embraced plant profusion and a sense of wildness, perhaps harking back to their pregarden pantheistic, nature-worshipping Celtic and Germanic roots. Today many people see gardens as a haven for the natural world, a return to a wilder place, and hope to invite as much diversity of flora and fauna as possible in order to recapture a different lost Eden. Ironically, the ugliness, danger, and chaos perceived to lie beyond the garden now often is wrought by ourselves.

So as we turn to gardens not just for sensory delight, joyful activity, and aesthetic pleasure but also for refuge or even salvation from a world ever more disconnected from nature, the question is how to choose plants and make a garden that fills this longing. Patterns, placement, and process learned from the natural world give plants presence in the garden beyond their innate character. Plants certainly create much of their power to engage us through their individual attributes. However, without thoughtful context, they remain merely a collection of curiosities to tend, study, and admire. It is their context that ultimately shapes our overall experience, both of their innate character and of the garden as a whole. Patterns, placement, and process create a context that allows plant-driven design to combine wonderful plants and a particular space into a Garden of

Eden for this day and age. When natural patterns are mirrored, when placement is considerate of both site and plant, and when process is evoked and respected, the response of a person in such a garden is strongly emotional, personal, and yet quite universal—one of being immersed in and united with a welcoming, comforting, and subliminally familiar beauty.

Natural models for design

Going to natural places, whether a small woodland or prairie nearby or a distant destination of a grand-scale mountain or canyon, is what many of us do for pleasure, escape, and rejuvenation. These places have much to teach a gardenmaker. It is often passive assimilation more than conscious observation that educates us (though both offer important lessons), as the lay of the land, the forms and patterns made by the vegetation, soil, and stone, and all the colors and effects of light join to create experiential memories. These are for the most part visual, but by no means underestimate the other senses and their recognition of such places—sounds, smells, how things feel underfoot, how the air feels on one's skin, the way one's body moves to traverse the terrain, the sense of openness or enclosure and such all blend into an experience of place.

It is these things that a garden's design needs to address to make connection possible, not the rote imitation of plant communities and habitats so often suggested as a way to bring nature and a sense of wildness back into the garden. Surely plant communities in the wild can serve as inspiration: choosing plants and placing and combining them in ways resembling natural communities that match the garden's site and region immediately make it possible to create gardens that are ecologically and aesthetically sympathetic to place. On the other end of the design spectrum, a modernistic, formal, or otherwise antinaturalistic treatment of plants has much to gain from the inspiration of natural places as well.

Throughout this book we do not intend to imply that a naturalistic garden design is inherently more desirable than one based on a different organizing principle. Not in

OPPOSITE TOP LEFT Nature—in this case a January blizzard—softens and subdues the urban, wholly man-made world of Manhattan's Upper West Side.

OPPOSITE TOP RIGHT Sometimes the idea of not gardening a place at all deserves consideration. A beautiful site, such as this slope of native aspen, is often best left alone. Joyce and Schubert Ogden garden, Rollinsville, Colorado.

OPPOSITE BOTTOM A relaxed composition of dryland subshrubs and perennials adapted to the rigors of Colorado's semiarid Front Range feels natural yet shows enough organization and tending to also read as a garden. *Seriphidium filifolium, Oenothera fremontii, Phlox nana, Calylophus hartwegii, Nassella tenuissima, Festuca mairei*, and compact pine species, authors' garden, Fort Collins, Colorado.

ABOVE Spending time amid unspoiled natural beauty remains a cherished activity for many; these places also confer knowledge and inspiration on gardenmakers. Rod Saunders of Silverhill Seeds hiking, Sani Pass, southern Drakensberg, Republic of South Africa.

OPPOSITE TOP Plant communities have their own spirit. Here, on the top of the South African Drakensberg,

windswept grasses and subshrubs overlook a treeless montane grassland. Tiffindell, Republic of South Africa.

OPPOSITE BOTTOM Sited amid a western North American montane grassland, this garden draws inspiration from such places the world over, resulting in similar plants, patterns, and placement as well as shared colors and textures. Northern Colorado, Ogden design.

the least. Plant-driven design complements all so-called styles. What does seem to be true, borne out by many gardeners and designers before us and by our own experience of designing, planting, and gardening spaces along all parts of the bell curve of formality and naturalism, is that naturalistic compositions are more complicated to design, plant, and garden. Knowledge that seeps in from being in wild places is essential, and one needs to have direct familiarity and experience of that sort. It is through harnessing this knowledge that one can then purposely deemphasize the hand of the gardenmaker, something much more complex than more formal control or an intentionally artificial organization. Beyond the initial conceptual process, on-site nuancing of the design is imperative for naturalistic gardens. Their ongoing care, while often less labor-intensive than more formal styles, requires a deeper level of understanding and sensitivity in refereeing, editing, revising, all based on a strong grasp of horticulture and also of ecology.

That said, any kind of garden can gain by incorporating aspects of the natural world; actually, any garden should. Whether the style of a garden is naturalistic or more formal makes no difference, as long as somewhere plants are allowed to determine the lines of the layout and/or to cross over lines made by the architecture, and as long as one senses some echo of natural processes. This ensures that plants are equal partners in design and also gives a sense of continuity—plants have been allowed a chance to respond to the site. By their very nature, plants change; art and architecture don't. Therein lies much of the magic in plant-driven gardens of any style.

When we are in a garden and sense the jarring of certain plant-related elements, we can almost always explain the dissonance by looking to natural models of placement, pattern, and process, and finding how they have been disrespected, misunderstood, or ignored. For example, we have visited many gardens—naturalistic and not—that are inspired by the inherent beauty of the Southwest and desert plants the world over. One such garden attempts to bring the feel of a wild desert plant community into a gravel planting. The contrast of powerfully architectural

This garden evokes the essence of the desert by combining and contrasting boldly architectural plants with feathery, wiry, and fine-textured ones. *Hesperaloe parviflora, Stenocereus thurberi, S. marginatus, Parkinsonia* sp., Desert Botanical Garden, Phoenix, Arizona.

plants and finely textured ones so characteristic of the desert is given life in this garden with a melee of dramatic cacti and agaves nestled among a froth of flowering dryland annuals from American and African deserts. Yet something feels wrong. The gravel mulch is made of pebbles all the same size, hardly what one would expect from a desert floor. A bold grouping of half a dozen golden barrel cacti (*Echinocactus grusonii*), placed asymmetrically as is often done to achieve a casual, natural effect, jars nevertheless, for they are too evenly spaced. To make matters worse, these plants are all the same size—almost like bedding plants, so unlike how they would be found in nature where cacti of several ages would exist side by side. And some of the individuals are placed along a small berm, all facing straight up into the sky, whereas in the wild these would have oriented themselves at angles in response to the changing grade. The onlooker experiences dissonance through disruption of process—this is not the way plants grow. With individuals of different sizes spaced more randomly, and those on the berm slightly tilted to suggest they are responding to the change in slope, a fundamental shift occurs and the garden starts to take on the evocative power of time passed, of individual plant response to site, and of a settled plant community.

What is as important as discovering and rectifying the flaws in a garden design like the one just described is recognizing that none of these elements would jar if the planting did not attempt naturalism. An entirely different situation unfolds in the case of a modern design. Another desert-inspired garden we have visited veers strongly away from nature, using brilliantly hued walls as backdrops to an arresting sculptural event of cactus and agave species planted in large modernistic patterns, implying the rectilinearity of both agriculture and architecture. Here the former garden's issues of placement, pattern, and process become moot. What is missing in this bold garden, though, is that same essence of the desert and its plants that even the most far-flung, unnatural design using its denizens needs to respect to approach the same power and character one experiences in the wild—that contrast of

ABOVE This east coast courtyard, unusually hot in summer, invites experimentation. Silver ponyfoot and orange-flowered Mexican flame vine thread through and beneath bold agaves; a teacup-shaped fountain and profuse plantings join in to soften what might otherwise be a harsh, unfriendly spot. *Agave americana*, A. 'Sharkskin', *Dichondra sericea* 'Silver Falls', *Senecio confusus*, *Nicotiana* sp., Chanticleer, Wayne, Pennsylvania, Jonathan Wright design.

LEFT Multiple-sized barrel cacti placed at various angles convey the spontaneity of nature, giving this succulent garden a mature, settled feeling. *Echinocactus grusonii*, Ruth Bancroft Garden, Walnut Creek, California.

RIGHT Boldly repeating a coarse herbaceous perennial—in this case giant knapweed—throughout a planting sets up a rhythm the eye can follow. This leitmotif unifies the space, making it feel larger and more generous. *Centaurea macrocephala*, *Salvia nemorosa*, *Verbascum* sp., Great Dixter, East Sussex, England, Christopher Lloyd design.

BELOW Limiting the palette of plants and interlacing them as repeated guilds in this moist meadow lends natural repose. This creates a gentle transition from more horticulturally complex parts of the garden to the meadows and fields of the countryside beyond. *Actaea simplex* (syn. *Cimicifuga simplex*), *Molopospermum peloponnesiacum*, *Darmera peltata*, *Carex muskingumensis*, Bury Court, Surrey, England, Piet Oudolf design.

OPPOSITE TOP Thoughtful color gradation of seedling candelabra primroses gives this planting a graceful feeling of process. One senses that the plants have made themselves at home for some time and are merrily reproducing. *Primula* spp., North Hill, southern Vermont, Wayne Winterrowd and Joe Eck design.

OPPOSITE BOTTOM Although only four years old, this planting feels settled. Grasses thread through conifers of various shapes and sizes, giving a sense of natural process and time passed. These contrasting forms and textures play with afternoon light, creating a vivid scene without flowers. *Pinus sylvestris* 'Beuvronensis', *Pinus mugo* 'Mops', *Pinus nigra* 'Hornibrookiana', *Pinus ponderosa* 'Mary Ann Heacock', *Pinus edulis*, *Picea pungens* 'Procumbens', *Picea omorika* 'Pendula', *Cupressus arizonica*, *Festuca* sp., *Nassella tenuissima*, *Juncus tenuis*, *Festuca mairei*, *Atraphaxis* sp., *Seriphidium filifolium*, *Forestiera neomexicana*, authors' garden, Fort Collins, Colorado.

COMPANIONS TO BOLD SUCCULENTS AND FIBER PLANTS

These plants offer textural and floral contrast to strongly architectural dryland plants, such as cacti, other succulents, and yuccas, agaves, and kin, collectively known as fiber plants.

Shrubby plants

Atriplex spp., saltbush
Buddleia marrubiifolia, desert butterfly bush
Calliandra eriophylla, fairy duster
Calliandra 'Sierra Starr'
Cistus ×*skanbergii*, pink rockrose
Convolvulus cneorum, silver bush morning glory
Dalea bicolor subsp. *argyraea*, silver dalea
Dalea frutescens, black dalea
Encelia farinosa, brittlebush
Ericameria (syn. *Chrysothamnus*) spp., rabbitbrush, chamisa
Justicia californica, chuparosa
Krascheninnikovia lanata (syn. *Eurotia lanata, Ceratoides lanata*), winter fat
Leucophyllum spp., ceniza
Parthenium spp., mariola, guayule
Perovskia ×*hybrida*, Russian sage
Phlomis lanata, dwarf Jerusalem sage
Rosmarinus officinalis, rosemary
Salvia apiana, beebush
Salvia clevelandii, chaparral sage
Salvia dorrii, blue ball sage
Salvia greggii, autumn sage
Salvia pachyphylla, desert sage
Seriphidium filifolium (syn. *Artemisia filifolia*), threadleaf sage, sand sage
Teucrium fruticans, silver germander

Smaller companion plants

Acantholimon spp., spikethrift
Astrolepis sinuata (syn. *Notholaena sinuata*), bulb cloakfern
Baileya multiradiata, desert marigold
Bulbine frutescens, bulbine
Calylophus spp. (many), sundrop
Cheilanthes fendleri, Fendler's lipfern
Cheilanthes tomentosa, woolly lipfern
Chrysactinia mexicana, damianita
Datura wrightii, angel's trumpet
Eriogonum spp. (many), buckwheat
Euphorbia rigida, gopher plant
Melampodium leucanthum, blackfoot daisy
Mirabilis multiflora, desert four o'clock
Nierembergia spp., cup flower
Oenothera spp. (many), evening primrose
Penstemon spp. (many), beardtongue
Psilostrophe spp., paperflower
Salvia chamaedryoides, germander sage
Scutellaria resinosa, prairie skullcap
Scutellaria suffrutescens, pink skullcap
Scutellaria wrightii, Texas skullcap
Seriphidium frigidum (syn. *Artemisia frigida*), fringed sage
Sphaeralcea spp., globe mallow
Stachys coccinea, scarlet betony
Stachys inflata, silver betony
Tagetes lemmonii, Mount Lemmon daisy
Tetraneuris scaposa (syn. *Hymenoxys scaposa*), perky Sue
Thymophylla pentachaeta, golden dogweed
Thymus capitatus (syn. *Thymbra capitata*), conehead thyme
Zauschneria spp., hummingbird trumpet, California fuchsia
Zinnia acerosa, hardy white zinnia
Zinnia grandiflora, Rocky Mountain zinnia

Grassy companions

Hesperostipa spp. (many), needle and thread grass
Melinis nerviglumis (syn. *Rhynchelytrum nerviglume*), ruby grass
Muhlenbergia dumosa, bamboo muhly
Nassella tenuissima, Mexican feather grass
Pennisetum villosum, feathertop
Stipa spp. (many), needlegrass

Ground covers

Callirhoe althaeoides, C. involucrata, C. tenuissima, poppy mallow
Dalea greggii, trailing indigo bush
Dichondra sericea, silver ponyfoot
Erigeron karvinskianus, Santa Barbara daisy
Glandularia spp., desert verbena
Heterotheca jonesii,
ice plants (several genera: *Delosperma, Drosanthemum, Lampranthus, Carpobrotus, Malephora*)
Portulaca spp., moss rose
Salvia chionophylla, snowleaf sage
Sedum diffusum 'Potosinum', little gray stonecrop
Sedum reptans
Sedum sediforme, big blue spruce sedum
Setcreasea pallida, purple heart
Stemodia tomentosa, trailing ceniza
Tanacetum densum var. *amani*, partridge feather
Tradescantia sillamontana, velvet creeper

powerful plants with those of thin texture and fleeting but brilliant color. If the cacti and agaves, left carefully gridded as they are, were given an underplanting of smaller, finely textured annuals, subshrubs, ice plants, or the like—perhaps equally gridded and probably as neatly divided by species as are the succulents to follow the overall geometrical organization of the planting—one simple but all-important aspect of the desert would be vivified and celebrated, and all the plants would have more of an emotional impact. Left as is with just mulch between them, the plantings resemble a wax museum.

Plant leitmotifs

Plants in nature generally form guilds, or small-scale communities. Gardens do well to follow this model, but this by no means suggests that one needs to slavishly copy which plants grow with which. Simply noticing that in a natural guild some species dominate and others are less common, and allowing this pattern to inform garden planting is all that is necessary to change a hodge-podge collection into a composition of plants that relate to one another. With the repetition of one species, or even just a group of plants that shares similar physical traits, a sense of unity and cohesion emerges as it does in nature. We borrow a term from music and call this finding a plant *leitmotif*. The translation of the German word is "guiding pattern," and guiding is exactly what a leitmotif does, whether aurally in a piece of music or visually in a garden. A recognized, repeated plant or plant type, like a brief recurring rhythmic or melodic pattern in a piece of music, becomes a leitmotif that organizes and unifies the experience of the whole, making it easier for us to comprehend and enjoy. A simple way to do this in a garden is to choose favorite plants for leitmotifs—we often rely on grasses and sedges to weave a garden together into a guild, but it could be any plant.

Often a plant presents its own case for being a dominant player, either by reproducing itself abundantly or by growing well and pleasing the gardener. The plants you like best and the plants that like you best ought to be brought to the fore. For example, North American, Asian, and European species of pasque flowers have now seeded comfortably into all parts of our steppe garden in Colorado, making their own garden community with the grasses and forbs there. They have adopted us, and we are smitten by them and happy with their prolific progeny. Likewise, in our small, more irrigated front garden we planted a couple members of the *Sanguisorba* tribe early on, and these grew so lustily and looked so happy that we have since planted close to a dozen other species and selections.

Finding the essence of natural plant communities: Woodland lessons

So it is the elusive essence of a wild place that awaits discovery, and this then needs to be reinterpreted with plants through patterns, placement, and process. Dozens of plant communities exist, thousands depending on how one categorizes them. Learning from these natural models, not copying them directly, is a key to creating powerfully moving gardens. By looking at how and where plants grow and with what other plants, one can take the essence of these aspects and bring them to a human scale—augmenting or diminishing, emphasizing or playing down as necessary—to fit within the physical and emotional parameters of a garden, whether in a grand scene or just a small, intimate vignette, all the while conveying a sense of place. Here three well-known plant communities serve as crystalline examples of how to discover their distinctive soul and find ways to express it in a garden.

One of the most universally entrancing plant communities is the woodland. Collective memory seems to be at play: many people yearn for such an experience in their gardens, whether they grew up with anything remotely related to a forest or not. As with any broad habitat category, woodlands vary by region and climate: dense tropical or temperate rainforests, cool northern woodlands, swampy bayous, sultry piney woods, mossy coastal glens, and on and on. The dominance of deciduous or evergreen trees changes a forest's nature, and within the subset of evergreen forest, a broad-leaf canopy of hollies, oaks, and southern magnolias makes for a community and experience distinct from that

RIGHT Narrow light shafts, like those that stream through windows of a gothic cathedral, penetrate the canopy and make for an intimate experience amid dense white cedars. *Chamaecyparis thyoides*, Pine Barrens, southern New Jersey.

BELOW Diffuse light glows green in this damp West Coast woodland of moss and sword fern. *Polystichum munitum*, Bloedel Reserve, Bainbridge Island, Washington.

offered by coniferous or needled trees such as pine, spruce, and fir. First and foremost, it is important to discover the spirit that ties all woods together. The essence of woodland needs to be distilled in order to sensitively design and garden a space that takes its inspiration from such places. Talking to gardeners, hikers, and clients as well as exploring one's own responses makes this journey of discovery possible.

What emerges is that above all, a sense of peaceful privacy, quiet reflection, and comfortable solitude pervades the descriptions given by people attempting to evoke their experience of the woods. Why is this and how does it happen? Trees are the catalysts. They and the understory shorten views, making for smaller, more intimate spaces. Often a person has to pick a path through these plant obstacles, making for a present, active engagement with the surroundings. We see, smell, hear, and feel things close up. Trees dwarf not only views but also the person, yet on a measurable scale, unlike the sense of smallness produced by big skies or being at sea. Many trees' trunks suggest human girth; perhaps this is why one rarely feels lonely in the woods except at night, when vision is limited. More than any other group of plants, trees give the sensation of being among companions.

In a woodland, the still air created by the trees' enclosure heightens sound, yet generally there is less ambient noise, so the slightest movement by an animal, a rock dislodged by one's foot, or a pinecone dropping to the ground is noticed, adding to the immediacy of experience. Trees make light more subtle and complex: some is blocked; some filters through translucent leaves or reflects off shiny opaque ones; some penetrates the canopy entirely, making for infinite and constantly changing patterns. Its softness invites close inspection of one's surroundings, intensifying intimacy.

What's more, woodland immerses us in life in all its cycles, from the ground we walk upon to the trees above our heads. The forest floor breathes death, decay, and birth. We feel this in soft, often spongy decaying plant material underfoot; we smell it while walking through and dislodging

TOP Decay and rebirth coexist and intermingle on the forest floor. Leaves of *Acer sieboldianum* and mushrooms, Arnold Arboretum, Jamaica Plain, Massachusetts.

ABOVE Felted fern fiddleheads and broad skunk cabbage foliage grow lustily in spring deciduous woodland. Garden in the Woods, Framingham, Massachusetts.

these life-filled layers, releasing pungent, earthy aromas; we see it in tender fern fiddleheads and limpid mushrooms growing by stumps of long-dead trees. Higher off the forest floor, life competes for space and light. Shrubs and trees stretch and intermingle, vines clamber singlemindedly to brighter points in the canopy. Animals of all sorts consort on both vertical and horizontal planes offered by the trees and understory. More than any plant community the woodland feels primeval, with the web of life and death so close at hand.

The intimacy of a walk in the woods may be what generates an emotional response people have to both trees and delicate woodland perennials. Sheltered by the benign architecture of a mature canopy—an outdoor house of sorts—many of us have spent hours inspecting mosses, ferns, ephemeral wildflowers, and all sorts of greenery growing fresh and lush in the shade and rich duff provided by those same trees. With their often fine textures, soft forms, thin substance, and pale flower colors, woodland plants for the most part have a subtlety that invites close viewing. They rarely flower as profusely as their sun-loving counterparts and often bloom in winter or spring, when the understory is less dense and competitive and the canopy, if deciduous, lets in more light. This makes them all the more cherished and anticipated.

So how to take these essentials of the woodland experience and translate them to a garden? Some gardens are blessed with an existing woodland. In these cases stewardship rather than gardening is necessary at the outset, yet plant-driven design informs decision-making about the plants already there. Some aggressive, self-important tree species or understory vine, shrub, or herbaceous plant, often alien but sometimes a down-home native, may need discipline or removal for a garden to proceed with any success. Choices must be made about culling and thinning of trees to make way for paths and to encourage growth by the healthiest, most beautiful, least invasive individuals, and ones that have the most value for creatures. As paths are laid out, it is vital to remember that much of the woodland experience relies on intimacy and a sense of being in the present. If paths become too wide, there is less to discover.

OPPOSITE TOP Many plants of the woodland floor have delicate forms and textures: these lacy maidenhair ferns form a veil over squirrel corn and toothwort just above ground level. *Adiantum pedatum, Dicentra canadensis, Cardamine diphylla*, Garden in the Woods, Framingham, Massachusetts.

OPPOSITE CENTER Soaking up the sunlight before summer's canopy fills in, most plants growing under deciduous trees—whether in the wild woods or in a garden—are at their freshest and most colorful in spring. *Disporum sessile* 'Variegatum', *Phacelia bipinnatifida*, David Culp and Michael Alderfer garden, Downingtown, Pennsylvania.

OPPOSITE BOTTOM Differing textures, foliage forms, and shades of green rather than flowers—here sensitive fern and mayapple—create an appealing matrix for much of the forest's growing season. *Onoclea sensibilis, Podophyllum peltatum*, Susquehanna State Park, Maryland.

ABOVE Native and exotic woodland plants often make comfortable partners in a garden, sharing similar physical characteristics and growth habits. These are borne of evolution in similar conditions. Asian *Hosta* 'Emerald Tiara', *Primula kisoana, Epimedium perralderianum*, eastern North American spring beauty *Claytonia virginica*, Chanticleer, Wayne, Pennsylvania.

There should be opportunities to have close encounters with plants. If the path runs straight its whole length, we see everything at once, no tree trunks surround and frame the view, and much of the forest essence is lost. In an attempt to make access easier and walks shorter, many estate and public woodland gardens make these mistakes, sacrificing the very mood they seek to celebrate. The worst actually pave the paths, creating a road through the trees rather than a walk through the woods. Wheelchair access notwithstanding, there need to be times when visitors must go around a thicket to see what's ahead, when plants or organic mulches soften the experience underfoot, when walkers look through a panel of tree trunks.

Certainly most gardenmakers will want to add favorite trees to an existing woodland. For sites not bestowed with enough trees to be woods, lots of trees must be planted. Take a cue from that woodland essence of enclosure brought about by the pattern, placement, and process of trees' growth in the woods, and by the natural layers of plants of different sizes and ages. Don't plant trees with the intention of growing them into the perfect specimens you might want in a nonwoodland setting. Err on the side of placing them too closely and let them duke it out and respond to each other's presence as they would in the woods. Find healthy but irregularly grown specimens at nurseries to mix in with the more regular individuals. Woodland trees are not all symmetrical. Search for multiple sizes of the same species. Include some understory trees and large shrubs and place them intermittently near the path, so that the walker's eyes don't always meet just with trunks but also at times with twigs and leaves.

Remember how important a role texture plays in ground-level plants of the forest floor. When the fleeting moments of spring bloom have passed, foliage must carry that same sense of soft freshness. Many American gardeners provide for this instinctively in woodland gardens by mixing favorite shade-loving perennials that offer a bevy of beautiful textures. However, others fall in love with some of the showiest and easiest of these plants and select them to the exclusion of others, hostas being poster children for this overly focused passion. Offered as a sea of bold leaves

Under pines, this subtropical wooded garden evokes the spirit of the deep South with native needle palms (*Rhapidophyllum hystrix*) and much beloved azaleas. Peckerwood Garden, Hempstead, Texas, John Fairey design.

with no textural relief, the lovely hosta takes on the look of cabbage escaped from vegetable garden into the woods. The play of light patterns so characteristic of a woodland experience disappears into this sameness of leaves. Strongly textural matrices seen in forests, such as skunk cabbage (*Lysichiton americanus*) growing with horsetail (*Equisetum scirpoides*) in a damp swale, can be mimicked by more garden-friendly hostas combined with delicately textured companions such as ferns, meadow rues, sedges, and the like. Much of the woods' wild essence will be recaptured.

Plants in nature grow, respond, and reproduce in certain distinctive ways. These differ from site to site, from plant community to plant community, and from region to region, yet some basic patterns emerge. Plants seed and distribute themselves, age and die, move from one area to another, all over time. When plants seed themselves beyond their original place, they intermingle with other plants. This obvious hallmark of nature is lost in much of the so-called natural plantings—usually featuring vast sweeps of perennials—so popular today. While these designs make use of

a more diverse palette of plants than many and often highlight species associated with one another in nature, the massive panels meant to evoke wild prairies and spangled woodland floors meet up with one another in stark boundaries, as if plants observed the lines of political maps. Just a bit of feathering, blurring, and intermingling at these edges would transform these plantings into less static, more interesting spaces that evoke a sense of process. The plants' interplay would give each species more presence in a counterpoint of unity and contrast.

In our bistate attempts at woodland gardening, leitmotifs figure prominently, giving a sense of a unified community rather than a disjointed collection of favorite shade plants. Almost our entire Texas garden lies shaded beneath the canopy of several live oaks. These graceful characters make for quite dry conditions. Here the "ferns" we use repeatedly are hardy cycads that thrive in drought and shade: several scratchy *Dioon*, *Cycas*, and *Macrozamia* along with more benevolent *Zamia* and *Ceratozamia* species impart the visual if not tactile softness of ferns with added elegant evergreen structure. The woefully restricted area of shade in Colorado where we meagerly attempt to create a bit of forest magic has been rough on most ferns. The few consistently tough enough for this garden's high pH, heavy clay soil, and dry air have been mainly various *Athyrium* species, so we have assembled a sizeable number of these, along with several dozen *Epimedium* selections from cold limestone areas in Asia to add cohesion to our tiny Colorado "woodland floor." Rocky Mountain woodland plants have not done so well in this Colorado garden as they are mostly adapted to the more acidic pH and looser soils of the nearby mountains where forests are found. This is a fine example that exposes the misguided assumption that native plants are inherently better adapted and reiterates the need for careful interpretation of the word *native*.

Herbaceous plants in the woods grow both one-here-one-there and as large sheets of self-replicating individuals. These patterns—where prevailing sameness is punctuated by occasional contrast created by different species—are found in most natural plant communities. Mirroring these in spirit adds richness to a garden. Up close to a woodland garden path, one might want to put more unusual plants and more of a mishmash of slower-growing species, while in areas more distantly viewed from the path, one can establish guilds of just a few more readily available and/or more easily propagated woodlanders, for a stronger visual impact both of texture and bloom. Many woodland gardens in the British Isles fail to follow this nature-informed model. Both a high level of plantsmanship and a climate that allows so many different plants to thrive make it difficult for gardenmakers there to limit themselves, even if it means sacrificing the essence of a woodland experience. Yet one of this and one of that throughout, even when carefully placed to provide artistic contrast of foliage and flower, feels artificial and lacks liveliness. Where are the sheets of fresh ferns, blankets of heart-shaped shamrocks and wild gingers, clusters of saw palmettos, pools of pale phlox and foamflower? Groups of plants give the feel of a healthy woodland where self-perpetuating, fertile, productive plants thrive alongside fragile rarities.

Allowing plants to feather and intermingle with each other, rather than keeping stark boundaries between them as commonly practiced, expresses natural, graceful coexistence. Astilbe and *Iris pseudacorus*, Chanticleer, Wayne, Pennsylvania.

THE HARDIEST CYCADS

These cycads withstand winter frosts down to 20 degrees F and occasional lows in the teens (USDA zones 8–11).

Ceratozamia hildae, bamboo cycad
Ceratozamia kuesteriana, El Cielo
  horncone
Ceratozamia latifolia
Ceratozamia mexicana, Mexican
  horncone
Ceratozamia sp. Palma Sole
Ceratozamia sp. Tamazunchale
Cycas panzihuaiensis
Cycas revoluta, sago palm
Cycas taitungensis, Formosan sago palm
Dioon angustifolium
Dioon edule, Mexican sago, chamal
Dioon sp. Palma Sole
Dioon sp. Queretaro blue
Encephalartos cycadifolius
Encephalartos ghellinckii
Encephalartos lehmanii
Encephalartos princeps

Macrozamia communis
Macrozamia johnsonii
Macrozamia miquelii
Macrozamia moorei

Macrozamia stenomera
Zamia integrifolia (syn. *Z. floridana*),
  coontie
Zamia umbrosa, Palatka giant coontie

In dry shade under live oaks, fernlike cycads and purple heart look fresh and lively even in the hottest, most parched months. *Zamia integrifolia, Setcreasea pallida* 'Pale Puma', authors' garden, Austin, Texas.

PLANT GUILDS FOR WOODLAND GARDENS

Here are several suggested combinations of herbaceous plants for the woodland floor. These plants grow well and look good together, and are neither overly rare nor prohibitively expensive. This way, substantial numbers can be acquired and planted, avoiding the "one-of-each" collector's syndrome that can fight a woodland mood. Especially rare, pricey, and/or strongly variegated or otherwise visually dominant plants are often best given specimen status in the garden rather than integrated into guilds. Gardens in gentle climates such as the Pacific Northwest and the mid-Atlantic region can support all the combinations included in the cool-climate category and many in the warm-climate category as well.

Cool-climate guilds

Aconitum napellus (late monkshood), *Actaea simplex* (syn. *Cimicifuga simplex*, snakeroot), and *Anemone hupehensis* (Japanese anemone)

Aruncus dioicus 'Kneiffii' (dwarf goatsbeard), *Hosta lancifolia* (narrowleaf hosta), and *Carex morrowii* 'Ice Dance' (silver sedge)

Asarum canadense (wood ginger), *Thalictrum thalictroides* (syn. *Anemonella thalictroides*, rue anemone), and *Trillium grandiflorum* (wake robin)

Asarum europaeum (European ginger), *Carex eburnea* (bristle-leaf sedge), and *Galanthus nivalis* (snowdrop)

Athyrium nipponicum 'Pictum' (Japanese painted fern), *Lathyrus vernus* (spring vetchling), and *Hyacinthoides hispanica* 'Alba' (white Spanish bluebell)

Brunnera macrophylla (Siberian forget-me-not), *Doronicum orientale* (leopard's bane), *Stylophorum lasiandrum* (celandine poppy), and *Dryopteris filix-mas* (male fern)

Digitalis purpurea (great foxglove), *Aruncus dioicus* (goatsbeard), *Astilbe chinensis* (dwarf astilbe), and *Luzula nivea* (wood rush)

Diphylleia cymosa (twinleaf), *Actaea racemosa* (syn. *Cimicifuga racemosa*, black snakeroot), and *Lilium superbum* (Turk's cap lily)

Eurybia divaricata (syn. *Aster divaricatus*, white wood aster) and *Pulmonaria* 'Majeste' or 'Samourai' (silver lungwort)

Helleborus ×*hybridus* (Lenten rose), *Epimedium* ×*youngianum* (barrenwort), and *Narcissus* 'Filly', 'Toby the First', or 'W. P. Milner' (pale early-blooming daffodil)

Hepatica americana (liverleaf), *Tiarella wherryi* (Wherry's foamflower), and *Erythronium grandiflorum* (trout lily)

Iris cristata (crested iris) and *Sedum ternatum* (white wood sedum)

Polemonium reptans (creeping Jacob's ladder), *Trillium luteum* (yellow toadshade), *Luzula sylvatica* (wood rush), and *Primula elatior* (oxslip primrose)

Pulmonaria saccharata 'Roy Davidson' (lungwort), *Dicentra eximia* 'Alba' (white fernleaf bleeding heart), and *Narcissus* 'Thalia' (late white daffodil)

Thalictrum aquilegifolium (meadow rue), *Hakonechloa macra* (hakone grass), and *Lilium martagon* (Turk's cap lily)

Tiarella cordifolia (foamflower), *Phlox stolonifera* (creeping phlox), *Carex plantaginea* (plantain-leaf sedge), and *Narcissus* 'Hawera' (dwarf daffodil)

Warm-climate guilds

Ajuga tenori 'Valfredda' (chocolate chip bugleweed), *Freesia laxa* (painted petals), and *Kaempferia pulchra* 'Alva' (peacock ginger)

Asparagus macowanii (ming fern) and *Crinum moorei* var. *schmidtii* (white crinum lily)

Begonia grandis and *Dryopteris erythrosora* (autumn fern)

Carex morrowii 'Silk Tassel' (silver sedge), *Hexastylis shuttleworthii* (syn. *Asarum shuttleworthii* 'Callaway' (spotted ginger), and *Bletilla striata* (ground orchid)

Eomecon chionantha (snow poppy) and *Onoclea sensibilis* (sensitive fern)

Iris 'Nada', *Ophiopogon chingii* (curly mondo grass), *Oxalis regnellii* 'Jade' or 'Silver Shade' (silver shamrock), and *Hyacinthoides hispanica* (Spanish bluebell)

Lycoris radiata (red spider lily) and *Athyrium* 'Ghost'

Malvaviscus arboreus var. *drummondii* (Turk's cap) and *Alstroemeria psittacina* (parrot lily)

Reineckia carnea, *Curcuma longa* (*C. petiolata* hort.) 'Emperor', and *Zephyranthes atamasca* (Atamasco lily)

Tricyrtis formosana (toad lily), *Selaginella braunii* (arborvitae fern), and *Iris tectorum* (Japanese roof iris)

Woodwardia orientalis (mother fern), *Lilium formosanum* (Formosa lily), and *Farfugium japonicum* (syn. *Ligularia japonicum*) 'Giganteum' (giant groundsel)

Zingiber zerumbet (shampoo ginger), *Thelypteris kunthii* (syn. *Thelypteris normalis*, southern shield fern), and *Allium neapolitanum* (Naples onion)

Guilds for both warm and cool climates

Adiantum capillus-veneris (warm climate) or *A. pedatum* (cool climate) (maidenhair fern), *Aquilegia canadensis* (eastern columbine), and *Heuchera americana* 'Dale's Strain' (alumroot)

Arisaema triphyllum (Jack-in-the-pulpit), *Spigelia marilandica* (Indian pink), and *Carex platyphylla* (blue sedge)

Chasmanthium latifolium (wild oats), *Chrysogonum virginianum* (green and gold), and *Aquilegia chrysantha* (golden columbine)

Cyclamen hederifolium and *Carex appalachica* (Appalachian sedge)

Phlox divaricata (blue wood phlox), *Polygonatum odoratum* 'Variegatum' (Solomon's seal), and *Leucojum aestivum* (spring snowflake)

LEFT In this eastern woodland garden, a guild of foamflower, ferns, and golden groundsel colonizes a shaded hillside as might occur in the wild. *Tiarella cordifolia*, *Matteuccia struthiopteris*, *Senecio aureus*, *Phlox stolonifera*, Chanticleer, Wayne, Pennsylvania.

BELOW Species native to the Piedmont region of the mid-Atlantic states feature in this garden. Sheets of Quaker ladies make a pale blue froth through which other woodland plants grow easily, under a light canopy of eastern dogwood at wood's edge. *Hedyotis caerulea*, *Cornus florida*, *Polystichum acrostichoides*, Mount Cuba Center, Greenville, Delaware.

The serenity of open spaces holds allure for many people. Needle-and-thread grass (*Hesperostipa comata*) undulates oceanlike on the Sandhills, a region of mid-grass prairie in north-central and northwestern Nebraska.

Prairie as a natural model

In direct contrast to the intimate stillness of woodland are the broad views, big skies, and sunlit plants of prairies. Windblown and alive with birds and insects, prairies have natural rhythms that are strong and grand rather than soft and subtle. Growth and color peaks in high summer and autumn rather than the spring ebullience of the woods. As with forests, many people are drawn to these natural places; the term "open space," used these days for often degraded remnants of untamed land sandwiched between developments, speaks volumes about this longing for a more uncrowded, less claustrophobic experience. The North American prairie has moved many a soul and more than a few designers: during the first half of the twentieth century, Danish-American gardenmaker and landscape architect Jens Jensen pioneered a style in the American Midwest that was highly influenced by nature, making prairie plantings as well as woodland a dominant part of much of his work.

The rich soils of North America's heartland, now given over mostly to agriculture, have engendered an exceptional palette of herbaceous perennials and grasses, paralleling the richness of this continent's forest communities. For those who merely want a taste of great plants, not a prairie per se, these communities make for one fine menu. As we mentioned earlier, in the first half of the twentieth century, German plantsman Karl Foerster set the stage by promoting garden use of grasses and large, long-lived, easy-care herbaceous perennials, many North American prairie natives among them. On the purist end of the scale, prairie

ABOVE A wild meadow in south-central Texas bursts with paintbrush, blue sage, and prairie larkspur in April. The plants' colors mark their places well on into the distance, creating repeated patterns that serve as visual structure in an otherwise structureless matrix. *Castilleja indivisa, Salvia farinacea, Delphinium virescens, Gaillardia pulchella, Pyrrhopappus multicaulis,* Karnes County, Texas.

LEFT The North American prairie is home to many striking herbaceous perennials. These untamed beauties offer gardens form and texture as well as a long season of interest. North American giant and narrowleaf coneflowers mix with Eurasian star allium and feather reed grass. *Rudbeckia maxima, Echinacea angustifolia, Allium christophii, Calamagrostis ×acutiflora* 'Karl Foerster', Royal Horticultural Society Garden at Wisley, Surrey, England, Piet Oudolf design.

The classic northern European meadow, with its mix of cool-season grasses and showy forbs, has a softly domestic mood. Here ox-eye daisies draw the eye to a similarly chalky white bee skep in the distance. *Chrysanthemum leucanthemum*, Sticky Wicket, Dorset, England, Pam Lewis design.

restoration and planting have become possible even for the novice gardener and suburban homeowner, thanks in great part to Neil Diboll and his pioneering Wisconsin business, Prairie Nursery, which was pivotal in producing seed and small-size, vigorous starts of prairie plants along with practical information for this growing interest.

Prairies and meadows continue to inform and inspire much of recent planting style, both here and abroad. This is good news for plant-driven design. Most visible in this country through their commercial landscape work, Wolfgang Oehme and James Van Sweden spearheaded use of ornamental grasses and mass plantings of bold perennials with several seasons of interest, supported by the passion of nurserymen like Kurt Bluemel on the East Coast and John Greenlee on the West, who made diverse selections of beautiful grasses available to Americans for the first time. At the same time in Germany, municipal plantings using ecological models with an emphasis on steppes and prairies entranced many. Dutch designer Piet Oudolf has recently expanded the palette with more eclectic flowering perennials and bulbs. The large scale of his plantings, often with open views on flat terrain, fits comfortably with the Dutch landscape and tradition, and translates well to North American places with similar character such as the Great Plains and the northern tier states along the Great Lakes. In the Midwest, his work evocatively echoes the prairie once there and finds a suitable climate match for its hallmark plants. Oudolf's artistic eye and plantsmanship take the plantings farther than many before.

The prairie continues to spark evolution of new styles in Europe, and its ties to the North American landscape make it pertinent for many spaces and easy to respond to for Americans. Yet when prairie-style plantings are forced into a traditional English-style garden setting, where old stone walls, clipped hedges, and perfectly manicured lawns nip at their heels, the effects can seem contrived. Some praise this "artistic tension"; we more often find the marriage self-conscious and disagreeable. In rustic and agricultural settings, prairie-inspired plantings find a more comfortable home.

ABOVE In a dry meadow garden, a cosmopolitan mix of American, South African, and Mediterranean natives mingle. *Echinacea paradoxa*, *Penstemon cobaea*, *Nassella tenuissima*, *Kniphofia stricta*, *Echium lusitanicum*, *Verbascum densiflorum*, *Salvia pratensis*, Denver Botanic Gardens, Panayoti Kelaidis design.

LEFT This meadow receives twenty inches or less of moisture annually. Cool- and warm-season grasses from North America and Europe consort with western wildflowers. *Koeleria macrantha*, *Festuca idahoensis*, *Argemone polyanthemos*, *Delphinium virescens*, *Thelesperma filifolium*, *Echinacea pallida*, authors' garden, Fort Collins, Colorado.

RIGHT Autumn is kind to prairie-inspired gardens, highlighting the subtle, warm hues of the plentiful grasses. *Aesculus glabra*, *Amelanchier canadensis*, *Acer grandidentatum*, and *Euphorbia epithymoides* erupt in flaming red. Authors' garden, Fort Collins, Colorado.

BELOW Displayed in puzzlelike patches, the warm fall colors of both garden and natural landscape make a strong statement on this wide-open site of grass-oak chaparral. *Gaura lindheimeri* 'Siskiyou Pink', *Panicum virgatum*, *Hylotelephium spectabile*, *Calamagrostis brachytricha*, in the distance *Quercus gambelii*, Red Butte Botanical Garden, Salt Lake City, Utah.

Mirroring a quintessential North American prairie combination of grass with composite, native daisy and exotic grass make cheerful fall garden duets in the authors' meadow garden. Fort Collins, Colorado.

TOP *Helianthus salicifolius* 'Low Down', *Miscanthus sinensis* 'Nippon'.

ABOVE *Symphyotrichum oblongifolium, Sesleria autumnalis, Solidago ohioensis, Festuca mairei.*

Steppe versus prairie as model

The term *steppe*, usually applied to cold, dry grasslands of central Asia, is less familiar to Americans than *prairie*. What Europeans call steppe gardens are along the lines of the prairie style, but include plants from the Old World rather than using mainly North American natives. These plants and plantings are mesic, meaning they require regular moisture during their growing season, and they are adapted to temperate climates. For example, two of the signature grasses used for European steppe plantings are tufted hair grass (*Deschampsia caespitosa*) and prairie dropseed (*Sporobolus heterolepis*). These beautiful midsize bunchgrasses are ideally suited to interpretations of the prairie style, but as choices for the vast hot-summer, dry regions of this continent, they require more horticultural intervention in the form of irrigation and soil amendment than would a garden based on a natural plant community from drought-ridden regions.

Here what we call steppe is more like the true central Asian grasslands, and includes the short-grass prairies of North America along with other similar dry-climate plant communities where woody plants are excluded or reduced to scrub below knee height. Gray-green and blue tussock grasses and aromatic pewter and green subshrubs mingle with low-spreading silver forbs. Unabashed sunlight celebrates these fine-textured, shimmering plants. As the seasons wax and wane, low bulbs and perennials intermittently offer up blossoms that vibrate in the breeze on short, wiry stems, studding the steppe with jewel-like color. These plants and plantings are fit to endure significantly less than twenty inches of rainfall annually, as well as extremes of heat and sometimes cold.

Most modern gardening styles have been born and gone on to flourish in moister regions than those that support steppes. However, America's recent population shift to the interior West and Southwest makes steppes more relevant all the time. Many beautiful plants from tall-grass and midgrass prairies, as well as lush, large perennials and grasses from other moist, temperate parts of the world, do not grow as well in dry or very hot regions. In cool, dry climates an

RIGHT Still tawny in dormancy, warm-season-grower buffalo grass is festooned with late-winter blossoms of *Iris reticulata*, a small, naturalizing, drought-resistant bulb. This gives the lawn a more natural spirit and people a seasonal floral event to enjoy. Northern Colorado, Ogden design.

BELOW In moist, temperate climates, commonly used cool-season turf grasses such as Kentucky bluegrass and tall fescue dominate and suppress all but the most vigorous bulbs. Exposed rocks and prolific 'Hawera' narcissi romance this hillside lawn. Chanticleer, Wayne, Pennsylvania.

inordinate amount of water thrown on these plants and massive amounts of organic matter added to the soil can make them grow; where it is consistently hot—whether dry or humid—most prairie plants languish or at best look good for a fraction of the time they do in northern temperate regions.

Even when kept on life support in the form of water and soil amendments, such plants convey an image of temperate lushness that jars with the natural landscapes of hot or semiarid places. A garden in the beautiful scrubland near Santa Fe overflows with grand sweeps of Mexican feather grass (*Nassella tenuissima*) abutting large panels of purple garden sage (*Salvia nemorosa* 'Mainacht') in a classic prairie-inspired planting. While feather grass is certainly more drought tolerant than many, purple garden sage is not. What's more, the sage blooms for about a month in the harsh sunlight and dry air of high-elevation New Mexico and then looks coarse and weedy the rest of the year. Even if a better-suited perennial had been chosen, placing plants in broad swards fights with the texturally more intricate landscape all around. Perhaps if the planting were in town or surrounded by walls, separated from the natural land, it might sit more comfortably. In urban spaces or enclosed gardens, such artificially lush plantings look less out of place, but left out to blend with a xeric rural or native landscape, they become as prosaic-looking as a strip-mall planting of petunias.

Many prairie-inspired styles permit plants to guide compositions and celebrate their individual characteristics but often miss the mark regarding an equally important aspect of plant-driven design, that a garden's plants must have a dialog with and be a match for the site, visually and culturally. Coneflowers, veronicastrums, and tall grasses melding into a rough hay meadow; sheets of rudbeckias, foxtail grass, and 'Herbstfreude' sedums softening a world of inner-city concrete: this is prairie-inspired planting that embraces site. On the other hand, such plants clambering up a slope, hiding the terrain's bones and flopping as they fight gravity, or shouting out temperate profusion when their surrounds whisper the textural subtleties born of

BULBS FOR STEPPE PLANTINGS

The following bulbs and corms grow best in climates with cold winters and warm summers. They have proven perennial and continue to increase in numbers and bloom in our steppe garden in northern Colorado. Some are best in moister soil while others prefer to bake after going dormant. The ones requiring some extra moisture are marked with ✳.

Allium coryi
Allium drummondi
Allium flavum subsp. *nanum*
Allium fraseri
Allium karataviense
Allium maximowiczii ✳
Allium moly
Allium oreophilum (syn. *Allium ostrowskianum*)
Allium thunbergii ✳
Anemone blanda, Grecian windflower
Bellevalia spp.
Brimeura amethystina (syn. *Hyacinthus amethystinus*)
Bulbocodium vernum ✳
Chouardia litardieri ✳ (syn. *Scilla litardieri*)
Crocus ancyrensis
Crocus angustifolius
Crocus biflorus
Crocus chrysanthus
Crocus korolkowii
Crocus pulchellus

Crocus sieberi
Crocus speciosus
Crocus tommasinianus
Iris danfordiae
Iris histrioides
Iris reticulata, snow iris
Muscari spp., grape hyacinth
Narcissus 'Baby Moon', 'Fairy Chimes', 'Gipsy Queen', 'Hawera', 'Little Gem', 'Midget', 'Snipe', 'Segovia', 'Xit'✳, dwarf daffodil
Narcissus wilkommii ✳
Ornithogalum balansae
Ornithogalum fimbriatum
Ornithogalum oligophyllum
Scilla bifolia ✳
Scilla luciliae ✳ (syn. *Chionodoxa luciliae*), glory of the snow
Scilla sardensis ✳ (syn. *Chionodoxa sardensis*), squill, glory of the snow
Tulipa batalinii
Tulipa biflora
Tulipa hissarica
Tulipa humilis
Tulipa kolpakowskiana
Tulipa korolkowii
Tulipa linifolia
Tulipa 'Little Beauty'
Tulipa 'Little Princess'
Tulipa saxatilis
Tulipa sylvestris
Tulipa 'Titty's Star'
Tulipa urumiensis
Tulipa vvedenskyi
Tulipa wilsoniana

Bulbous plants, more than other plant types, have easily observable synchronicity with seasonal cycles. Their responsive bloom feeds our anticipation and expectation; their ephemeral blossoms make that time all the more special. Species that naturalize are a prime choice for steppe gardens, as they give a sense of untamed self-replication, and many have evolved to endure seasonal drought, poor soil, and the extremes of temperature characteristic of similar communities across the globe. Dozens of bulbous species and thousands of individuals bejewel the authors' steppe garden in northern Colorado.

OPPOSITE TOP Early spring: *Tulipa sylvestris* and *Narcissus* 'Segovia' with *Pulsatilla vulgaris*, *Phlox bifida* 'Betty Blake' blooming through still-dormant grass.

OPPOSITE BOTTOM Late spring: *Tulipa* 'Little Princess' and *Anemone blanda* with foliage of *Allium maximowiczii* and *Stachys iva*.

TOP LEFT Early summer: *Allium moly* and dwarf pussytoes (*Antennaria parvifolia*).

LEFT Autumn: *Allium thunbergii* and *Crocus speciosus* with grasses and *Artemisia frigida*.

Low-growing, drought-tolerant bunchgrasses make up the primary matrix of a steppe planting. Their soft textures and subtle color distinctions— greens, gray-greens, blues— lend a fresh yet restful serenity to a space as well as making it seem larger. Authors' garden, Fort Collins, Colorado.

drought, heat, and poor soil—such insensitivity confuses and confounds. Plant-driven design is informed by site and region; ignore this and even the most plant-rich garden will suffer. Once again, here is a case for regional interpretation of design, in this instance the suitability of some natural models over others. The Santa Fe garden would do well to look to steppes rather than prairies.

Our recent work has been devoted in part to developing an aesthetic and palette that draws inspiration from the steppe, because we love prairies but the regions where we live, garden, and design need and invite this plant community to undergo new interpretation. This emerging option is in its infancy, as many of the grasses and sedges we select as garden matrices and leitmotifs are not yet commercially available in quantity, and there is much yet to be learned about compatibility and longevity of the perennials and subshrubs with which we are experimenting. Like the prairie palette, many of these steppe-suited plants celebrate wind and light with their textures and ability to move. They also retain their form once dormant and dried. Small bulbous plants are interspersed and allowed to naturalize to add winter and early spring color; some species flower with monsoonal rains later in the year. We hope to inspire others to experiment with the impressive array of lovely, drought-tolerant, adaptable species that can give hotter, drier gardens of North America that same feeling of serenity and openness that endears the prairie to so many.

These steppe-adapted plants offer a more ecologically sound alternative to resource-intensive mesic species not just in terms of water and soil additives. There is the conundrum of garden cleanup. Prairie gardens create an immense amount of vegetation that dies down annually and, in the absence of large herbivores or fire, that must be dealt with by gardeners. Not all gardeners or gardens can deal with a bush hog, an industrial-strength chipper-shredder, or even a compost heap that is large enough to accommodate the debris. And far from all communities have municipal composting. Once the onerous cleanup is completed, does it all get carted off to the landfill? In a steppe garden plants grow more slowly, to a much smaller ultimate height, and many are partially woody and don't die down to the ground each year. The result is far less annual work cutting the planting back in late winter, and far less debris.

Beyond cleanup practicalities, steppe plantings offer an alternative to lawn spaces not used for traffic. Unlike typical ground cover and shrub alternatives trotted out to replace unused lawn, steppes retain much of the visual openness and calm of lawn—that pool of seeming sameness against which more complex and busy plantings of a garden can contrast. Using low plants with similar fine textures creates an overall effect that conveys in microcosm the repose of a grassy horizon even if the area is quite small. In contrast, a prairie-inspired planting needs more room to give that sense of generous space, because individual plants operate on a much larger and coarser scale. Up close and in a constrained area, prairie plants and plantings look gawky and, to some, even intimidating. So-called pocket prairies— diminutive urban or suburban prairie gardens—generally look like weed patches. On the other hand, steppe plantings offer a superb new idiom in scale with smaller home gardens as well as a beautiful and diverse alternative to the overused, environmentally unsound response of covering all bare ground with highly uniform, resource-intensive turf.

Alpine communities as models for rock gardens

One more natural community to look to for inspiration in plant-driven design is found in alpine regions. In traditional Asian cultures, mountains and their plant communities have enthralled people for hundreds, even thousands of years, and influenced horticulture and gardens. Bonsai and Pen Jing that echo the gnarled, windswept forms of mountain trees, and large stones placed to recreate mountains in microcosm both reflect the powerful influence of high places on these cultures' sense of beauty. As leisure travel became an option for a much larger number of people in the last century and a half, high mountains inevitably lured many. Northern Europeans, more prone to romanticizing the wild than their southern counterparts, fell hard

In a rock garden fashioned by nature, blue mountain columbines—the state flower of Colorado—grace a boulder field above tree line. *Aquilegia caerulea, Mertensia ciliata*, Mount Audubon, north-central Colorado.

and hopelessly for high-elevation flora and its varied rocky haunts. The rock garden was born, in all its loveliness and eccentric excesses.

Alpine communities are so distinctive, both in their endemic plants and in their romantic appeal, that their essence deserves exploration. Rock gardens, for better or worse, have taken their place as a viable garden style for much of North America. It is no accident that so many people come away from a trip to the mountains with the burning desire to recreate a bit of what they saw there. Above tree line the world over, strange and beautiful land-scapes unfold, briefly and gloriously bursting to life each year between months of entombment in snow and cold. This intensity of delicate growth and bloom, in such stark contrast with the harsh climate and unyielding stone that engender it, melts the heart. Not unlike the large-eyed cuteness of baby mammals thought to be an evolution-ary development to foster maternal behavior toward these rather helpless young, a comparable ploy of alpine plants exploits extra large, profuse, and pretty flowers perched atop diminutive stems and leaves to ensure attracting an often elusive pollinator on the few days they can. Puppies, kittens, moss pinks and gentians. Most of us are lost once we see them.

Many of these plants share small stature and tidy growth habits with their lower-elevation compatriots in difficult climates, the steppe plants. We find there is even some overlap of actual species. This is a big help, as the great-est challenge for many rock gardeners is to find plants that impart the distinctive look of alpines yet tolerate the often hotter, more humid, and less well-drained conditions of

TOP LEFT Dwarf in stature, with comely rounded form and over-sized flowers, cushion phloxes make adaptable, tractable rock garden subjects in many climates, even those not remotely similar to high mountains. *Phlox bifida* seedlings, Rock Alpine Garden, Denver Botanic Gardens.

LEFT Crammed into a rock crevice, a tiny congested bun of moss campion ekes out a harsh existence, blooming prolifically to attract whatever pollinator might chance by in the brief, windy summer at twelve thousand feet in elevation. *Silene acaulis*, Mount Audubon, north-central Colorado.

most lower-elevation gardens. It helps to generalize, scouting for any and all plants that may tolerate one's specific conditions and remain short in stature with relatively large flowers; ones with cushion, mounding, rosette, or cascading habit; dwarf forms of species, and the like.

As in gardens modeled after desert plant communities, the unusual form and compelling character of many alpine plants invite museum-piece placement. In some desert- and mountain-inspired collections, plants never touch. Even worse, they often have prominent labels, as their obscurity makes their names harder to remember and their rarity as well as their sometimes difficult cultivation inspire a bit of showing off. This static, overcontrolled situation where plants are not allowed to mingle and respond to one another and are placed more as trophies than as garden denizens is, we believe, one of the reasons that rock gardens have not been wholly embraced by the general public. Certainly there are places in the wild mountains where plants grow so sparsely that they do not touch, but it is easily as common to see rich communities of alpine species clustered and woven together into a tight-knit mix. Most people enjoy profusion in their gardens, not just a clumsy unrelated series of intimidating rarities, and want the same among their rocks.

Placement, as with the bold succulents in desert gardens discussed earlier, also should relate to any and all changes in grade: planting at an angle reflects the response a plant would have in nature to such a slope. Rock gardens are typically built on a change in grade. We would like to suggest that this is not as important an element in capturing the spirit of high places as it would at first seem. Certainly a hillside offers a grand spot to delve into an alpine-inspired planting, but often a gentle slope, a rock wall, or even a series of troughs will do beautifully. In fact, where drainage allows, we promote the idea of essentially flat rock gardens as a wonderful alternative to the difficult-to-construct and often unattractive man-made berms and mini-mountains that dominate rock garden style. For purists, a jog of their memory to gently flattened mountaintops in the wild, strewn with beautiful stones and plants, should

In a highly creative design for a difficult site, this backyard rock garden is built up against and hides a massive concrete retaining wall that is part of adjacent road construction.

The verticality offers extra surface area for gardening and close encounters with all sorts of plant treasures as well as interesting stone. Stireman garden, Salt Lake City, Utah.

OPPOSITE TOP Rock gardens need not be limited to a small scale or strictly alpine spirit. Bulky boulders and plants with stature serve larger, more naturalistic sites and gardens well. *Yucca baccata*, *Tulipa whittallii*, *T. clusiana* var. *chrysantha*, *T. linifolia*, *Nepeta mussinii*, northern Colorado, Ogden design.

OPPOSITE BOTTOM Rock garden plants have a demure quality that appeals to many, especially when juxtaposed with hard, immutable stone. The rocks offer warmer or cooler, wetter or drier aspects that meet the needs of a diverse array of cosmopolitan species. *Clematis columbiana* var. *tenuiloba*, *Primula saxatilis*, *Bergenia cordifolia*, Laporte Avenue Nursery display garden, Fort Collins, Colorado, Kirk Fieseler and Karen Lehrer design.

TOP LEFT Springtime is magical in the rock garden, with most species bursting into exuberant bloom. *Pulsatilla vulgaris*, *Arabis ferdinandi-coburgii*, *Picea pungens* 'R. H. Montgomery', Laporte Avenue Nursery display garden, Fort Collins, Colorado, Kirk Fieseler and Karen Lehrer design.

LEFT Bucking tradition, this dryland rockery takes on a southwestern spirit with larger plant species and unconventional stonework. *Penstemon palmeri*, *Eriogonum umbellatum*, *Eschscholzia californica*, cacti, Scott Skogerboe garden, Fort Collins, Colorado.

invite more gardens of this sort. It is delightful to walk into and through a horizontal rock garden, hopping from rock to rock, inspecting lovely plant treasures as one goes, something not usually possible in more vertical renditions.

In our Colorado backyard we do just that. A grade change of merely two feet seemed hardly inspiring for a rockery. We built one anyway, using blocky local sandstone. It has turned out surprisingly well, more inviting than many refined, plant-rich rock gardens. The relatively flat terrain provides easy access and joins effortlessly with the rest of the garden.

So many gardens, alpine-inspired or otherwise, are fraught not only with the overstuffed-attic syndrome of the collector but also with the gardenmaker's compulsion to create plantings with different themes that he or she doesn't put much thought into unifying. So a rock garden abuts a water feature that sits near the vegetables, which in turn adjoins a perennial border, which runs alongside a rose garden, which faces a vine-covered pergola, which is surrounded by lawn. In an ambitious garden, these might go on to be divided into "rooms." This Disney World–like collection of unconnected themes often makes the entire space feel constraining, manipulative, and discordant.

We managed to avoid most of these pitfalls by carefully integrating our rock garden. Otherwise it could easily have

BELOW Blending a rock garden into its surroundings can often be a challenge. Repeating similar plants in adjacent areas—bulbs, conifers, and grasses in this garden—help make the transition less abrupt and dissonant. *Tulipa sylvestris*, *T. whittallii*, *Thermopsis lupinoides*, *Euphorbia epithymoides*, *Sesleria glauca*, jonquilla daffodils, authors' garden, Fort Collins, Colorado.

OPPOSITE TOP AND BOTTOM Compact and dwarf selections of conifers are stalwarts in rock gardens and sustain beauty from spring and early summer's floral explosion to the subtler seasons of late summer, fall, and winter. The evergreen stems of yellow-flowered broom do the same. Authors' garden, Fort Collins, Colorado.

turned out to be hopelessly lost, set adrift as it is on a flat bit of suburbia. First we chose the most expansive space on the property; contrary to what one might think, small spaces are not better for small plantings, as a dollhouse-like effect takes over. Also, we are blessed with a view of the foothills from our backyard, so it seemed natural to tie the real mountains to our mini version of them. Many of the plants we selected are reiterated in form and texture in the adjacent steppe. The rock garden's dwarf conifers mirror larger needled evergreens that mingle throughout our property. Gravel mulch covers the rock garden as well as the xeric plantings behind it, and the secondary paths that interweave throughout the entire backyard. And the low-profile stone sits well on the flat site, sharing texture, grain, and color with the buff flagstone of our patio, firepit, and primary paths.

Rock gardens, whether of the wild sort or fashioned by human hands, have the distinction of adding the enticing element of stone. It is easy to become as obsessed with rocks as with plants. Not just alpine gardeners fall for this: witness the "meteor" plantings so common in commercial landscape work, where large rocks are plopped incongruously on a site with no relation to place, to plants there, or to each other. The key to incorporating stone in a garden is not to lose sight of its essence in the wild. It may vary in size, shape, texture, color, and the way it protrudes from the earth, whether as linear strata or massive irregular forms,

Rock formations and their plant communities in the wild offer a bounty of lessons in design and cultivation of rock gardens. Sani Top, southern Drakensberg, Republic of South Africa.

but its interplay with plants more than any of its intrinsic qualities is what makes the real magic. As do plants, stones display patterns, placement, and process in nature. Ignoring this in a garden, as is often done by eager rock gardeners, creates a dissonance even more acute than when plants miss the mark. Boulders lying precariously on the soil, rather than partially settled into it, err in placement. Too much larger rock at the top of a slope, rather than moving toward the base as gravity would demand, ignores process. Too many small stones placed like fruit in a fruitcake on confined, steep berms flies in the face of both scale and pattern. These are just a few "stone sins" often encountered.

Learning from natural stone formations, generalizing one's plant palette to include adapted species not necessarily from high elevations that still capture the essence of alpine plants' distinctively charming attributes, and loosening the parameters of slope and scale to include tiny troughs and flat spaces all help make rock gardens rewarding for anyone enchanted by the world's high places and their plants. Observing patterns, placement, and process with both rock and plant ensures that one can truly savor a bit of these special places close at hand in the front or backyard.

Romantic human models for gardens

After all this, one would think nature is the only place to find the essence of patterns, placement, and process so vital to plant-driven design. Not so. Some of the most compelling places to find inspiration are man-made. These feature strong architecture overrun by plants. Ruins,

walls, and rooftops where plants have been permitted to take equal standing with the built elements all express the sense that nature is taking back some control over the human-made world—a romantic softening of the hand of man. The charming but constraining architecture of many central and southern European cities—built four, five, or even more centuries ago with narrow cobbled alleys and blocks of attached three- and four-story buildings—engendered a green revolt of sorts. People grew all kinds of plants and continue to do so to this day: vines clamber up walls; trailing plants spill over balconies and arcades; shrubs and small trees grow shoehorned into cracks in courtyard paving. Equally appealing, the green jungles of New York City's rooftop gardens bring gentle reprieve to one of the modern world's most overbuilt places.

Some romantic garden styles deliberately recreate such

situations, the ruin gardens famous in parts of the British Isles and Italy being the most obvious of these. In these kinds of gardens, placement, pattern, and process once again figure prominently, and plants are placed to respond to the built environment. A tree may be intentionally planted close to a dilapidated building to make it grow and bend away for more light and space. Vigorous vines are allowed to have their way with walls, arches, arbors, and trellises, cloaking and in some cases engulfing the architecture. Plants are also selected and planted to celebrate their response to time—self-seeding selections create patterns of slow dispersal over space as their progeny falls into and moves down the cracks of a wall and onto an adjoining pathway, giving a sense of continuity and process.

These effects can be created more quickly by mimicking plants' natural growth, response, and reproduction. So

PLANTS FOR BETWEEN STEPPING STONES

These plants are flat mat-forming species that tolerate some foot traffic.

Plants needing some shade

Lysimachia japonica 'Minutissima', tiny creeping Jenny

Ophiopogon japonicus 'Bluebird', 'Kyoto Dwarf', 'Nana', dwarf mondo grass

Sagina subulata, Irish moss

Plants tolerant of hot and dry conditions

Antennaria spp., pussytoes

Artemisia caucasica

Heterotheca jonesii

Paronychia spp., nailwort

Penstemon procumbens, mat penstemon

Sphaeromeria capitata

Plants for average sun and moisture

Acaena pusilla (syn. *Leptinella pusilla*), brass buttons

Bolax glebaria, plastic plant

Campanula cochlearifolia, dwarf bluebell

Carex caryophyllea 'Beatlemania'

Chamaemelum nobile, Roman chamomile

Draba repens

Erigeron scopulinus

Herniaria glabra, rupturewort

Lotus corniculatus, dwarf trefoil

Mazus reptans

Thymus spp. (prostrate species), thyme

Veronica liwanensis, *V. oltensis*, *V. repens* 'Sunshine', Turkish speedwell, creeping speedwell

Ruins strike deep emotional chords, especially when plants are growing and thriving in and among their skeletal structures and tumbling rubble.

OPPOSITE This ruin and its garden stand in place of a former residence but are wholly artificial—built from scratch rather than from the house once there. Their romantic power remains the same. *Corylopsis* sp., *Pieris japonica*, *Scilla luciliae*, cyclamineus daffodils, *Nyssa sylvatica*, Chanticleer, Wayne, Pennsylvania, Chris Woods design.

ABOVE In older cultures, artifice is rarely necessary as aged architecture abounds and true ruins are not uncommon. The benevolent climate of the British Isles encourages plants to colonize and engulf structures in very little time, and the romantic marriage of old masonry with rampant plants finds an easy home. *Geranium* spp., *Astilbe* spp., *Campanula* spp., *Filipendula purpurea*, The Garden House, Devon, England, Keith Wiley design.

RIGHT A small dry-stack stone wall, when stuffed and seeded with plants that enjoy such spaces, gives a visually appealing sense of process. It makes the case that architecture and the natural world can indeed coexist. *Geranium renardii*, *G. cinereum*, *Corydalis lutea*, *Gypsophila repens*, *Campanula* sp., Royal Horticultural Society Garden at Wisley, Surrey, England.

BELOW Located on a college campus, this outdoor amphitheater draws human activity of all sort, from solitary study to friendly chatter, lunches, theatrical and musical events, and clandestine seductions. The popularity of the space is no doubt due in part to its inviting combination of strong yet welcoming natural and architectural elements. Scott Arboretum, Swarthmore College, Swarthmore, Pennsylvania, Thomas W. Sears design.

instead of waiting for a tree to bend, one might select a crooked tree specimen to plant right next to the building, aging it immediately. The self-sowing plant in the wall might be joined by smaller individuals of the same species, planted as if they had sown themselves there. Of course, given time these effects happen of their own accord. We generally mix the two approaches, thinking about what our selected plants will possibly do and allowing them to grow, respond, and reproduce over time with our gentle guidance, yet also often at the outset choosing some plants and placing them so that they look as if they have already settled in for some time. Time is the ultimate master of the garden, yet all but the most patient gardenmaker is compelled to make strong marks of his or her own.

PLANTS FOR DRY-STACK STONE WALLS

These are plants that enjoy growing in tight quarters on vertical surfaces, with attractive cushion or cascading habits that enhance a wall. Many are classic rock garden plants, and other more obscure and/or more challenging species from that tradition serve as excellent wall plants as well. The following are generally available; these rock-lovers are undemanding when matched to climate.

Plants needing some shade

Adiantum spp., maidenhair fern
Androsace spp., rock jasmine
Aquilegia spp., dwarf columbine
Asarina procumbens, creeping snapdragon
Asplenium spp., spleenwort
Begonia sutherlandii
Carex spp. (many), sedge
Chiastophyllum oppositifolium, golden drops
Codonopsis spp.
Corydalis spp., fumitory
Cymbalaria muralis, Kenilworth ivy
Edraianthus spp.
Haberlea spp.
Heuchera spp., coral bells
Lewisia spp.
Oxalis spp.
Pellaea spp., cliff brake
Ramonda spp.

Rosularia spp., hen and chicks
Saxifraga spp.
Selaginella spp., spike moss
Semiaquilegia spp.
Telesonix jamesii
Thalictrum kiusianum, dwarf meadow rue

Plants tolerant of hot and dry conditions

Achillea ageratifolia, *A.* ×*kelleri*, *A. serbica* (and others), dwarf yarrow
Aethionema spp., stone cress
Alyssum spp.
Anacampseros spp.
Ballota pseudodictamnus 'Nana'
Bulbine frutescens, bulbine
Cotyledon orbiculatus, pig's ear
Dalea frutescens, black dalea
Delosperma spp., ice plant
Dianthus spp., pinks
Drosanthemum spp., ice plant
Dudleya spp.
Echeveria spp., hen and chicks
Erigeron spp. (many of the smaller ones), fleabane
Eriogonum spp., buckwheat
Glandularia spp., ground cover verbena
Graptopetalum spp., ghost plant
Graptoveria spp.
Marrubium globosum, dwarf round-leaf horehound

Melampodium leucanthum, blackfoot daisy
Nierembergia spp., cup flower
Origanum spp. (small species with large bracts), oregano, marjoram
Othonna spp.
Penstemon baccharifolius, *P. californicus*, *P. crandallii*, *P. davidsonii*, *P. purpusii*, *P. teucrioides* (and other small mat-forming or mounding species)
Pterocephalus spp., dwarf pincushion flower
Ptilotrichum spinosum
Ruschia spp., ice plant
Satureja spp., savory
Scutellaria spp., skullcap
Stachys chrysantha, *S. iva*, *S. lavandulifolia* (and other small species), betony
Talinum spp., flameflower
Teucrium aroanium, *T. cossonii*, *T. majoricum*, *T. marum*, *T. orientale* (and other dwarf species), germander
Thymophylla pentachaeta
Zauschneria spp., hummingbird trumpet, California fuchsia
Zinnia acerosa
Zinnia grandiflora, Rocky Mountain zinnia

Plants for average sun and moisture

Alchemilla alpina, dwarf lady's mantle
Antirrhinum molle, creeping snapdragon

PLANTS FOR DRY-STACK STONE WALLS, continued

Arabis spp., rock cress

Aubrieta spp., purple rock cress

Aurinia saxatilis, basket of gold

Campanula elatines, C. garganica, C. 'Birch Hybrid', *C. kemulariae, C. portenschlagiana, C. poscharskyana,* bellflower

Cerastium spp., mouse ears

Ceratostigma plumbaginoides, leadwort

Chaenorrhinum spp. dwarf snapdragon

Cheilanthes spp. (some like shade, some prefer full sun), lip fern

Cotula spp.

Crassula spp. (many of the smaller ones)

Diascia spp., twinspur

Draba spp.

Erinus alpinus

Erodium spp., storksbill

Erysimum kotschyanum, creeping wallflower

Geranium cinereum, G. dalmaticum, G. renardii, G. sanguineum (and other small species), dwarf cranesbill

Globularia spp.

Gypsophila aretioides, G. cerastioides, G. repens, dwarf baby's breath

Helichrysum spp.

Hylotelephium pachyclados (syn. *Sedum pachyclados*)

Hylotelephium sieboldii (syn. *Sedum sieboldii*), autumn daphne

Hylotelephium tatarinowii (syn. *Sedum tatarinowii*)

Hypericum spp., (dwarf) St. John's wort

Iberis spp., candytuft

Omphalodes luciliae, navelwort

Orostachys spp.

Petrophytum caespitosum, rock spirea

Petrorhagia saxifraga

Phedimus spp. (syn. *Sedum* spp.), ground cover sedum

Phlox bifida, P. kelseyi, P. subulata (and other small cushion phlox species)

Primula auricula, primrose

Saponaria ocymoides 'Nana' (syn. *Saponaria ocymoides* 'Compacta'), dwarf soapwort

Schivereckia podolica

Sedum spp. (many), stonecrop

Sempervivum spp., hen and chicks

Thymus spp. (some), thyme

Tradescantia sillamontana, velvet creeper

Veronica spp. (many small ones), speedwell

UNDERSTORY TREES & SHRUBS FOR WOODLAND GARDENS

While a multitude of herbaceous and ground-covering perennial plants for woodland gardens are well known and much loved, gardeners have a more difficult time coming up with the intermediate layer for the shaded garden—the understory shrubs and small trees. Here are some options.

Deciduous trees

Acer barbatum, southern sugar maple

Acer capillipes, snake bark maple

Acer circinatum, vine maple

Acer crataegifolium

Acer davidii, stripebark maple

Acer forrestii

Acer griseum, paperbark maple

Acer palmatum, Japanese maple

Acer pensylvanicum, moosewood

Acer pseudosieboldianum, dwarf Korean maple

Acer rufinerve, redvein maple

Acer sieboldianum

Alnus spp., alder

Amelanchier spp., serviceberry

Aralia spp., Hercules club

Asimina triloba, pawpaw

Carpinus caroliniana, ironwood

Cercis canadensis, eastern redbud

Chionanthus virginicus, fringe tree

Cladrastis kentukea, yellowwood

Cornus spp., dogwood

Davidia involucrata, handkerchief tree

Euonymus bungeana

Halesia spp., silverbell

Hamamelis spp., witch hazel

Magnolia kobus

Magnolia salicifolia, willowleaf magnolia

Magnolia sieboldii

Magnolia sinensis

Magnolia wilsonii

Nyssa sylvatica, tupelo

Ostrya virginica, hop hornbeam

Populus tremuloides, aspen

Stewartia spp.

Styrax spp., snowbell

Viburnum prunifolium, blackhaw

Viburnum rufidulum, rusty blackhaw

Evergreen trees

Arbutus menziesii, madrone

Cephalotaxus spp., plum yew

Clethra pringlei, Mexican summersweet

Magnolia delavayi

Magnolia ernestii (syn. *Michelia wilsonii*)

Magnolia grandiflora, southern magnolia

Magnolia maudiae

Maytenus boaria
Pseudopanax delavayi (syn. *Metapanax delavayi*)
Taxus spp., yew
Thujopsis dolabrata
Torreya spp., nutmeg yew
Trachycarpus spp., windmill palm
Trochodendron aralioides
Tsuga spp., hemlock
Umbellularia californica

Deciduous shrubs

Abelia chinensis
Abelia mosanensis
Abutilon spp., flowering maple
Alangium platanifolium var. *macrophyllum*
Aesculus californica, California buckeye
Aesculus parviflora, bottlebrush buckeye
Aesculus pavia, red buckeye
Callicarpa spp., beautyberry
Calycanthus spp., sweetshrub
Chimonanthus praecox, wintersweet
Clethra spp., summersweet
Corylopsis spp., winter hazel
Deinanthe spp.
Edgeworthia spp.
Eleutherococcus sieboldianus, fiveleaf aralia
Fothergilla spp.
Holodiscus spp., rock spirea
Hydrangea spp.
Kerria japonica, kerria
Lindera spp., spicebush

Lonicera spp., honeysuckle
Neillia spp.
Paeonia spp., tree peony
Rhododendron spp., deciduous azalea
Rhodotypos scandens, jetbead
Ribes spp., flowering currant
Rubus spp., bramble
Sinocalycanthus orientalis (syn. *Calycanthus orientalis*)
Sorbaria spp., false spirea
Stachyurus spp.
Staphylea spp., bladder nut
Symphoricarpos spp., snowberry
Vaccinium spp., blueberry
Viburnum spp. (many)

Evergreen shrubs

Andromeda spp.
Ardisia japonica
Aucuba japonica
Azara spp.
Camellia spp.
Chimonanthus nitens, Chinese evergreen wintersweet
Cleyera japonica
Cryptomeria japonica, dwarf cultivars
Daphne laureola
Daphne odora
Daphne tangutica
Daphniphyllum spp.
Drimys spp., winterbark
Enkianthus spp.

×*Fatshedera lizei*
Fatsia japonica
Gardenia spp.
Garrya elliptica, coast silktassel
Guihaia argyrata, Asian needle palm
Ilex pernyi, perny holly
Illicium spp., star anise
Itea spp., sweetspire
Juniperus communis, mountain juniper
Juniperus squamata
Kalmia spp., mountain laurel
Loropetalum chinense, Chinese witch hazel
Mahonia spp., grape holly
Magnolia figo var. *skinneriana*, banana shrub
Microbiota decussata, Siberian arborvitae
Nandina domestica
Osmanthus spp., sweet olive
Pieris spp., andromeda
Pittosporum spp.
Podocarpus spp.
Prunus lusitanica, Portuguese cherry laurel
Rhapidophyllum hystrix, needle palm
Rhododendron spp., rhododendron and evergreen azalea
Ruscus spp., butcher's broom
Sabal minor, dwarf palmetto
Sarcococca spp., sweetbox
Skimmia spp.
Taxus spp., yew
Vaccinium spp., blueberry
Viburnum spp. (many)

5

CONNECTING
Creating gardens that embrace people, places, and the natural world

PLANTS IN A GARDEN extend a strong connection to the natural world, through both their individual spirit and their deeply rooted relationship with one another and the site. Just as powerful is their ability to touch us, sensually and emotionally. These connections arise from physical experience through the five senses and emotions these sensations kindle, be they memories, fantasies, strong associations, or simple bodily pleasure. Perhaps the most basic is the sensory thrill of a garden's food, something strangely missing in many of the otherwise rich gardens we have visited over the past couple of decades. Our five children have all grown up delighting in the impulsive pleasures of snapping up sun-warmed cherry tomatoes, velvety raspberries, eye-wateringly piquant peppers, ambrosial peaches, and the like while wandering through our home gardens.

Plants, exceptionally diverse living beings that they are, grant a richness that architecture or artifact cannot. The power to elicit a sensory or an emotional response gives plants presence. A garden that allows them their full potency makes all sorts of experiences possible, from the universal down to the highly personal. Through our senses' interaction with the green world, we connect with nature, with the uniqueness of the place, and with the gardenmaker. In this way, a garden becomes more than a mere snapshot or viewing place. It passes into transcendence.

A sense of place through human connections

A garden that in some way—whether subtle or obvious—evokes its region's natural places, leaves a unique imprint on the senses, mind, and heart. This identity grounds the garden: a sense of place grows organically from a design that follows the plants' leads and respects natural patterns, placement, and process. Similarly, a sense of place emerges when plants in a garden call forth a human connection. A planting that evokes agricultural, historical, and/or cultural traditions links people across continents and across time; it connects us to one another.

Sometimes this experience is so dramatic and immersive that it feels like a trip to a faraway place. Such was the day we spent in the Classical Chinese Garden in downtown

OPPOSITE Plants are intriguing. They have the power to connect us with the natural world, with other people, and with ourselves. *Artemisia versicolor, Santolina chamaecyparissus* 'Nana', *Perovskia* ×*hybrida, Nepeta racemosa, Agastache rupestris, Eschscholzia californica, Zauschneria garrettii,* daughter Daphne in authors' garden, Fort Collins, Colorado.

Pond and willow are framed by a latticework window, presenting an intimate view. Classical Chinese Garden, Portland, Oregon.

Portland, Oregon. This small public garden combines authentic architecture with a huge array of Asian plants, both traditional garden plants and newer introductions. With an hour to spare before a meeting, we thought we would stop in and check out the garden, which fits into less than a city block. We almost missed our meeting and returned immediately thereafter to spend the rest of the day exploring this engrossing place. Neither of us has ever been to China, nor do we have much experience with Chinese art or tradition, so there was no sense of familiarity or belonging. Yet the universal sensory delight of this garden welcomed and drew us in. At every turn extraordinary architecture met with equally extraordinary plants. It didn't matter that we had never before peered though an intricately carved window at the branches of a weeping willow, nor heard the rustle of bamboo against latticework, nor smelled the flower of a rare species of magnolia. Learning later that Chinese craftsmen had come over to help create the garden, that the Chinese-American community of Portland had donated plants, time, and money to the project, and that expert plantsman Sean Hogan had helped select the vast and striking array of Asian flora here added another layer of connection to our experience. By visiting this garden, we felt we had come to know a bit of China and its people, and sensed a kinship through our shared love of the intrinsic beauty of plants and nature.

Certainly a great deal of the power of place that this public garden puts forth is due to its architecture as well as its plantings. In most gardens this is unnecessary, yet people go to great lengths to mirror culture with artifact, putting endless effort and money into architectural features and hard elements to evoke a sense of place without giving equal or greater weight to plants. Iconic species like Italian cypresses, southern magnolias, hollyhocks, or old garden roses make connections with traditions, culture, and history as well as or better than any statue, fountain, column, wrought-iron gate, or piece of pottery. Nonliving components certainly contribute to gardens but too often they do so at the expense of plants. The many Mexican-inspired gardens popping up all over southwestern cities often fall prey to this mistake. Lots of bright tile and pottery, colored masonry walls, and quirky shrines to the Virgin of Guadalupe meet up with bare gravel or paltry suburban American plant fare. A simple display of affection for plants—adding a few brightly colored roses, oleanders, bougainvilleas, potted geraniums, and voluptuous spineless prickly pears—would give these spaces a lively sense of Mexican culture and transform them into real gardens.

Sometimes a garden develops a sense of place by creating strong associations with aspects of the immediate site and traditions of the region. A striking garden at Matanzas Creek Winery in rural Sonoma County, California, accomplishes this beautifully with plants alone. Designer Gary Ratway placed lavender in rows to be harvested yet also to be enjoyed as a garden, with silver germander and santolina sheared into great billows and strong counterpoints of wheatlike ornamental grasses throughout, calling forth Mediterranean plant colors and fragrances along with agrarian patterns, textures, and placement. These combine into a thoroughly modern garden with a strongly grounded identity in keeping with its bucolic surroundings.

ABOVE Agriculture has transformed much of the inhabited regions of this planet, and we feel strong subliminal comfort and familiarity with its intrinsic patterns and textures. Barley field, Surrey, England.

LEFT Rows of sheared lavender in modern forms echo agrarian patterns, settling this winery garden into the rolling rural land and Mediterranean climate of north-central California. *Lavandula ×intermedia, Stipa gigantea*, Matanzas Creek Winery, Sonoma County, California, Gary Ratway design.

A wooded hillside and simple two-hundred-year-old house inspired a garden with a rich sense of place. The quiet grace of native deciduous woodland finds a match in the plantings created beneath it; garden surrounds house in a heartfelt embrace. Silverbell (*Halesia* sp.) blooming over bench, hellebores, ferns, David Culp and Michael Alderfer garden, Downingtown, Pennsylvania.

Any garden ought to relate to structures on site. Few come into being before the existence of a house or main building, or for that matter, an immediate neighborhood. This does not mean that if one's home is English Tudor, Spanish villa, or generic suburban style, the garden must closely follow suit. Yet the strongest dialogs are those that truly unify a garden with the building—spatially, visually, and emotionally. One person's taste prejudices often accomplish this synchronicity through highly personal decisions that influence both house and garden in similar ways. A person who revels in the intricate detail and old-fashioned charm of a Victorian home is often drawn to equally intricate, old-fashioned flowering plants. Someone who purposely builds a spare, strong-lined modern house rarely favors the same plants as the owner of the Victorian.

Often gardenmakers begin with a house and/or neighborhood far removed from personal predilections and dreams. Lauren bought a run-down yet charming Craftsman bungalow in a small farming town as home to her first Colorado garden and then hemmed in her strong desire to create a naturalistic rock garden on the small front lawn, opting instead for a more congruent cottage garden. This compromise helped connect house with garden, garden with site, and garden with neighborhood. With similar care, designer Will Fleming imitates the banked azaleas and formal lawns typical of front gardens in traditional upscale neighborhoods of Houston. Yet instead of placing azaleas as foundation plantings, he often shifts them out from the house to enclose and disguise a path with diverse naturalistic plantings set behind their greenery, and a picturesque mix of plants continuing out of view into the backyard. In this way he creates highly personal gardens that still fit comfortably within their formal neighborhoods.

One of the finest examples of a garden having a deep resonance with place is David Culp's and Michael Alderfer's two-acre homesite in the pastoral hills just west of Philadelphia. Both men have Pennsylvania Dutch (German) roots and a sense of unaffected, simple beauty. A derelict 1790s farmhouse situated on a flat piece of land skirted by wooded hillsides entranced David. Two decades later, house, garden, site, and region all blend seamlessly, reflecting nature, culture, history, and the personalities of the gardeners. In the flat, vaguely rectangular backyard, a low white picket fence encloses a traditional German foursquare garden filled with vegetables and flowers, echoing the whitewashed masonry walls and straightforward lines of the house and giving the space an authentic Pennsylvania country garden feel. Casual beds brimming with shrubs, perennials, and bulbs outline the perimeter.

As the terrain abruptly rises, a rustic dry-stack stone wall foots a wooded slope. This distinct area revels in a naturalistic treatment where hundreds of species of shade-loving plants consort comfortably. Narrow meandering paths run crisscross up the hill, inviting immersion; native trees and shrubs mingle with planted newcomers that enjoy the deciduous canopy. In late winter, David's passion for hellebores and snowdrops paints the browns of sleeping flower beds and slope with subtle floral colors that softly murmur the coming of spring. Thousands of daffodils herald its arrival in earnest, under a spangle of pale blossoms of magnolias, silverbells (*Halesia* spp.), and dogwoods.

Seasonality and a sense of place

While this Pennsylvania country garden entices its owners and visitors at any time of year, late winter and spring are clearly highlights. Celebrating the most rewarding seasons of one's region engenders a strong sense of place and evolves naturally in a plant-driven garden because the climate of the region enforces its rhythms on plants. In Pennsylvania, a slow, steady, moist transition from winter to spring allows for a long early-season display, and then the weather abruptly shifts into a less benevolent, hot, humid, and often dry summer. David and Michael are in tune with these cycles and augment them with plants that respond accordingly. Their deciduous woodland, like others on the eastern half of the continent as well as similar forests across the globe, fosters early bloom before the canopy fills in, so on the wooded hillside these early seasons are celebrated.

Honoring and delighting in seasonality goes against a commonly expressed desire of gardeners, designers, and plant breeders for year-round performance from a plant. We claim to long for extended bloom, evergreen foliage, and a shapely plant that holds up all year. Were we to fill our gardens exclusively with such creations, we would quickly lose interest, for it is the change and response inherent to plants, and the anticipation, expectation, and hope for surprise we feel as nature's rhythms affect the garden's denizens along with those in nature that compel us to go out and look in the first place.

Every region has specific plants that mark the seasons. Every gardenmaker has a relationship with plants that have done this during his or her lifetime. After twenty years in the West, Lauren glibly claims not to miss the burning fall colors that transformed the landscapes of her East Coast

Seasonal moments . . .

TOP Tender spring sunlight teases forth precocious beech and oak catkins, a display not as showy as daffodils and tulips but surely as evocative of the season, especially when backlit. Chanticleer, Wayne, Pennsylvania.

ABOVE An ephemeral spring moment late in the day catches Christmas fern fronds unfurling. *Polystichum acrostichoides*, eastern Pennsylvania woods near Philadelphia.

ABOVE RIGHT Wet snow accentuates branch patterns on spruce. *Picea pungens*, northern Colorado.

OPPOSITE TOP LEFT Filaments on the edge of *Yucca baccata* leaves hold a dusting of snow. Authors' garden, Fort Collins, Colorado.

OPPOSITE TOP RIGHT In certain favored regions of the world, senescing foliage paints canopy and then ground below

in vibrant color. Japanese maple leaves, Arnold Arboretum, Jamaica Plain, Massachusetts.

OPPOSITE BOTTOM Late spring thunderstorms bring rain lilies into bloom in the Texas hill country. *Zephyranthes drummondii, Gaillardia pulchella*, Llano County, Texas.

LEFT When good fall and winter rains precede, a sea of brilliant annual flowers washes over the stark Sonoran desert in March. *Eschscholzia mexicana*, west of Tucson, Arizona.

ABOVE AND OPPOSITE TOP Taking a cue from glowing wild sumacs and buff-toned grasses in nearby foothill ravines, a Colorado garden offers this evocative autumnal combination on a scale to be appreciated up close and intimately. *Rhus typhina* 'Laciniata', *Calamagrostis ×acutiflora* 'Karl Foerster', *Saccharum ravennae*, *Miscanthus sinensis*, *Helianthus maximiliani*, Denver Botanic Gardens. In nature, *Rhus trilobata*, near Horsetooth Mountain, northern Colorado.

LEFT In autumn, flowers and foliage sometimes create surprising color pairings: peony leaves go golden while late-blooming *Allium thunbergii* sends up rose-purple umbels. With *Diascia integerrima* and *Carex plantaginea*, authors' garden, Fort Collins, Colorado.

ABOVE In April, bluebonnets—the state flower of Texas—and other wildflowers bestow the region's countryside with sumptuous color. Sheets of brilliant navy blue are set off by the chartreuse of mesquites and darker greens of live oaks, prickly pear, and juniper. *Lupinus texensis, Opuntia lindheimeri, Prosopis glandulosa, Quercus fusiformis, Juniperus ashei*, Llano County, Texas.

OPPOSITE To celebrate this special season, a rustic hill country garden invites wildflowers to invade and self-sow. Bluebonnets (*Lupinus texensis*), Abell garden, Llano, Texas.

childhood. After all, we grow a bevy of trees and shrubs that color up quite respectably in our garden in Colorado, and the nearby foothills and mountains glow with golden aspen, ruddy gambel oak, and orange three-leaf sumac. Yet on an eastern visit a couple of autumns ago, she was caught off guard while walking through moist fallen leaves on the way back to a friend's house. The sweet smell brought forth homesick tears from the subconscious. These associations run so deep, to ignore them is a disservice to one's psyche and one's identity. Including plants that mark a region's seasonality connects a garden to its surroundings; including, where climate and soil permit, a smattering of plants

associated with the seasons of one's childhood helps maintain connection with a unified self.

Plants that most obviously relate to seasonal cycles are those that grow and bloom exuberantly in response to a beneficial change in temperature or moisture. On the other end is senescence, accompanied by a last, profuse bloom or by colorful dying foliage. Not all parts of the world share equally in breathtaking cyclical events. Spring wildflowers or those that bloom in response to monsoonal rains paint deciduous woodlands, steppes, and deserts at distinct times of the year; mountain meadows wait until summer to burst forth in evanescent splendor; taller flowers

and grasses color prairies in late summer, after their full growth is achieved; brilliantly hued foliage briefly burnishes some forests in autumn. Gardens have much to gain by following nature's lead in seasonal generosity.

Plants with bulbs, corms, tubers, and other underground storage organs (collectively defined as geophytes) also respond dramatically to seasonal cycles, showing sparsely clothed yet often disarmingly lovely, fleeting flowers, and slipping back into dormant obscurity soon after. Take for example a daffodil, or its warm-climate cousin, a paperwhite narcissus. Surely flower and fragrance endear it, but equally important to the heart is its much-anticipated

ABOVE In winter 'Grand Primo' narcissi send up welcome fragrant blossoms. *Artemisia* 'Huntington', *Yucca filifera*, authors' garden, Austin, Texas.

ABOVE RIGHT A sun-warmed, wind-protected spot coaxes midwinter bloom from *Crocus ancyrensis*. Too tidy an autumn cleanup would spoil the emotional power of seeing this forceful sign of life amid last year's debris. Allowing dead and living to mingle connects us with the annual cycle of renewal. Authors' garden, Fort Collins, Colorado.

RIGHT Highly responsive to changes in barometric pressure, aptly named barometer bush or ceniza marks the approach of summer thundershowers with profuse bloom. *Leucophyllum langmaniae* 'Lynn's Legacy', central Texas.

brief yet dependable appearance, year after year, marking floral time, in a season when little else has yet awoken. The contrast of turgid green foliage thrusting through bare brown earth, and of translucent ivory or yellow blossoms nodding pliantly against a backdrop of last season's parched, bleached, fallen foliage connects us to the cycles of seasonal renewal and return of life.

In our Austin garden, long hot summers are often punctuated by thunderstorm reprieves. A few days following such an event, one can see an obvious response in the garden and in the wild. Plants plump up, becoming greener, and a number of bulbs as well as xeric shrubs take the opportunity to flower. Pastel rain lilies dot the green tangle of our native sedge lawn, fat flower spikes of crinums emerge with the promise of opulent bloom, and twiggy branches of gray-leafed cenizas swell with lavender buds.

The flush of new growth on woody plants—in springtime, and in warm climates, in response to rain—envelops the land in a fresh green haze. In some species, new growth is preceded by precocious flowers. Among these are many favorite garden plants, filling a void after a dreary dormant season. Some of these leafless bloomers, like redbuds,

DECIDUOUS WOODY PLANTS WITH PRECOCIOUS FLOWERS

These trees, shrubs, and vines are especially showy in bloom because the flowers are not hidden by foliage. They also hold a special place in many gardeners' hearts for their courageous early appearance, a welcome sign that the life cycle is once again renewing. Some have the added bonus of fragrance.

Trees

Acer rubrum, red maple (bronzy red)

Amelanchier spp. (many), serviceberry (white)

Cercis canadensis, eastern redbud (pink, rose, white)

Cornus florida, flowering dogwood (white, pink, rose)

Cornus mas, Cornelian cherry (yellow)

Cornus officinalis, Japanese Cornelian cherry (yellow)

Forestiera neomexicana, New Mexico olive (yellow, fragrant)

Hamamelis mollis, *H.* ×*intermedia*, witch hazel (yellow, orange, red, fragrant)

Jacaranda mimosifolia (blue), sometimes before leaves unfurl, sometimes after

Magnolia spp. (some) (white, pink, rose, yellow, some fragrant)

Malus spp. and hybrids (some), crabapple (white, pink, rose, some fragrant)

Paulownia fortunei (white, fragrant)

Paulownia tomentosa, Empress tree (lavender-blue, fragrant)

Prunus spp. (many), cherry, plum, peach, apricot (white, pink, rose, some fragrant)

Pyrus spp. (many), pear (white, some fragrant)

Salix spp., willow (yellow, white)

Xanthoceras sorbifolium, yellowhorn (white, fragrant)

Shrubs

Abeliophyllum distichum, white forsythia (white, fragrant)

Acacia tortuosa (golden orange, fragrant)

Cercis chinensis, Chinese redbud (rose, white)

Chaenomeles spp., flowering quince (white, pink, rose, coral, red)

Chimonanthus praecox, wintersweet (maroon, yellow, fragrant)

Corylopsis spp., winter hazel (pale yellow, fragrant)

Corylus avellana, filbert (yellow, pink)

Daphne genkwa, lilac daphne (lavender)

Daphne mezereum, February daphne (pink, white, fragrant)

Edgeworthia papyrifera, paperbush (pale yellow, rusty red, fragrant)

Forsythia spp. (yellow)

Fothergilla spp. (cream, fragrant)

Jasminum nudiflorum, winter jasmine (yellow)

Lindera spp., spicebush (yellow, fragrant)

Lonicera fragrantissima, *L.* ×*purpusii*, *L. standishii*, winter honeysuckle (pale yellow, fragrant)

Prunus spp. (many), plum (white, pink, some fragrant)

Rhododendron spp. (many), azalea (pink, rose, lavender, white, orange, yellow, some fragrant)

Salix spp., willow (yellow, white, gray, rose, black)

Spiraea prunifolia, old-fashioned bridal wreath (white)

Stachyurus praecox (yellow, fragrant)

Ungnadia speciosa, Mexican buckeye (pink, rose)

Viburnum ×*bodnantense* (white, pink, rose, fragrant)

Viburnum farreri (pink, fragrant)

Vines

Wisteria floribunda, Japanese wisteria (lavender, purple, white, fragrant)

Wisteria sinensis, Chinese wisteria (lavender, purple, white, fragrant)

ocotillos, and dogwoods, are superbly showy, drawing whatever pollinator might brave the yet inconsistent weather. Others, like witch hazels and wisteria, also use fragrance to enhance their chances of reproduction. More subtle species still make their mark: red maples that dot woodland edges throughout much of the eastern half of the continent are enveloped in a distinctive bronzy-red haze of bloom at winter's end.

Spontaneity versus control

Exuberant seasonal events owe much of their appeal to apparent spontaneity and abundance. At any time, however, a gardenmaker walks the fine line between plants' bursts of self-determination and the need or desire to intervene. Each climate supports, each gardener promotes, and each garden consequently finds a particular balance of chaos and control. There is no right or wrong in this process; plants speak for themselves in how they want to grow, and the gardenmaker responds in a uniquely personal manner. As two distinct people, we see our own individual differences find ironic expression when we garden together. Scott is much more comfortable with more casual maintenance: a few weeds, senescing plant parts, and some unruly growth don't send him into a tailspin of anxious action as they do Lauren. Yet he is much more likely to shear a plant into a formal shape or stake a stem to assure vertical stance than is Lauren, the tidier gardener.

Some of the most compelling plant-driven gardens display the counterpoint of spontaneity and control, where nature and the gardener's hand seem engaged in an ongoing dance rather than an unending battle. Traditional examples of this spirited tension are ebullient English-style perennial borders set off by shorn box, yews, and perfectly mown lawn. Dutch designer Piet Oudolf often includes shrubs pruned into unconventional shapes with his signature

The counterpoint of clipped plants with unshorn makes for a visual contrast as well as a comforting sense of balance between nature and the hand of the gardenmaker. *Santolina rosmarinifolia, Artemisia versicolor, Eryngium maritimum, E. bourgatii, Lavandula angustifolia, Salvia officinalis* 'Berggarten', Bury Court, Surrey, England, Piet Oudolf design.

pastiche of charismatic perennials. In many home gardens, self-sown seedlings grow on in unexpected places, and plants thread and mingle into one another, yet now and again a carefully placed specimen plant or an arresting group of containers gives testimony to the hand of the gardenmaker. In more formal gardens, allowing plants to depart just a bit from perfect geometry gives lightness and relief without sacrificing the calm, elegant, and comforting beauty inherent in planned shapes and spaces. Another way to bring an impromptu touch is to allow or introduce a seemingly spontaneous interloper into an otherwise uniform, more controlled planting. In part of our steppe, we filled one area almost entirely with a particularly pale blue cultivar of sheep's fescue (*Festuca glauca*). This patch of sameness lends serenity, giving the eye a cool blue pool on which to rest. Yet a small native white-flowered *Asclepias* species hitchhiked in at some point and is now mingling into the grass a bit, a welcome surprise to our plans.

The more spontaneity one allows in the garden, the more chance for surprises. These may be joyful or require extra effort to eradicate. How much of a chance the gardenmaker is willing to take is a matter of prior experience and personal temperament. Again, our own personal differences illustrate this well. Scott is completely at ease sowing seed around in dense clutches, and planting trees and shrubs closely, knowing full well that within a few years' time they will be affecting each other's growth, probably adversely. The answer then is to let the plants grow into one another and "duke it out," or remove and transplant those determined to be superfluous. Lauren hates to dig and move most anything in the garden, especially larger plants, and avoids this possibility at all costs, which sometimes means not planting a particular plant at all, no matter how lovely. Were it up to her, our garden would have much less diversity and we would have learned about and enjoyed much less. She, however, is the one who most confidently edits

EVERGREEN PLANTS FOR SHEARING

These woody plants respond well to shearing and can be shaped into hedges or more creative forms.

Abelia ×*grandiflora*, glossy abelia
Acca sellowiana (syn. *Feijoa sellowiana*), pineapple guava
Berberis spp. (many), barberry
Buxus spp., boxwood
Camellia sasanqua
Carissa macrocarpa, Natal plum
Citrus spp.
Cocculus laurifolius
Cotoneaster buxifolius, grayleaf cotoneaster
Cupressocyparis ×*leylandii*, Leyland cypress
Dodonaea viscosa, hopbush
Elaeagnus ×*ebbingei*, silverberry
Elaeagnus pungens, silverthorn
Eugenia uniflora, Brazilian cherry
Euonymus japonicus 'Microphyllus', littleleaf euonymus

Ficus microphylla, Indian laurel
Forestiera segregata, Florida privet
Grevillea rosmarinifolia
Ilex spp. (many), holly
Illicium parviflorum, Ocala anise
Juniperus spp. (many), juniper
Laurus nobilis, bay
Leptospermum scoparium, tea tree
Leucophyllum spp., ceniza
Ligustrum spp., privet
Lonicera nitida, *L. pileata*, box-leaved honeysuckle
Loropetalum chinense, Chinese witch hazel
Myrica cerifera, wax myrtle
Myrsine africana, African box
Myrtus communis, myrtle
Nandina domestica
Olea europaea 'Montra' (sold as Little Ollie), dwarf olive
Osmanthus spp., sweet olive

Photinia ×*fraseri*, red-tip photinia
Pittosporum spp.
Platycladus spp., arborvitae
Podocarpus spp. (many)
Prunus caroliniana, cherry laurel
Prunus lusitanica, Portuguese cherry laurel
Pyracantha spp., firethorn
Raphiolepis umbellata
Rhamnus alaternus, Italian buckthorn
Rhus lancea, African sumac
Taxus spp., yew
Teucrium fruticans, silver germander
Thuja spp., arborvitae
Tsuga spp., hemlock
Viburnum awabuki
Viburnum obovatum
Viburnum suspensum
Viburnum tinus, laurustinus
Xylosma congestum (syn. *Xylosma senticosum*)

and discards seedlings self-sown in the wrong places and other plants not up to muster. This ensures a more visually enticing experience and allows individual plants to flourish that would not were the competition left in place. Gardens where plants are allowed to grow exuberantly and in abundance invite immersion; how much of this growth is spontaneous and how much intervention and gentle guidance take place are up to the gardenmaker.

Light and its effects on color

As anyone who has lived in a garden for a period of time knows, plant compositions look different over the years, over the seasons, even over a single day. This is not just because plants have wills of their own; much of this change reflects the mercurial properties of natural light. Over the course of a week we once watched an indecisive client repaint her wooden pergola six times in a futile

attempt to get just the right tone of eggshell; each day she eagerly coated the upright posts of her arbor anew, only to be disappointed in the slightly altered off-white seen in fresh sunlight the following day. This former client made a mistake common to novice gardenmakers who approach design with color first on their minds: she forgot, or perhaps never knew, that hue and tone are aspects of light that change in response to the strength and quality of the sun. These shifting effects influence not only plant growth but also how we visually experience plants, masonry, and other components of a garden scene.

Thousands of words and dozens of tomes have been written on the subject of color in the garden. In our opinion, most of these words are wasted. In spite of innumerable comparisons that portray garden design as an outdoor stepchild of painting, combining living plants into a garden demands more than skill with mixing tints. What's

more, color is ever changing, and each gardenmaker's taste as well as his or her physical perception of color are infinitely complex. Attempting to turn color selection and use into science is as futile as trying to define every garden and gardenmaker's mood across the globe.

Surely color is and will remain one of the most important aspects of a garden since people respond so strongly to it. Human beings can't help themselves; their eyes and brain are wired to take notice of color over most other aspects of the perceived physical world. Interviewed at Denmans, his texturally and spatially complex garden, English designer John Brookes expressed his frustration with this reality: "I follow (visitors) around and watch what they photograph. It's almost always the flowers" (*BBC Gardens Illustrated*, December 2006).

OPPOSITE LEFT An unexpected interloper—a diminutive but spreading western milkweed—adds spry spontaneity to a grass-dominated area in this steppe garden. *Asclepias pumila, Festuca glauca, Bouteloua gracilis*, authors' garden, Fort Collins, Colorado.

OPPOSITE RIGHT Colors of all hues and values consort unselfconsciously in the wild, as on this Oklahoma roadside. *Monarda citriodora, Dracopis amplexicaulis, Gaillardia pulchella*, near Stillwater, Oklahoma.

ABOVE Unabashed color combinations play in this flower meadow modeled loosely after a South African springtime wildflower display. *Dierama* sp., *Papaver rhoeas, Silene armeria, Kniphofia* sp., *Lagurus ovatus, Tanacetum niveum, Eschscholtzia californica*, The Garden House, Devon, England, Keith Wiley design.

ABOVE Like a translucent green parasol, banana leaves at once shade and illuminate a quiet seating corner in this tropical garden. *Musa acuminata* 'Dwarf Cavendish', *Heliconia* sp., *Russelia equisetiformis*, Hotel Escalante, Naples, Florida. Jorge Sanchez and Phil Maddux design.

ABOVE RIGHT Opaque in spring and summer when in their blue-green hues, the leaves of shrubby western oak become translucently red in autumn. *Quercus undulata* with *Ericameria nauseosa* var. *hololeuca* 'Santa Fe Silver', authors' garden, Fort Collins, Colorado.

Modest color-themed plantings are often charming in gardens, but organizing a design first or exclusively around color has proved a mistake in many spaces we have visited, and ones we have created ourselves. Color is light, and light is infinitely mutable. And neither color nor any other isolated attribute deserves to determine a design for most gardens: rather, the unique spirit of plants—both individually and collectively—and the site should suggest a direction. Color brings its joy to gardenmaking by indulging personal delight. A set of supposedly universal principles will not guarantee a pleasing result; a better plan is to observe colors' local behavior, and when the gardenmaker discovers something pleasing, to replicate its most desirable aspects. Not just plant selection but also basic approach to design warrants a regional filter. Different climates favor different uses of color; some garden climates don't support a color-themed approach to design at all.

The lovely color effects of classic English flower borders and the vivacious, sometimes shocking contrasts of ruby-tinted and variegated leaves popular in gardens along the Pacific coast depend on muted light, a product of coastal fogs and the low angle of the sun at high latitudes. The gentle, filtered sunlight common to these maritime climates promotes steady growth and flowering; it also encourages the perception of warm hues and delicate pastels. Through mists and under cloudy skies, soft pinks glow, chartreuses fluoresce, ambers warm, whites glisten. Under such conditions a plant-driven design can exploit subtleties of color found in both leaves and flowers.

In contrast, our own two gardens experience some of the strongest light in the Northern Hemisphere because of a preponderance of fair weather, elevation (five thousand feet in Colorado), and low latitude (thirty degrees in Texas). Under this potent, relentless sun, plant growth proceeds quickly and buds expand rapidly to often fast-fading blooms. Although not all of North America is this extreme, most of the continent basks in fierce brightness at some times of the year. Many American gardeners deal with harsher light than their British counterparts, as anyone on this side of the Atlantic can see by the futility of taking a Royal Horticultural Society color wheel outside on a bright day: before one's eyes subtle differences in hues become unpredictable, then moot as the sun moves across the sky.

Blessed with cool nights and the sparkling ultraviolet spectrum common to high elevations, our Colorado garden makes the most of brightly colorful summer flowers. At altitude floral colors take on iridescence in the vivid light of summer; such conditions especially flatter warm hues, sympathize with vibrant combinations, and preserve pastel tones that would otherwise fade in the strong sun. Although blooming plants and colors may tire a bit on hot afternoons, bottomless blue skies provide a prevailing backdrop to enhance color effects.

In the sweltering lowland climate of our Texas garden, however, high summer temperatures bring challenges. Pastel hues bleach and flatten, and bright colors can seem strident, clashing with each other in the sometimes brutal illumination; even the blue of the sky turns milky white when temperatures approach 100 degrees F. Some plants adopt a strategy of replacing blooms each day: richly-hued new flowers of shrimp-toned tropical sage (*Salvia coccinea* 'Pink Nymph'), soft yellow pondoland mallow (*Hibiscus calyphyllus*), light pink Mexican petunia (*Ruellia brittoniana* 'Chi-Chi'), and lavender bush violet (*Barleria obtusa*) expand freshly each morning. When these same blooms lose their vibrant colors in the afternoon as temperatures spike upward, they wither and shed. New flowers open in their place the following morning. Plants with light-trapping or translucent green foliage and those with blue or white blooms are among the few that hold up visually during this annual heat wave; together these provide a visual reprieve for sunworn eyes. During this season strong gold, orange, red, and magenta often seem overbearing unless they possess a shining, transparent quality: backlit, the fluorescent bracts of cerise bougainvillea appear vibrant and alive; viewed in flat light these same bright blooms wear on observers, looking harsh and inert, more like colored fabric than living plant. Likewise, waxy-leaved evergreens that shine reflectively—pleasant and lively looking in the winter dormant season—may start to resemble masses of molten plastic in the unrelenting heat and high-angled rays of summer.

Light effects beyond color

Designing in response to natural light begins with understanding different luminous effects in plants. The polished needles of many pines, the shiny leaves of hollies, boxwoods, myrtles, and cherry laurels, and the silken petals of ice plants, purslanes, cacti, and Guernsey lilies (*Nerine* spp.) all glisten in strong sun. Other species are so silvery as to appear almost white. In the searing light of southwestern gardens the felted gray leaves of cenizas (*Leucophyllum* spp.) and silver senna (*Senna artemisioides*) shimmer against masonry walls or among feathery acacias. Likewise, in the crystalline light of the upland West, silver sage (*Artemisia ludoviciana*) and white-leafed forms of rabbitbrush (*Ericameria nauseosa*, syn. *Chrysothamnus nauseosus*) gleam.

Although silver-foliaged plants such as these are typical of strongly sunny climates, some varieties also thrive in temperate, mist-prone regions: scalloped-leafed dusty miller (*Senecio cineraria* 'Cirrhus') offers pale beacons to brighten cloudy coastal regions as well as sunny gardens. Plants whose silvery leaves reflect light diffusely look their brightest when light shines directly on them rather than from behind. The beautiful silver wormwood *Artemisia* 'Huntington', for example, is so pale that it shines even on the dullest days; given a straight shot of sunshine, it radiates white light. When backlit, however, silver plants such as this blur to muddy gray.

Both shining and silver plants exemplify reflectivity—plant surfaces bouncing light back into the landscape as either glittering highlights or diffuse brightness. Other leaves and flowers, such as the delicate blossoms of spring bulbs, the watery summer leaves of cannas, and the diaphanous fall foliage of maples, glow in sunlight. This is translucence—light passing through the plants' leaves, flowers, or—as in the case of the colorful maple *Acer tataricum* 'GarAnn' (offered in the nursery trade as Hot Wings)—its ruby-toned paired samaras, and radiating into the garden.

Reflectivity and translucence are not static; they vary in response to changing light and also with growth cycles of plants, as can be felt walking in a deciduous forest at different times of the year. The luminous fresh green light of the spring canopy passes to quiet, more somber summer shadows made by the mature matte or reflective foliage. Those same leaves once again transmit light, in warmer tones of gold and red, as they senesce in the brilliant sunlight of fall.

One of the most interesting design effects mixes plants that glitter with those that glow—in other words, combining reflectivity with translucence. Along our front walkway

TOP Most ice plants—South African succulents with daisylike flowers—have glittering, reflective petals that sparkle in brilliant sunshine. *Delosperma* 'Kelaidis' (sold as Mesa Verde), Denver Botanic Gardens.

LEFT Autumnal light is characterized by a golden warmth and low angles that backlight plants readily. With a silver skirt of *Veronica incana*, fall-blooming *Crocus speciosus* basks in this treatment. Authors' garden, Fort Collins, Colorado.

backlit tufts of prairie dropseed (*Sporobolus heterolepis*) smolder in autumnal tones of copper and amber next to gleaming emerald rosettes of bergenia. Although glittering plants such as bergenia can be placed anywhere, glowing subjects such as the grass deserve thoughtful placement to catch low morning or evening light. Harnessing natural sunlight for backlighting effects requires siting translucent plants east and/or west of the main viewing points so that they are enjoyed with the sun behind them.

Fine textures such as feathery foliage, surface hairs, spines, and gossamer seed heads also trap light when backlit. Near a walkway along the south side of our Colorado home we replaced a poorly positioned deck with a garden featuring bold rosettes of hardy century plants (*Agave havardiana*) among wispy Mexican feather grasses (*Nassella tenuissima*), numerous cacti with white-frosted spines, blue-violet Rocky Mountain penstemons (*Penstemon strictus*), and orange-red California poppies (*Eschscholzia californica* 'Tequila'). In the setting sun the light-trapping cactus spines and gossamer blooms of the grass create luminous halos; these mix with glowing floral colors, highlighting the stolid, sculptural agaves.

By their nature, architectural plants host plays of light and shadow. Agaves, palms, yuccas, sotols, cacti, and other bold plants not only grow well in strong sun but also look their best. Some of these, such as sotols and cacti, have small prickles along edges of foliage or stems that trap or transmit light, outlining their striking form. Filaments or translucent margins on leaves also ignite dramatic effects. Sculpted by ever-changing sunlight, these textural plants fill the void when flowers ebb. In our Texas garden, while blossoms wane in punishing midsummer heat, rays of sun catch fishbone silhouettes of cycad fronds, softly radiant plumes of bamboo muhly grass (*Muhlenbergia dumosa*), and fresh, exuberant foliage of bananas and elephant's ears. Over the day quite different scenes arise as sunlight alternately reflects off and passes through this foliage.

Light emphasizes not only textures and bold forms but also variegation. Interspersed in a garden, variegated plants make a fine backdrop to ephemeral colors of seasonal

Backlighting accentuates blond Mexican feather grass and translucent new growth on manzanita, while casting opaque subjects such as agaves, yuccas, and cacti in shadows. *Yucca harrimaniae, Nassella tenuissima, Arctostaphylos ×coloradoensis, Opuntia macrorhiza, Agave havardiana*, authors' garden, Fort Collins, Colorado.

DESIGNING WITH LIGHT

Plants interact with light in different ways; the following lists introduce several distinct effects and species that lend themselves to designs intended to showcase light in the garden.

Reflective plants
(plants that glitter and shine)

Asarum europaeum, European ginger (foliage)

Bergenia spp., pigsqueak (foliage)

Buxus spp., boxwood (foliage)

Camellia spp. (foliage)

Carex spp., sedge (some, foliage)

Coprosma spp., mirror plant (foliage)

Farfugium japonicum 'Giganteum', giant groundsel (foliage)

ice plants (many, flowers)

Ilex spp., holly (most, foliage; some, fruit)

Magnolia grandiflora, southern magnolia (foliage)

Pinus spp., pine (most, foliage)

Prunus caroliniana, cherry laurel (foliage)

Sciadopitys verticillata, umbrella pine (foliage)

Ternstroemia gymnanthera, Japanese cleyera (foliage)

Viburnum awabuki 'Chindo' (foliage)

Translucent plants
(plants that glow)

Acer spp., maple (many, foliage and samaras)

Acorus calamus 'Variegatus', striped sweet flag (foliage)

Anemone hupehensis and hybrids, Japanese anemone (flowers)

Bulbine frutescens (flowers)

bulbs (flowers)

cacti (flowers)

Cercidiphyllum japonicum, katsura tree (foliage)

Chionanthus virginicus, fringe tree (flowers and foliage)

ferns (young foliage)

Hesperaloe parviflora, red yucca (flowers)

Ilex vomitoria, yaupon (fruit)

Iris spp. (many, flowers and foliage)

Kniphofia spp., red hot poker (flowers)

Metasequoia glyptostroboides, dawn redwood (foliage)

Nelumbo spp., lotus (flowers)

Nymphaea spp., waterlily (flowers)

Papaver spp., poppy (flowers)

Portulaca grandiflora, moss rose (flowers)

Light-trapping plants

Amsonia hubrichtii, willow-leaf bluestar (foliage)

Aruncus spp., goatsbeard (flowers)

Asparagus spp. (foliage)

Cotinus spp., smokebush (flowers)

Crambe cordifolia, *C. orientalis*, sea kale (flowers)

Echium spp. (flower stalks and foliage)

Fallugia paradoxa, Apache plume (foliage and seed heads)

Foeniculum vulgare, fennel (foliage)

grasses (most, flowers; some, foliage if very fine)

Limonium spp., sea lavender (flowers)

Otatea acuminata, Mexican bamboo (foliage)

Papaver triniifolium, Armenian poppy (foliage, stems, flower buds)

Pulsatilla spp., pasque flower (flowers, stems, seed heads)

Salix spp., willow (some, flowers)

Salvia argentea, silver sage (foliage and flower stalks)

Stachys byzantina, lamb's ears (flower stalks and foliage)

Symphyotrichum ericoides, *S. lateriflorum*, heath aster (flower panicles)

Architectural plants sculpted by light

Agave spp., century plant (especially species with filamentous leaves)

Alocasia and *Colocasia*, elephant's ears

bamboos

bananas

bromeliads (sun-tolerant species such as *Aechmea blanchetiana*, *Androlepis skinneri*, *Portea petropolitana*, *Puya* spp.)

cacti

cannas

Cordyline australis, New Zealand cabbage tree

cycads

Dasylirion, sotol

gingers

Nolina, bear grass

palms

Phormium, New Zealand flax

Yucca

ABOVE LEFT Watery canna foliage transmits sunlight readily, accentuating the lush forms of the leaves. *Canna warscewiczii*, Austin, Texas.

ABOVE Fuzzy bumblebee and frothy meadow rue play a sensual duet in lingering afternoon sunlight. *Thalictrum aquilegifolium*, Fritz Creek Gardens, Homer, Alaska.

LEFT Seep muhly grass (*Muhlenbergia reverchonii*), a little-known Texas treasure, offers fine mounded foliage and a late-season treat of ruddy flowers and is hardy into zone 5 to boot. Authors' garden, Fort Collins, Colorado.

RIGHT Bright floral colors and curious shapes revel in the clear light of the West. Cacti, especially *Echinocereus ×lloydii* in bloom and bristly *Opuntia* 'Peter Pan' with spines outlined by backlighting, shine. With *Eriogonum umbellatum*, *Eschscholzia californica*, *Penstemon strictus*, *Penstemon alamosensis*, *Agave havardiana*, *Nassella tenuissima*, authors' garden, Fort Collins, Colorado.

BELOW Light endows a prickly *Opuntia acicularis* with a spiny halo while dramatizing the sculptural, sinuous foliage of *Agave weberi*. Boyce Thompson Arboretum, Superior, Arizona.

bloom. Luminous throughout the growing season in back-lit situations, the swordlike leaves of striped bearded iris (*Iris pallida* 'Aureovariegata') are joined in early summer in our Colorado garden by gleaming poppies, creating fluorescent punctuation that responds to morning and evening sunlight.

Light changes over the seasons and so do plants that respond to its shifting qualities. Autumn in Colorado is gilded by a mellow, warmly hued sun that makes the lavender and purple of asters and fall crocuses glow, deepens the gold of the ubiquitous composites, and animates the tawny hues of grasses in our garden and on the hills beyond. In Texas, low-angled winter light washes across somber green live oaks and our shiny sedge lawn, moving on to catch white, parchmentlike petals of tazetta narcissi and burning orange torches of *Kniphofia* 'Christmas Cheer'. As spring returns to Colorado and sun intensifies, crocus, snow iris, and species tulips are teased from the ground, their rich hues illuminated as they open to the warmth. Silvery pussy willow buds and red-infused unfurling peony shoots harness the strong yet pale light of March and April. Such fleeting light effects create moments of incandescent beauty that may be planned for but still remain largely beyond the gardenmaker's control.

Dusk, dawn, and darkness

The end of the day often brings a special hour when the setting sun ignites in a fiery red sphere. Even as the sky darkens, landscapes warm. In the fading rays, flowers of all types reflect a reddish glow. This ephemeral festival of radiant light and its rosy-hued morning imitator, dawn, bracket the hours of darkness when much of a garden slips from view.

As important as light may be to the experience of a garden, so too is its absence. As the sun sets and light and vision fade, a paradox is revealed: a darkened garden becomes even more strongly sensual. With disempowerment of vision comes heightened awareness of other senses: hearing, touch, and smell assume new importance. Chirping crickets, ratcheting katydids, and whirring moths; the first cool, gravid breezes of dusk; and the mysterious scents of

Sun sets and moon rises; everything in the garden is transformed. Escarpment live oak (*Quercus fusiformis*) and ball moss (*Tillandsia recurvata*), authors' garden, Austin, Texas.

unseen flowers, dampened leaves, and fresh grass flood the senses.

The potency of a night garden comes in part from unfamiliarity: the dim light that remains omits color and allows only ghostly shapes and glittering stars to be seen. Favorite plants, well-trodden paths, and familiar arbors acquire eerie, ill-defined boundaries. The visitor to a darkened garden—even his or her own—remains on alert, for everything about the landscape seems strange and uncertain. Perhaps we feel a measure of primordial fear, listening for unseen predators that prowl in the night.

Beyond imagined predators, night-blooming flowers and creatures that pollinate them become active in darkness. This is a common strategy for plants in climates with torrid daytime temperatures: in the South, Southwest, and the Great Plains and prairies of North America a number of native wildflowers exhibit night-blooming habits. When one of the objectives of a garden is nocturnal enjoyment, its design showcases such blooms and invites the hovering hawk moths and other night creatures that visit them.

The soft, reflective white pelt of woolly mullein (*Verbascum bombyciferum*) is equally seductive day or night. Lemon yellow flowers open at dusk to lure moth pollinators. With *Glaucium* spp., *Linum perenne*, Rob Proctor garden, Denver, Colorado.

Compositions using pale stones, crunchy gravels, reflective or trickling water, and contrasts between light and dark blossoms and foliage engage the senses, creating gardens to be enjoyed in moonlight or near darkness. Waxy, reflective leaves and light-trapping foliage or spines also respond to dim illumination, adding interest to darkened landscapes. From a practical standpoint, gardens to be visited at night benefit from bold, obvious shapes and clearly defined layouts that bring visitors comfortably close to plants, water, and other features.

The well-known concept of the white garden, made popular in England and often copied in America, follows the essential themes of a night garden: a mix of silver and gray foliage among white and pale-colored flowers with darker green foliage for contrast. Gardens of ancient Persia—featuring sweet jasmines and musk roses, and allees of pale-barked sycamores along central canals—and of Song Dynasty China—with fragrant magnolias, sweet olives, and fanciful pavilions sited near reflecting pools, moon gates, and oddly weathered limestone boulders—were designed to celebrate nocturnal experience as well.

In the half-light of a darkened garden, round, plate-like, and cupped floral shapes—obvious during daylight hours—may blur into unrecognizable masses. Some of the most apparent flowers are elegantly slender: tubular blooms such as jasmine tobacco (*Nicotiana sylvestris*) or tuberose (*Polianthes tuberosa*), and flowers borne on tall, skinny spikes like mullein (*Verbascum* spp.) or plantain lily (*Hosta plantaginea*) silhouette pale outlines against the darkness. Likewise, blossoms with slim, dangling, or feathered petals such as spider lilies (*Hymenocallis* spp.), night-fragrant daylilies like the old pale yellow *Hemerocallis* 'Hyperion', fringe-petaled pinks (*Dianthus superbus*), and starry pinwheels of Confederate jasmines (*Trachelospermum jasminoides*) shine out of the night with attenuated forms. Oversized, funnel-shaped blooms of datura, brugmansia, crinum, and night-flowering cacti join these to draw pollinators, most often nectar-feeding moths that hover over open flowers like hummingbirds. Although day-flowering, the airy, insubstantial sprays of *Gaura lindheimeri* show up well at dusk and draw hawk moths as light fades. Any white, pale yellow, or greenish blossom that stays open at night—even those of common daisies or yarrows—might feature in an evening garden, but plants specialized for night flowering often offer intense perfumes as well.

Fragrance

More than the sight of their opulent blossoms, a whiff of fragrance from an old-fashioned lilac conjures images of springs past. People who grew up with these iconic cold-climate shrubs—but who presently garden in balmy Florida, southern Arizona, or California—often willfully forgo gardenias, jasmines and other sweet-scented flora suited to their gardens in mostly futile quests for a few pathetic blossoms bearing the treasured smell of childhood. Scents access deep memory and revive primeval feelings; this gives fragrance special powers in a garden, for the emotions awakened by aroma change, augment, and sometime overpower reality. Eleagnus, sarcococca, and osmanthus—pedestrian shrubs that provide little more than evergreen furniture most of the year—bear inconspicuous flowers that release penetrating fragrances just as a garden goes to sleep in autumn. The mind's eye paints away these ordinary-looking plants along with the tawdry browns of spent perennials and fallen leaves, replacing them with imagined (smelled) spring. It is not always necessary to view plants to see them, for their aromas convey images that trump the visual world. The putrid scents of aroids accurately duplicate rotting meat, convincing unwitting flies to pollinate somber-colored blooms as they lay their eggs. As much as any visual reality, experiences created by fragrance become key to perceiving gardens. Describing a landscape at night, Louise Beebe Wilder expressed this truth: "We seem to have had no hand in fashioning the vast purple gloom, the pearly visions, the sharp, pale shapes that part the shadows. . . . Only the fragrances of the night are familiar—Honeysuckle, White tobacco, Stock seek us out like the warm pressure of a hand" (*Color in My Garden*, 1918).

Scent rather than color is the tactic many night-blooming plants employ to attract pollinators, and—because cooler, denser, more humid air readily transmits fragrance—such flowers become most potent at night. Fresh buds time their openings and schedule their release of aromas to take

TOP RIGHT Muskily fragrant *Crinum bulbispermum* opens new flowers each evening and has proven hardy in zone 5. It is backed here by spirals of a native Kansas selection of willowleaf sunflower, *Helianthus salicifolius*. Authors' garden, Fort Collins, Colorado.

RIGHT Sultry-scented dwarf Formosa lilies (*Lilium formosanum* var. *pricei*) give a tropical air to wiry sheep's fescue, *Festuca glauca*. Authors' garden, Fort Collins, Colorado.

TOP At dusk, sweetly scented white gumbo lily and silver threadleaf sage, both western natives, take on new animation as the rest of the garden slips into gray oblivion. *Oenothera caespitosa, Seriphidium filifolium, Dianthus ×allwoodii, Festuca glauca,* northern Colorado, Ogden design.

ABOVE We selected this extra silver, ultra-narrow-leaved form of western plains native *Oenothera fremontii* in our Colorado garden. We named it 'Shimmer', as both flowers and foliage reflect light during the day as well as at night.

advantage of the greatest effects. On summer evenings in our Texas garden new flowers of prairie lilies (*Zephyranthes drummondii*), four o'clocks (*Mirabilis jalapa*), blush-colored *Crinum* 'Mrs. James Hendry', and dwarf butterfly gingers (*Hedychium* 'Luna Moth') expand at dusk, admitting pollinators just as their fragrance becomes strongest, while night jessamine (*Cestrum nocturnum*)—with green tubular blooms that remain entirely unscented during the day—radiates narcotic sweetness. As night approaches in Colorado, creamy white evening primroses or "gumbo lilies" (*Oenothera caespitosa*), hardy ice plants like miniature tiger jaws (*Stomatium* spp.), summer-bedded acidantheras (*Gladiolus callianthus*), and jasmine-scented pinks (*Dianthus petraeus* subsp. *noeanus*) open fresh, fragrant blooms. Near our deck dwarf Formosa lilies (*Lilium formosanum* var. *pricei*) and *Daphne burkwoodii* 'Carol Mackie' perfume the air from already-open tubular flowers; along the fence clustered blossoms of hardy noisette rose 'Darlow's Enigma' emit a honeyed aroma. A scented evening bloom we discovered as a chance seedling of native sundrop, *Oenothera fremontii* 'Shimmer', combines soft yellow freesia-scented flowers with mats of silver-toned, ribbony leaves. Showy day and night but noticeably sweet smelling only in the evening, this sprawls in a pale froth beside a gravel-covered path.

Some plants produce fragrance that carries widely on the air, an effect encouraged by partially enclosed nooks and placement against walls or hedges that offer shelter from wind. The thick atmosphere of courtyard gardens in New Orleans and Charleston is famously redolent with scents of gingers, jasmines, citrus, gardenias, sweet olives, henna, saw palmettos, and other subtropical flowers. These luxuriate in the humid, sheltered environment, permeating the dense coastal air with heady aromas.

Although some plant fragrances pervade still air, others are better appreciated close-up by smelling individual flowers. In the case of aromatic foliage, touching and rubbing the leaves releases fragrant oils. These distinct fragrant plant experiences call for different placement in gardens. As with color, not all climates are equally good for

EVENING-FRAGRANT AND NIGHT-FRAGRANT PLANTS

Plants included here are most fragrant at or after dusk; some continue to have fragrance during the day.

Trees and shrubs

Abelia chinensis
Albizzia julibrissin, mimosa
Aloysia gratissima, sweet brush
Bauhinia forficata, white orchid tree
Brugmansia spp., angel's trumpet
Brunfelsia spp., yesterday, today, and tomorrow
Carica papaya, papaya
Carissa macrocarpa, Natal plum
Cestrum nocturnum, white jessamine
Citrus spp.
Clerodendron spp., glory bower
Daphne spp.
Eleagnus spp., silverberry
Eriobotrya japonica, loquat
Gardenia spp., Cape jasmine
Lawsonia inermis, henna
Lonicera caprifolia, L. fragrantissima, L. hildebrandiana, honeysuckle
Magnolia figo (syn. *Michelia figo*) var. *skinneriana*, banana shrub
Magnolia grandiflora, southern magnolia
Magnolia virginiana, sweet bay
Melia azederach, chinaberry
Osmanthus spp., sweet olive
Philadelphus spp., mock orange
Pittosporum spp.
Plumeria spp., frangipani
Rhododendron spp. (many deciduous azalea species)
Ribes aureum, R. odoratum, clove currant
Rosa moschata and hybrids, musk rose
Sarcococca spp., sweetbox
Serenoa repens, saw palmetto
Tabernaemontana divaricata, crape jasmine
Viburnum ×*bodnantense*
Viburnum ×*burkwoodii*
Viburnum ×*carlcephalum*
Viburnum carlesii
Viburnum farreri
Viburnum grandiflorum
Viburnum ×*juddii*

Vines

Anredera cordifolia, Madeira vine
Calonyction aculeatum, moon vine
Gelsemium sempervirens, Carolina jessamine
Jasminum spp. (many, especially white-flowered), jasmine
Lagenaria siceraria, birdhouse gourd
Lonicera japonica, honeysuckle
Momordica charantia, bitter melon
Quisquallis indica, Rangoon vine
Solandra guttata (syn. *Solandra maxima*), cup of gold
Thunbergia fragrans
Trachelospermum jasminoides, star jasmine, Confederate jasmine
Vitis spp., grape

Herbaceous perennials, bulbs, annuals, succulents

Abronia spp., sand verbena
Aethionema schistosum, fragrant stonecress
Amsonia spp. (white-flowered)
Begonia odorata
Brassavola nodosa, lady of the night orchid
Cardiocrinum spp.
cereus, night-blooming (*Epiphyllum* spp., *Hylocereus* spp., *Nyctocereus* spp., *Peniocereus* spp., *Selenicereus* spp.)
Cleome hassleriana, spider flower
Crinum spp.
Datura spp., angel's trumpet
Dianthus petraeus subsp. *noeanus*, jasmine pinks
Dianthus superbus, fringed pinks
Dracaena spp.
Fraxinus cuspidata, fragrant ash
Fraxinus ornus, flowering ash
Gladiolus callianthus (syn. *Acidanthera bicolor*), Abyssinian gladiolus
Gladiolus tristis, marsh Afrikaner
Hedychium spp., butterfly ginger
Hemerocallis altissima
Hemerocallis citrina (syn. *Hemerocallis lilioasphodelus*)
Hemerocallis flava
Hemerocallis multiflora
Hemerocallis 'Hyperion'
Hesperaloe funifera
Hesperaloe nocturna
Hesperis spp.
Hosta plantaginea and its hybrids such as 'Royal Standard', plantain lily
Hymenocallis spp., spider lily
Iris dichotoma (syn. *Pardanthopsis dichotoma*), vesper iris
Lilium candidum, madonna lily
Lilium formosanum, Formosa lily
Lilium longiflorum, Easter lily
Lilium regale, regal lily
Manfreda maculosa, rattlesnake master
Matthiola longipetala subsp. *bicornis*, evening-scented stock
Mentzelia spp., sticky stars
Milla biflora
Mirabilis jalapa, M. longiflora, four o'clock
Nicotiana spp., flowering tobacco
Nymphaea odorata, N. rubra, waterlily
Oenothera spp. (many), evening primrose
Petunia spp. (old-fashioned strains)
Polianthes tuberosa, tuberose
Sansevieria spp., mother-in-law's tongue
Saponaria officinalis, bouncing Bet
Stomatium spp., miniature tiger jaws
Valeriana officinalis, valerian
Victoria amazonica
Zephyranthes atamasca, Z. chlorosolen, Z. drummondii, rain lily

ABOVE Wafting sweetness into the air, jonquils are naturalized over much of the lower South and Gulf states. Their early blossoms speak of spring to people raised in those parts, who call them little sweeties. *Narcissus jonquilla*, *Claytonia virginica*, Sisters' Bulb Farm, Gibsland, Louisiana.

RIGHT Although its medicinal and culinary properties remain a mystery to most gardeners, adaptable southwestern sunset hyssop now graces gardens all over the world with heady root beer aroma and profuse orange-peach flowers. Hummingbirds and hawk moths appreciate it as well. *Agastache rupestris* with *Helianthus maximiliani* 'Dakota Sunshine', *Perovskia* ×*hybrida*, *Pinus heldreichii* var. *leucodermis* 'Iseli Fastigiate', *Achnatherum calamagrostis*, *Festuca mairei*, authors' garden, Fort Collins, Colorado.

transmitting scent: windblown alpine flowers in the thin, chill atmosphere above timberline must attract pollinators with colorful, oversized blooms rather than aromas.

Dry or frosty air discourages perfumes, but moderately cool weather can be ideal for carrying fragrance. Several plants put forth pleasant (or sometimes rather clinical, chlorine- or anise-like) scents during fall, winter, and early spring to draw pollinators to otherwise inconspicuous blossoms: the mostly unseen flowers of chimonanthus, winter honeysuckle, witch hazel, and boxwood release penetrating perfumes. With sweet scents and somewhat larger, clustered winter and early spring blossoms, mahonias, loquats, pittosporums, Carolina jessamines, and Korean spice and Burkwood viburnums attract hungry early-flying bees and moths; golden currants lure early-arriving hummingbirds as well as insects. Perhaps because they also bloom so early in the season, bulbs such as daffodils, dwarf irises, snowdrops, and grape hyacinths put forth especially fragrant flowers, guiding insects with concentrated honeyed scents any sunny moment the changeable, early-season weather allows. Hyacinths and jonquils radiate perfumes detectable over short distances. Many other early bulbs need to be cupped in the hands to be smelled; raised beds, rockeries, and slopes bring them nearer to the nose.

It would be a shame if a heavy-scented peony like the old clear pink 'Sarah Bernhardt' or a richly aromatic rose like the choice white damask 'Madame Hardy' were set at the back of a bed where it could not be readily approached and enjoyed. Lilacs, mock oranges, daphnes, brooms, dianthus, wallflowers, and other especially fragrant subjects ought to be placed where they can be smelled as well as seen. Magnolias, crabapples, witch hazels, Texas mountain laurels, sweet acacias, and other aromatic flowering trees merit consideration for their scent at the same time they are added to gardens to provide beauty and structure. Spots near entries and along paths and walls foster both fragrant and visual encounters. Remarkably pungent in autumnal demise, katsura trees (*Cercidiphyllum japonicum*) and Joe Pye weeds (*Eutrochium maculatum*) scent the air with intense sweetness released from fading leaves and old flower stalks; these unusual plants warrant casual spots where their fallen foliage can lie and spent flower stems can be left standing.

Sweet-scented vines such as wisterias, roses, honeysuckles, and jasmines deserve walls that allow them to grow up and surround windows, or arbors where they can envelop passersby with scented bloom. The word *arbor*—contrary to supposition that it derives from Latin *arbor* or tree—comes from Middle English *herber*, recalling the use of these structures to showcase collections of fragrant plants during the Middle Ages. Scented herbs cultivated in these gardens—mint, sage, lavender, costmary, rosemary, tarragon, and thyme, among others—provide fragrance with aromatic foliage rather than blossoms. Positions in strong sun cause their oils to volatilize, releasing scent on warm days. Planting these often nondescript plants between stepping stones or other places where their foliage might occasionally be bruised also promotes release of fragrance. Although commonly isolated in gardens unto themselves, herbs and other aromatic perennials—especially those endowed with showy blooms such as many of the agastache clan, or with valuable evergreen foliage like rosemary—mingle happily with almost any planting; like other fragrant plants they warrant forward placement where they can be touched and smelled.

Texture

Bringing plants close encourages touching. Brushing by a grassy tussock, bending down to feel the soft pelt of a mullein or to pat a hummock of moss invites immersion. For better or worse, all plants are potentially tactile. Their physical texture also determines much of their visual power. Leaf, petal, and bark surfaces; stem thickness and branching; foliar, floral, and branch patterns; and overall form join together to create a unique textural imprint.

In our own gardens and many of those we create for others, we've learned to rely more on plants' forms and textures than on colors to create dependable, lasting beauty. Fortunately, when plants are chosen and placed to highlight and allow interplay among their varied textures, a garden becomes as complex and satisfying as—and arguably

Lush textures of temperate shade plants reflect the gentle climates to which they are best suited. *Pulmonaria* 'Majeste', *Corydalis flexuosa*, *Dryopteris affinis* 'Cristata', Bosvigo, Cornwall, England.

petals drop is what counts for most of the year. Human eyes, primed for colorful seduction, need retraining to think in terms of texture. Recent interest in foliage for design has gone a long way in bringing textural interest to gardens, yet once again magnetic color often leads these attempts astray. Prominent placement of a specimen plant with dramatically contrasting foliage color—one purple beech, one golden locust, or one ice blue spruce amid a sea of green—rarely has the desired effect. Similarly, lurid combinations of bronze, yellow, striped and spotted, as well as purple foliage, particularly common in maritime and tropical climates that encourage such plants to flourish, deserve the scathing label of "contrastifolia style." These compositions may be exciting at first glance but quickly become overbearing and, in the end, tedious and one-dimensional.

How to overcome our innate prejudice toward color and learn to consider texture as equal or more important? One of our friends, a talented landscape designer, is color blind to distinctions between red and green as well as orange and blue. Yet he creates complex, inviting, beautiful gardens. Imagining a garden in black and white, or even actually photographing it this way, offers a lesson in texture and form. When plants look good drained of all color, when a garden remains lovely awash in only grays, there's little doubt that with the return of color, something delightful is at hand.

As with all aspects of plant-driven design, plant textures vary with site and region. Dry, sunny climates engender fine, twiggy textures and stiff, powerful forms, as exemplified by desert-inspired, herb-filled, and chaparral-themed gardens. Warm, moist climates promote soft, lush textures and often exuberant, somewhat amorphous forms, reflected in both subtropical and temperate gardens. When Lauren first moved to Colorado, she was jarred by the strange lushness of people's gardens in the interior West, so incongruously green and juicy compared to the sere grassland and scrubby chaparral pushed back by the outskirts of cities and towns. Much of this has changed in the intervening two decades, thanks to reduced water use and the growing popularity of xeriscape. As more drought-tolerant plants

more dynamic than—one based solely on intricate color harmonies and contrasts. Sensitivity to texture often suggests placement to enhance light effects that change over the day and over the seasons. Paying attention to textures also helps a design honor plants' individual spirits, something commonly sacrificed in compositions that value floral color over other characteristics.

Flowers, for the most part, are fleeting gifts to a garden, to be anticipated and cherished. What remains after the

SHRUBS FOR A CHAPARRAL GARDEN

These dryland shrubs offer varied textures, forms, and colors over the year and can be used alone or together with xeric perennials, cacti, other succulents, fiber plants, and grasses to create diverse, low-maintenance gardens.

For hot summer climates with mild winters

Acacia berlandieri, guajillo
Acacia rigidula, blackbrush
Acacia tortuosa, catclaw acacia
Aloysia gratissima, sweetbrush
Anisacanthus spp., chuparosa
Arctostaphylos spp., manzanita
Bauhinia lunareoides, Anacacho orchid tree
Buddleia marrubiifolia, woolly butterfly bush
Caesalpinia gilliesii, bird of paradise bush
Caesalpinia pulcherrima, dwarf poinciana
Calliandra spp., fairy duster
Cistus spp., rockrose
Condalia hookeri, bluewood
Convolvulus cneorum, silver bush morning glory
Dalea spp., indigo bush
Encelia farinosa, brittlebush
Forestiera angustifolia, wild privet
Garrya spp., silktassel
Justicia californica, chuparosa
Larrea tridentata, creosote bush
Lavandula spp., lavender
Leucophyllum spp., ceniza
Mahonia trifoliolata, *M. vaseyi*, agarita
Myrsine africana, African boxwood
Myrtus communis subsp. *tarentina*, dwarf myrtle
Phlomis spp., Jerusalem sage
Punica granatum 'Spanish Beauty', dwarf pomegranate
Quercus turbinella
Rhus aromatica, shrubby sumac
Rosmarinus officinalis, rosemary
Salvia ballotaeflora, mejorana
Salvia clevelandii, chaparral sage
Salvia greggii, autumn sage
Salvia regla, royal sage
Senna artemisioides
Senna wislizenii
Tecoma stans var. *angustata*, esperanza
Teucrium fruticans, silver germander

For cold winter climates

Amorpha spp., leadplant
Arctostaphylos spp., manzanita
Atriplex spp., saltbush
Caryopteris ×*clandonensis*, blue mist spirea
Cercocarpus spp., mountain mahogany
Chamaebatiaria millefolium, fernbush
Cowania mexicana, cliff rose
Cytisus spp., dwarf broom
Ephedra spp., joint fir
Ericameria (syn. *Chrysothamnus*) spp., rabbitbrush, chamisa
Fallugia paradoxa, Apache plume
Fendlera rupicola, cliff fendlerbush
Forestiera neomexicana, New Mexican olive
Genista spp., dwarf broom
Gutierrezia sarothrae, broom weed
Hypericum frondosum, *H. kalmianum*, shrubby St. John's wort
Mahonia fremontii, *M. haematocarpa*, desert grapeholly
Perovskia ×*hybrida*, Russian sage
Philadelphus microphyllus, littleleaf mock orange
Prunus andersoniana, desert peach
Quercus gambelii, *Q. turbinella*, *Q. undulata*, shrub oak
Rhus microphylla, *R. trilobata*, littleleaf sumac
Ribes aureum, golden currant
Ribes odoratum, clove currant
Salvia dorrii, *S. pachyphylla*, desert sage
Seriphidium (syn. *Artemisia*) spp., sagebrush
Shepherdia spp., buffaloberry

TOP With barely a flower in bloom, Denver Botanic Gardens' Water-Smart Garden nevertheless holds its own during the molten days of August with textures and colors of stalwart foliage. *Opuntia macrorhiza*, *Achillea* 'Moonshine', *Eriogonum jamesii*, *Artemisia ludoviciana*, *Seriphidium tridentatum*, *Fallugia paradoxa*, Ogden design.

ABOVE Also at Denver Botanic Gardens, an abundant midsummer composition of western natives belies drought and poor soil. Textures lend an air of profusion. *Chamaebatiaria millefolium*, *Artemisia ludoviciana*, *Gaillardia pinnatifida*, *Gutierrezia sarothrae*, *Erigeron divergens*.

Happy in dry soil and ferocious sunlight, statuesque eremurus hybrids and whimsically gnarled *Yucca thompsoniana* stand up to harsh, heat-reflecting architecture and concrete paths. With *Allium aflatunense*, Denver Botanic Gardens, Dan Johnson design.

dominate, gardens better reflect the textures and colors of the region's natural landscapes.

Different seasons also emphasize distinct textures. Winter in our garden in Texas hosts an interplay of relatively inert, evergreen, sculptural cacti, aloes, nolinas, and palms with the fresh, somewhat ungainly foliage and satiny, delicate flowers of ephemeral bulbs. Summer sees a profusion of luxuriant subtropical growth as gingers, cannas, crinums, and rice-paper plant burst forth with such energy that they relegate most other plants to the background. By contrast, summer lushness in our Colorado garden is characterized by grasses and sedges, planted as great feathery swards and as diaphanous veils to soften the spiky flowers of kniphofias and penstemons, along with vertically ambitious mulleins and foxtail lilies.

Our northern winter scene reveals a dried filigree of flowerheads and tawny grasses, intermingled with the evergreen intricacy of dwarf conifers and manzanitas. In neither place do the much-heralded "bones" demand hardscape, artifact, or strongly sheared plants to hold up the garden through the waxing and waning seasons. Plants themselves, through their texture, can provide structure, cohesion, and unity as flowers come and go. Certainly some beautiful stonework, a well-placed trough or urn, or an intriguing sculpture may add a new and perhaps welcome dimension to either garden, but this is hardly essential. In Colorado, where we feel strong cravings for the curvaceous succulents hardy in our warm-climate Texas garden, we tend an inordinate collection of potted specimens that spend most of their lives indoors in our sunroom and along south- and west-facing windows, with a short four-month summer vacation in the garden. These container plants help diminish our winter boredom and lend their lovely textures to the garden in summer, adding contrast to the multitude of fine-textured plants growing in the ground. But in plant-driven design they are not the necessary crutches that containers and other artifacts or hardscape are in landscapes where plants are not considered partners in the design process.

VEIL PLANTS

These plants have diaphanous flowers and thin stems rising above relatively low foliage, making it possible to use them as a visual screen or veil in front of other plants. This effect loosens a planting, adding spontaneity, mystery, and surprise to the experience.

Actaea racemosa (syn. *Cimicifuga racemosa*), black snakeroot

Actaea simplex (syn. *Cimicifuga simplex*), snakeroot, bugbane

Anemone hupehensis, *A.* ×*hybrida*, Japanese anemone

Anethum graveolens, dill

Aruncus dioicus, *A. sylvester*, goatsbeard

Asparagus spp.

Blepharoneuron tricholepis, mountain mist grass

Consolida orientalis, cloud larkspur

Crambe cordifolia, *C. orientalis*, giant sea kale

Deschampsia caespitosa, tufted hair grass

Dianthus giganteus, pinks-on-a-stick

Dierama spp., fairy's fishing rod

Eragrostis spp., lovegrass

Foeniculum vulgare, fennel

Gaura lindheimeri, apple blossom grass

Heuchera spp., coral bells

Heucherella spp.

Linaria purpurea

Molinia caerulea var. *arundinacea*, tall moor grass

Muhlenbergia capillaris, Gulf muhly

Muhlenbergia reverchonii, seep muhly

Origanum laevigatum, ornamental oregano

Patrinia scabiosifolia

Salvia cyanescens

Sanguisorba spp., burnet

Senecio aureus, *S. obovatus*, golden groundsel

Sporobolus spp.

Stipa extremorientalis

Stipa gigantea, giant feather grass

Tellima grandiflora, fringe bells

Thalictrum spp., meadow rue

Valeriana officinalis, valerian

Verbena bonariensis, verbena-on-a-stick

Veronicastrum spp. and hybrids, culver's root

Diaphanous yet strong stems of tall Japanese anemones and *Verbena bonariensis*, placed unconventionally as a foreground veil, loosen this stolid late-summer border of shorter sedum and bee balm. Weihenstephan Garten, Freising, Germany.

HERBACEOUS PLANTS WITH GOOD-LOOKING SPENT FLOWERS

This list includes herbaceous perennials and a few annuals and biennials that have the bonus of looking good with their blossoms gone over. This extends their ornamental life, makes for a different textural mood in a planting, and allows the gardener to wait a while before cutting them back. Most of these plants are mid- or late-season bloomers, not because early bloomers have less attractive spent flowers but because it is difficult to integrate browning and tawny plant parts into a freshly green early-season garden. As plants expand over the year's growing cycle, their mature forms become larger and less precise, and their colors tend to deepen or fade to a less brilliant green, so senescing flower heads don't jar like they do earlier in the season.

Acaena spp., New Zealand burr
Acantholimon spp., spike thrift
Acanthus spp., bear's breech
Actaea (syn. *Cimicifuga*) spp., baneberry, snakeroot, bugbane
Alchemilla spp., lady's mantle
Allium spp., ornamental onion
Ammi spp., annual Queen Anne's lace
Anaphalis spp., pearly everlasting
Anemone hupehensis, A. ×*hybrida, A. tomentosa*, Japanese anemone
Anethum graveolens, dill
Angelica spp.
Anthriscus spp.
Artemisia lactiflora, ghost plant
Aruncus spp., goat's beard
Asclepias spp.
Aster spp. (fine-textured ones)
Astilbe spp.
Astrantia spp., masterwort

Ballota spp.
Baptisia australis, false blue indigo
Belamcanda spp., blackberry lily
Berlandiera lyrata, paper flower
Bupleurum spp.
Caryopteris spp., blue mist spirea
Catananche caerulea, Cupid's dart
Centranthus ruber, Greek valerian
Cephalaria spp., giant pincushion flower
Ceratostigma spp., leadwort
Crambe spp., sea kale
Crocosmia spp., montbretia
Dalea spp.
Daucus spp., Queen Anne's lace
Dianthus carthusianorum, D. giganteus, D. pinifolius, pinks-on-a-stick
Digitalis spp., foxglove
Echinacea spp., coneflower
Echinops spp., globe thistle
Eriogonum spp., buckwheat
Eryngium spp., sea holly
Euphorbia epithymoides, cushion spurge
Eutrochium spp., Joe Pye weed
Filipendula spp., meadow sweet
Foeniculum spp., fennel
Geum triflorum, prairie smoke
grasses (most)
Helleborus spp., hellebore
Heuchera spp., coral bells
Hylotelephium spp., stonecrop
Glaucium spp., horned poppy
Gomphrena spp., globe amaranth
Knautia macedonica spp., burgundy pincushion flower
Lavandula spp., lavender
Liatris spp., gayfeather
Limonium spp., sea lavender
Lunaria spp., money plant
Monarda spp., bee balm, horsemint

Nigella spp., love-in-a-mist
Nolina spp., beargrass
Origanum spp., ornamental oregano
Osmunda cinnamomea, cinnamon fern
Osmunda regalis, royal fern
Papaver spp., poppy
Parthenium integrifolium, wild quinine
Patrinia spp.
Penstemon digitalis 'Husker Red'
Perovskia spp., Russian sage
Persicaria spp.
Phlomis spp., Jerusalem sage
Polygonum spp.
Prunella spp., self-heal
Psilostrophe spp., paper flower
Pulsatilla spp., pasque flower
Ratibida spp., prairie coneflower
Rheum spp., ornamental rhubarb
Rudbeckia spp., black-eyed Susan
Ruta spp., rue
Salvia spp. (several)
Sanguisorba spp., burnet
Saponaria ×*lempergii* 'Max Frei', soapwort
Scabiosa spp., pincushion flower
sedges (most)
Sedum spp., stonecrop
Seseli gummifera, moon carrot
Solidago spp., goldenrod
Stachys spp.
Symphyotrichum ericoides, heath aster
Symphyotrichum oblongifolium, aromatic aster
Symphyotrichum lateriflorum
Symphyotrichum sericeum, silky aster
Thalictrum spp., meadow rue
Valeriana officinalis, valerian
Verbascum spp., mullein
Verbena bonariensis, verbena-on-a-stick
Veronicastrum spp., culver root

ABOVE LEFT Plants that "die well" deserve high praise as long-playing garden members. *Eryngium bourgatii, Astrantia major, Allium christophii,* Royal Horticultural Society garden at Wisley, Surrey, England, Piet Oudolf design.

ABOVE Ripening seedpods and slightly tawdry foliage can be beautiful, especially in the gentler light of late summer. *Penstemon digitalis* 'Husker Red', *Sedum ×luteolum* 'Blue Spruce', *Iris pallida* 'Argenteomarginata', *Catananche caerulea, Helictotrichon sempervirens,* authors' garden, Fort Collins, Colorado.

LEFT Many grasses and alliums look good long after their growth and bloom cycles have finished, as do some mulleins. *Nassella tenuissima, Allium aflatunense, Verbascum bombyciferum,* Denver Botanic Gardens.

PLANTS FOR SIMPLE INDOOR-OUTDOOR CONTAINERS

The following plants have passed our rough-and-tumble personal testing for ideal container plants. They are stunning in form and relatively compact, need very little water (except the palms and ferns) or fertilization, and don't grow too large or too fast to make them ungainly to move, nor do they require repotting or repropagation by cuttings more than every three to five years to keep them looking good. Our cats leave them alone. They are rarely plagued by pests or disease unless stressed by overwatering or incorrect light exposure. We enjoy these plants outside for part of the year and inside for the colder months. Without strong indoor sunlight for at least half a day, choices are more limited: plants tolerant of indirect light while inside and shade-tolerant while outdoors are marked ✳. Note that light intensity varies in different parts of the country; we are reporting our experiences in sunny climates with strong light.

Agaves

Agave attenuata 'Nova', 'Hummel Hybrid', 'Blue Flame'✳
Agave bracteosa ✳
Agave colorata
Agave desmettiana 'Joe Hoak', 'Variegata'✳
Agave sp. Felipe Otero (syn. *Agave* sp. Sierra Mixteca)
Agave filifera
Agave geminiflora
Agave guadalajarana
Agave horrida
Agave isthmensis
Agave lophantha 'Univittata'
Agave macroacantha
Agave multifilifera
Agave murpheyi 'Variegata'
Agave ocahui
Agave parrasana
Agave parryi var. *truncata*, 'Cream Spike'

Agave parviflora
Agave pelona
Agave polianthiflora
Agave polyacantha var. *xalapensis*
Agave potatorum
Agave schidigera 'Durango Delight'
Agave 'Sharkskin' (*A. asperrima* × *A. fernandi-regis*), sharkskin agave
Agave shawii
Agave striata
Agave stricta
Agave titanota
Agave victoriae-reginae

Aloes

Aloe aristata
Aloe aristata × *A. variegata*
Aloe brevifolia
Aloe cameronii
Aloe deltoideodonta
Aloe harlana
Aloe humilis and hybrids
Aloe nobilis
Aloe peglerae
Aloe polyphylla
Aloe reitzii
Aloe variegata
Aloe vera
small hybrids of mainly Madagascan species

Cacti

Only larger barrel and clustering types are listed—strongly columnar cacti get top-heavy in pots, making them difficult to move around, and the little ones don't show up when placed outside in the garden for the summer.

Astrophytum capricorne
Astrophytum myriostigma
Astrophytum ornatum
Echinocactus grusonii, golden barrel
Echinopsis hybrids
Ferocactus latispinus, wide-spined fire barrel

Mammillaria geminispina, *M. parkinsonii*, nipple cactus
Mammillaria spinosissima, redheaded Irishman
Notocactus magnificus
Schlumbergera hybrids, Christmas and Easter cactus ✳

Palms

Brahea armata, Mexican blue palm
Chamaedorea elegans ✳
Chamaerops humilis, Mediterranean fan palm
Howeia fosteriana, Kentia palm ✳
Phoenix roebelinii, pygmy date palm
Rhapis excelsa, lady palm ✳
Rhapis multifida ✳

Other great performers in pots

Aechmea 'Burgundy'
Aglaonema spp. ✳
Astrolepis sinuata ✳, bulb cloak fern
Beaucarnea spp., ponytail palm
Cotyledon orbiculata
Crassula arborescens, silver dollar plant
Crassula ovata (syn. *C. argentea*), jade plant
×*Cryptbergia* 'Rubra'✳, burgundy bromeliad
cycads ✳
Deuterocohnia lorenziana (syn. *Abromeitiella lorenziana*)
Dracaena spp.✳
Dudleya spp.
Dyckia spp.✳
Euphorbia aeruginosa
Euphorbia horrida
Euphorbia tirucalli 'Sticks on Fire'
Furcraea spp.✳
Haworthia spp.✳
Kalanchoe thyrsiflora
Phlebodium pseudoaureum (syn. *Polypodium pseudoaureum*), blue rabbit's foot fern
Sansevieria spp.✳, mother-in-law's tongue

ABOVE Containers make mobile problem solvers in sagging garden areas. When planted with textural subjects needing little water or fertilizer, they serve as living portable sculpture, with more appeal than most inanimate items that usually go by that name. *Agave gentryi, A. parryi, Aloe cryptopoda, Crassula ovata*, with *Penstemon pinifolius* and *Centranthus ruber* blooming, Ogden design, northern Colorado.

LEFT Indoors or out, containers allow the gardenmaker to explore plants otherwise unsuited to the year-round climate and/or soil of a site. Well over two hundred are trotted around house and garden by the authors. They bridge the gap between indoor and outdoor realms. *Crassula arborescens, Mammillaria spinosissima, M. parkinsonii, Agave lophantha* 'Univittata', *Yucca thompsoniana, Dasylirion quadrangulatum, Aloe cameronii, Ferocactus latispinus*, with flowering *Tanacetum niveum*, Ogden design, northern Colorado.

Rhythm and musicality in the garden

Grasses, among the most texturally compelling of plants, also bring an added element often missing in gardens, that of motion and rhythm. These plants, along with their cousins the bamboos, animate a space with their exquisite responsiveness to air movement. Few other plants, except those with foliage borne on pliant petioles such as poplars, quaking aspen, and many palms, or those with long, bending stems and branches such as dieramas and some willow species, move much save in the event of gale-force winds.

In open, exposed sites where wind often plays a strong role, grasses make ideal choices, celebrating the breezes. When dry and more brittle toward the end of their yearly growth cycle, grasses make soothing sounds as they sway. In the subtropics, palms—a great boon in urban areas for their powerful visual vitality—also help mitigate traffic noises with their year-round rustling in the same way moving water can.

Plants introduce rhythm into a garden. They do not necessarily have to move to lend such musicality to a space,

Repeating plants, whether in a formal or naturalistic manner, gives gardens cohesion, unity, and a sense of motion.

OPPOSITE Fine-textured, lithe bunchgrasses wend their way down this path, creating windswept movement and rhythmic repetition, while echoing wild grassland beyond the garden's perimeter. *Nassella tenuissima*, *Helictotrichon sempervirens*, *Echium lusitanicum*, *Eremurus* spp., Ogden design, northern Colorado.

LEFT Sheared boxwood punctuates this formal walk, moving the visitor down the path from one garden room to the next. *Buxus sempervirens*, Tintinhull, Somerset, England.

ABOVE Sinuous octopus agave (*Agave vilmoriniana*) sets up lively motion under crooked, equally sensual tree trunks of Texas ebony and eucalyptus. Boyce Thompson Arboretum, Superior, Arizona.

RIGHT Amaryllis dance beneath curvaceous branches of live oaks. *Hippeastrum* 'Mead Strain', *Ajuga reptans*, *Quercus fusiformis*, authors' garden, Austin, Texas.

however. Repetition of texture, form, and even color creates patterns that are often experienced bodily as music. Curved or strongly linear forms awaken distinct responses, often felt as romantic legato or bold staccato. Rhythm and musicality greatly influence the pace and mood of a garden experience. A path or road lined with pleached lime trees or Italian cypresses gives a sense of intent and drives one to move along; sinuous live oak branches arching over tiered azaleas and rounded camellias encourage lingering. Walking along a linear hedge clipped with sharp angles feels more purposeful and hurried than at the side of one left unshorn or trimmed in rounded, billowing forms. Along narrow garden paths, we often intersperse a series of small or mid-size fine-textured grasses. As one looks down such a path, similar textures set up an inviting rhythm. When a breeze blows, these repeated textural notes—garden leitmotifs—move, beckoning yet more strongly.

Seduction, exploration, arrival

Some gardens effortlessly draw people through their spaces, bringing visitors—even those unfamiliar with the place—into encounters with individual plants and scenes composed of plants, architecture, and terrain. The design tools that build this sense of flow play on universal human instincts: they repeat similar elements through a garden, developing visual familiarity and anticipation, as with the grass-dotted path just described. They also periodically hold back a bit of the view ahead or focus attention forward to an intriguing plant, object, or vista, alternating between intimate spaces and more expansive openings. This creates a series of transitions that provoke human curiosity, impelling people forward to each discovery.

In one planting lush bamboos line a gravel walk with their overarching stems, forming a dark, leafy tunnel; at the end a small patio bathes in sunlight, enticing visitors. Another garden lures people down a rustic flagstone path that curves out of view; glimpses of exotic amaryllis, vibrantly colored annuals, and groupings of bold succulents hint at further horticultural treasures beyond. By a still pool an overhanging angel's trumpet (*Brugmansia* 'Charles Grimaldi') suspends pendant funnels of volup-

Seduction by flower and water—what could be better than an evening soak beneath a redolent brugmansia? With *Macleaya* sp.,

Tom Hobbs and Brent Beattie garden, Vancouver, British Columbia, Canada.

tuous apricot-tinted bloom, promising potent fragrance as night falls. These vignettes exhibit the power of seduction: they draw people in by suggesting and inviting close, personal contact with individual plants and richly planted outdoor spaces.

Repeating plants, paving, and artifacts or themes endows a garden with a comfortable, unified identity that leads the eye to pick out familiar forms. Yet, too much direction or rote repetition abandons diversity, abundance, and the opportunity for individual exploration and response. More subtle use of plants with similar shapes or colors—not necessarily the same species or formally placed—are all that most people's eyes need to build, often subliminally, a sense of anticipation for what lies ahead. Likewise, a narrow path surrounded by lush foliage, opening onto an expansive lawn or patio is all that is required to announce transition to a new space. An urge to immediately inspect

one's surroundings upon entering a clearing may derive from some forgotten instinct to check for danger when leaving the safety of the forest; even without an architectural cue like a gate for reinforcement, this mostly subconscious experience provokes a definitive moment for many people. Garden spaces that arc gently away from intersection with a path reveal views that coincide roughly with limits of peripheral vision, and this also seems to subconsciously place people on alert, producing a sense of arrival as they look about to ascertain boundaries of new, unfamiliar surroundings.

ABOVE A bright opening beckons beyond the gate in this tropical-themed, summer-bedded courtyard garden. *Xanthosoma* sp., *Ensete ventricosum* 'Maurelii', *Coleus ×hybridus, Equisetum hyemale, Cyperus alternifolius, Canna* 'Bengal Tiger', vines, Chanticleer, Wayne, Pennsylvania, Dan Benarcik design.

OPPOSITE TOP Partially obscuring an entry and its destination—in this case with New Mexican olive—feeds on our natural curiosity. *Forestiera neomexicana, Papaver triniifolium, Penstemon strictus, Tanacetum niveum, Salvia sclarea*, northern Colorado, Ogden design.

RIGHT Looking from a place of enclosure to a well-lit opening entices. Crabapples, daffodils, and lawn, Chanticleer, Wayne, Pennsylvania.

Such innate human responses have much to do with how it feels to be in a garden and relate strongly to scale and proportion. A path three feet across feels ideal and encouraging to one person exploring a landscape; four feet accommodates two astride; wider still, and the experience takes on the generosity of a public park; less than three feet—perhaps only a few stepping stones—invites an intimate, solitary adventure among plants. These responses—tied directly to human scale—shape experience and color our connection with a garden.

Architects pay careful attention to proportion when designing buildings, maintaining set dimensions for windows, doors, and other features so that these comfortably relate to people, to one another, and to the building as a whole. Landscape designers likewise often employ grids when laying out gardens; these relate to some feature of the house that extends its scale onto surrounding grounds. Yet where large trees, natural rocks, distant views, grade changes, and other nonarchitectural features figure strongly, these native geometries—not necessarily those of buildings—deserve consideration and reflection. The complex proportions of gardens—and more important, our perceptions of them from various perspectives in actual landscapes—are better judged in person than on paper. Applying arbitrary rules of scale such as those in the Chinese feng shui tradition may improve confidence for inexperienced designers but often produce results that are just that: arbitrary. Likewise, architectural formulas like the golden

ratio (A/B=A+B/A) and golden angle (137.5 degrees)—although commonly present in nature and helpful for designing buildings and interior spaces to give a feeling of natural progression—offer little promise for a wide-open outdoor world where proportional relationships succeed from one angle of view but fail from another.

As with color, the sense of scale in gardens remains frustratingly within the realm of individual interpretation, yet at times proportionality becomes important for the interplay and experience of plants and people. A walkway that circles widely around a mature tree appears to respond to its size and majesty, encouraging several distinct views and experiences of its presence. One that travels straight

OPPOSITE TOP Slightly out of kilter, young hornbeams move in playful semi-unison, driving the visitor down this hosta-lined path to the gate and beyond. Hadspen House, Somerset, England.

OPPOSITE BOTTOM LEFT The repetition of fresh ostrich ferns down this path encourages further exploration. The ferns also impart a welcome woodland spirit to an otherwise staid space. *Matteuccia struthiopteris*, *Pieris japonica*, Chanticleer, Wayne, Pennsylvania.

OPPOSITE BOTTOM RIGHT An intimate path melds into a quiet clearing, pacing pause and reflection and then inviting one to proceed. Such subtle guidance through a garden preserves a chance for individual experience. *Tetrapanax papyrifera*, *Chasmanthium latifolium*, branches of live oak, and lawn, Ogden design, Austin, Texas.

RIGHT A path meant to accommodate only one person provides rich encounters with plants. *Crambe cordifolia*, *Alchemilla mollis*, *Papaver orientale* 'Helen Elizabeth', *Dianthus ×allwoodii*, *Penstemon digitalis* 'Husker Red', *Onosma echioides*, Ogden design, northern Colorado.

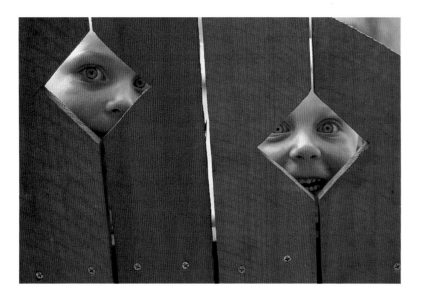

Curiosity drives *Homo sapiens* to great heights and depths of experience. Gardens can play off this insatiable instinct. Daughter Daphne and son Russell, authors' garden, Fort Collins, Colorado.

by—even though approaching closely beneath—hardly allows one to notice the tree, hastening passage and minimizing opportunities and angles to observe its form and power. Where a garden path goes determines whether one looks at, over, through, down on, or upward to a subject, or whether one looks at it at all, celebrating or diminishing certain plants and views. Paths also divide gardens and in so doing influence their potential. Designed to make a quick, convenient transition from car to house, the original walkway of our suburban Colorado residence hardly allowed comfortable space for adjacent planting; like many garden-loving homeowners, we chose to remove this unacceptable path, replacing it with a more leisurely, less direct walk whose interplanted flagstones and surrounding exuberantly planted beds create more of an invitation and sense of immersion in the garden.

Yet no two individuals see a garden in the same way. People naturally choose different routes through plantings: one turns away from plants or elements attractive to another or may be drawn to an enclosed or expansive space depending on personal preference. Landscapes that appeal to many visitors do so because they offer layers of experience that can be appreciated in multiple ways over varied

seasons. For gardens, richness and diversity offer a design recipe that serves both people and nature, and success in a plant-driven composition is best measured ecologically as well as aesthetically: while nurturing human beings, such a garden supports other living things as well.

Connecting with other living creatures

As it happens, the same alternations between open and enclosed spaces that develop interesting landscapes also benefit wildlife. Edges and transitions between garden spaces offer varied habitats inviting to birds, butterflies, and other creatures. Sheltering trees, dense plantings along perimeters, and successions of actively flowering and fruiting plants over the year—components that endow gardens with comfortable scale and enduring beauty—also provide food and shelter for animals.

Feisty, whirring, iridescent hummingbirds and lazily fluttering butterflies draw people as much as or more than the most beautiful flower. The arrival of these magical creatures can at times eclipse all else in the garden. Plantings dedicated to attracting these delightful interlopers include their favorite flowers—typically long-tubed red or orange blooms for hummingbirds, and flattened or daisylike flowers or open blossoms with projecting, feathery stamens for butterflies—along with twiggy trees and shrubs that provide habitat and shelter. For certain butterflies, gardens can incorporate larval food plants: senna and other legumes for sulfurs; milkweeds for monarchs; pipevines, members of the citrus family such as rue or hoptree, and carrot relations like dill, fennel, and parsley for swallowtails; passionflowers for zebra longwings and Gulf fritillaries. Positioning favored plants near windows brings ordinarily shy butterflies closer; likewise, a well-placed coral honeysuckle or sunset hyssop draws skittish hummingbirds to where they can be watched. These vitamin- and mineral-rich flowers—healthier for the birds and more attractive than artificial feeders—are self-replenishing.

Gardens created with wildlife in mind include not only sources of food—plants with berries and small seeds, nectar- and pollen-rich flowers, and diverse plantings to support an array of prey or forage species—but also sources

TOP LEFT With their amazing migratory feats, monarch butterflies engender wonder and sympathy when stopping in for a drink or a sip of nectar on their journeys. Spanish iris (*Iris xiphium*), authors' garden, Austin, Texas.

LEFT Fiercely territorial anoles claim their own plants in the garden before mating season. This one has chosen a flashy variegated agave as its hotel suite. *Agave americana* 'Marginata', *Arctotis fastuosa* 'Zulu Prince', *Asparagus* sp., Tom Peace garden, Lockhart, Texas.

ABOVE A shaded bowl filled with water reflects variegated dogwood foliage and provides for thirsty wildlife. *Cornus controversa* 'Variegata', hostas, ferns, iris, *Corydalis* sp., Penelope Maynard garden, Bedford, New York.

of water. Small, shallow bowls are just as good for birds as grand fountains; almost any type of water in a garden increases wildlife presence. In Colorado we periodically fill ceramic saucers or small natural basins created by sandstone boulders to offer water for birds, insects, and toads; in the hotter climate of Texas deeper Asian water jars provide shaded reservoirs that keep water cool, protecting it from evaporation, while their narrow-lipped openings present perches for thirsty birds visiting our plantings. Gardeners who appreciate mosquito-eating toads, lizards, and other small creatures encourage them not only with water but also by edging plantings, stabilizing slopes, and building garden spaces with rough-angled or irregular stones set loosely to leave damp, shaded hiding places. Allowing leafy debris or fallen logs to remain in wooded areas also preserves homes for tiny slithering animals.

Surprise, discovery, and playfulness

Connecting to a garden inevitably blurs the supposedly separate realms of people and nature. For people this blurring sometimes finds expression in a sense of play. The leafy paths and spaces we create offer opportunities to place surprises where they may later be discovered by visitors: perhaps a cherished specimen fern by a still, reflective pool or a serene statue set in a secluded grove offer unexpected reward for someone. Sections of petrified wood or flattened spirals of ammonites, casually laid among plantings, speak to connections with their specific regions—large ammonites make iconic accents for many ranch-house gardens in Texas and are often incorporated in walls and garden paving in southern England, both places where these fossils abound—and also say much about the passions of the gardenmakers.

Art that whimsically imitates or merges with plantings offers further evidence of a playful human spirit. Such compositions honor plants by echoing forms and colors of leaves, flowers, or other attributes; these nods to nature from the built world are charming when they leave plants in the lead but sometimes feel overbearing or surreal when artifice dominates planting. In either instance these fits of human playfulness stand as testimony to the desires of people to restore connections with nature.

It probably will take another several millennia before that ancient mark of our former wild surroundings and our

A gate fashioned of bamboo canes flanked by live bamboo makes for an appealing insider's joke at the home of nurseryman, designer, and bamboo enthusiast John Greenlee and his wife, Leesa. With variegated phormiums, Brisbane, California.

longing to be reunited with them are entirely obliterated from our souls. Gardens where plants are celebrated reconnect us with the exuberance, generosity, and abundance of the natural world. We can hope this connection will never break entirely, for in it lies much of our humanity. When we see ourselves as a part of a larger whole, one that we can influence but that also influences us in even greater ways, we recapture a sense of grace and humility that enables us to treat political foe, next-door neighbor, bird, tree, stone, soil, water—any and all living and nonliving elements of the earth and the universe—with respect. In creating and tending a plant-driven garden, unlike the Eden where we fell from grace, we may find a part of our lost divinity.

ABOVE LEFT In the garden and outdoor gallery of artists George Little and David Lewis, a quiet surprise awaits those who look closely and wander beyond the obvious—their own reflection in a sculpted mirror set among ferns and a cool blue concrete wall. *Adiantum pedatum, Asplenium nidus* var. *plicatum*, ivy, Little and Lewis garden, Bainbridge Island, Washington.

ABOVE In a plant-driven garden, we rediscover our connection with plants and nature, and feel our place in the universe. Daughter Hope, authors' garden, Fort Collins, Colorado.

PLANTS WITH FLOWERS THAT ATTRACT BUTTERFLIES & HUMMINGBIRDS

Plants included here offer nectar in floral shapes and presentations that make feeding easy for these creatures. These characteristics bring butterflies and hummingbirds with regularity. Hummingbirds pre- fer flowers in red, orange, magenta, or deep blue, with just a few pastel and yellow exceptions. Note a preponderance of daisy, verbena, and mint family members preferred by butterflies. Many plant species grown only in tropical and frost-free climates are not included here.

Flowers that commonly attract butterflies

Acacia spp.
Achillea spp., yarrow
Ageratina spp.
Ageratum spp., mist flower
Allium spp., ornamental onion
Aloysia spp., sweet brush
Amorpha spp., leadplant
Anaphalis spp., pearly everlasting
Anthemis spp., marguerite
Arabis spp., rock cress
Aralia spp., Hercules club
Armeria spp., sea thrift
Aruncus spp., goatsbeard
Aster spp.
Aubrieta spp., purple rock cress
Baccharis spp.
Baileya multiradiata, desert marigold
Bauhinia mexicana, goatfoot tree
Berlandiera lyrata, chocolate flower
Calendula officinalis, pot marigold
Caryopteris spp., blue mist spirea
Centaurea spp., knapweed
Centranthus ruber, Greek valerian
Cephalanthus occidentalis, buttonbush
Cephalaria spp., giant pincushion flower
Ceratostigma spp., leadwort
Cirsium spp., thistle
Clethra spp., summersweet
Conoclinium spp., mist flower
Cordia boissieri, wild olive

Coreopsis spp., tickseed
Cosmos spp.
Cynara spp., artichoke, cardoon
Dalea spp.
Dianthus spp., pinks
Duranta erecta, golden dewdrop
Ebanopsis ebano, Texas ebony
Echinacea spp., coneflower
Echinops spp., globe thistle
Echium spp.
Ehretia anacua, anacua
Encelia spp., brittlebush
Ericameria (syn. *Chrysothamnus*) spp., rabbitbrush, chamisa
Erigeron spp., fleabane
Eriogonum spp., buckwheat
Eryngium spp., sea holly
Eutrochium spp., Joe Pye weed
Farfugium japonicum, giant groundsel
Fendlera rupicola, cliff fendlerbush
Gaillardia spp., firewheel
Gomphrena spp., globe amaranth
Hedyotis (syn. *Houstonia*) spp., bluets
Helenium spp., sneezeweed
Helianthus spp., sunflower
Heliopsis spp.
Heliotropium arborescens, cherry pie
Hylotelephium spp., stonecrop
Knautia macedonica, burgundy pincushion flower
Lavandula spp., lavender
Leucaena retusa, golden ball lead tree
Leucanthemum spp., ox-eye daisy
Liatris spp., gayfeather
Ligularia spp.
Ligustrum spp., privet
Limonium spp., sea lavender, statice
Lindera spp., spicebush
Lithospermum spp., puccoon
Lunaria spp., money plant
Lobularia maritima, sweet alyssum
Machaeranthera spp., Tahoka daisy
Malpighia glabra, Barbados cherry
Mentha spp., mint
Origanum spp., oregano

Passiflora spp., passion flower
Pavonia spp., rockrose
Philadelphus spp., mock orange
Phyla nodiflora, frogfruit
Plumbago spp.
Primula spp., primrose
Prunella vulgaris, selfheal
Pycnanthemum spp., mountain mint
Ratibida spp., prairie coneflower
Rosmarinus officinalis, rosemary
Rudbeckia spp., black-eyed Susan
Sambucus spp., elder
Saponaria spp., soapwort
Scabiosa spp., pincushion flower
Senecio spp., groundsel
Silphium spp., compass plant
Solidago spp., goldenrod
Spiraea spp.
Stachytarpheta, porterweed
Stokesia laevis, Stoke's aster
Symphyotrichum spp., aster
Tagetes spp., marigold
Tanacetum spp., tansy
Tetraneuris (syn. *Hymenoxys*) spp.
Thelesperma spp., greenthread
Thymophylla spp.
Thymus spp., thyme
Tilia spp., linden
Tithonia spp.
Trixis spp.
Verbesina spp.
Vernonia spp., ironweed
Viburnum spp.
Viguiera spp.
Viola spp., pansy, violet
Vitex spp., chaste tree
Valeriana officinalis, valerian

Flowers that commonly attract hummingbirds

Abutilon megapotamicum, red flowering maple
Agapanthus spp., lily of the Nile
Agave spp., century plant
Alcea rosea, hollyhock

Aloe spp.
Alstroemeria psittacina, parrot lily
Anisacanthus spp., hummingbird bush
Antigonon leptopus, rosa de la montana
Antirrhinum majus, snapdragon
Aquilegia spp., columbine
Arbutus spp., madrone
Arctostaphylos spp., manzanita
Begonia spp.
Beschorneria spp.
Bignonia capreolata, cross vine
Bougainvillea spp.
Bouvardia ternifolia
bromeliads
Caesalpinia spp., bird of paradise bush
Callistemon spp., bottlebrush
Camellia spp.
Campsis spp., trumpet creeper
Canna spp.
Caragana spp.
Castilleja spp., Indian paintbrush
Cestrum spp.
Chaenomeles spp., flowering quince
Chorisia speciosa, floss silk tree
Cleistocactus spp.
Clematis texensis
Cleome spp., spider flower
Correa pulchella, Australian fuchsia
Crocosmia spp.
Cuphea spp., firecracker flower
Dicliptera suberecta
Digitalis spp., foxglove
Dudleya spp.
Dyckia spp.
Echeveria spp., hen and chicks
Embothrium coccineum, Chilean flame tree
Epilobium angustifolium, fireweed
Eremophila spp.
Erythrina spp., coral bean
Fouquieria splendens, ocotillo
Fuchsia spp.
Galvezia spp., bush snapdragon
Gilia (syn. *Ipomopsis*) spp.
Gladiolus spp.
Grevillea spp.
Hemerocallis spp., daylily
Hesperaloe spp., red yucca
Hippeastrum spp., amaryllis

Heuchera spp., coral bells
Ixora spp.
Jasminum spp., jasmine
Jatropha spp., coral plant
Justicia spp., chuparosa
Keckiella spp.
Kniphofia spp., red hot poker
Lagerstroemia spp., crape myrtle
Leonotis spp., lion's ears
Leucophyllum spp., ceniza
Lilium spp. (especially Turk's cap types)
Lobelia spp.
Lupinus spp., lupine
Lychnis spp.
Lycoris radiata, red spider lily
Mahonia spp.
Malvaviscus arboreus subsp. *drummondii*, Turk's cap
Manfreda spp.
Maurandya spp., snapdragon vine
Mertensia spp.
Mirabilis spp., four o'clock
Nicotiana spp., flowering tobacco
Odontonema stricta, firespike
Pedilanthus spp., redbird
Pelargonium spp., florist geranium
Petunia spp.
Physostegia virginiana, obedient plant
Polianthes spp., tuberose
Poliomintha maderensis, Mexican oregano
Puya spp.
Quamoclit coccinea, cypress vine
Ribes spp., currant, gooseberry
Robinia spp., locust
Scrophularia macrantha, red birds in a tree
Scutellaria spp., skullcap
Sophora spp.
Spigelia marilandica, Indian pink
Sprekelia spp., Aztec lily
Stachys albotomentosa, Hidalgo sage
Stachys coccinea, scarlet betony
Tecoma spp., esperanza
Tecomaria capensis, Cape honeysuckle
Tropaeolum speciosum, flame nasturtium
Watsonia spp.
Weigela florida
Wisteria spp.
Zauschneria spp., hummingbird trumpet, California fuchsia

Flowers that attract both
Abelia spp.
Aesculus spp., buckeye
Agastache spp., anise hyssop
Albizzia julibrissin, mimosa tree
Asclepias spp., milkweed, butterfly weed
Buddleia spp., butterfly bush
Calliandra spp., fairy duster
Ceanothus spp., wild lilac
Cercis spp., redbud
Cheiranthus spp., wallflower
Chelone, turtlehead
Chilopsis linearis, desert willow
Consolida spp., larkspur
Delphinium spp.
Echinocereus coccineus, *E. triglochidiatus*, claret cup cactus
Erysimum spp., wallflower
Glandularia spp., moss verbena
Hamelia patens, firebush
Hesperis spp., dame's rocket
Hibiscus spp.
Iberis sempervirens, candytuft
Impatiens spp.
Ipomoea spp., morning glory
Kolkwitzia amabilis, beauty bush
Lantana spp.
Lonicera spp., honeysuckle
Matthiola spp., stock
Mimulus spp., monkey flower
Monarda spp., bee balm, horsemint
Nepeta spp., catmint
Penstemon spp.
Pentas lanceolata, Egyptian star
Phacelia spp.
Phlox spp.
Rhododendron spp., deciduous azalea
Rondeletia spp.
Ruellia spp., wild petunia
Russelia spp., coral blow
Salvia spp., sage
Silene spp., catchfly
Syringa spp., lilac
Trichostema spp., blue curls
Verbena spp.
Wedelia (syn. *Zexmenia*) spp.
Zinnia spp.

6

PLANTS HONORED
A gallery of gardens in the spirit of plant-driven design

THE GARDENS FEATURED in this chapter all take their lead from plants, not architecture or artifice. Bold or subtle, traditional or modern, naturalistic or formal, they represent gardenmaking from many diverse regions in the United States and also from other parts of the world.

An immersive matrix

We begin this chapter with a German garden, for while we have learned a great deal from and continue to admire English plantsmanship, it is in Germany where we have been inspired by approaches more synchronous with plant-driven design. The German public garden Weihenstephan allows for an unusually intimate experience. Located in Freising, a medieval university town on the outskirts of Munich, Weihenstephan takes as its mission to experiment with changing plantings and to teach university students through active involvement. Open to all, it doubles as a town park.

In one particular area, a restricted palette of herbaceous perennials and subshrubs forms a matrix on a flat, rectangular, approximately quarter-acre space. The entire planting is criss-crossed with narrow turf paths, allowing one to walk around, into, and through the garden rather than just alongside, museum-style, as is typical for most herbaceous plantings. Plants are mostly ankle- to waist-high and

fine-textured, inviting immersion without physically overwhelming the visitor.

The green paths serve as visual unifiers—tidy bright ribbons through a haze of powder blue, silver, white, and chartreuse. The space seems enlarged yet well defined by repetition of frothy textures and limited colors, dominated by pale blue Russian sage, chartreuse euphorbia, white pearly everlasting, and a host of silver-leaved plants. Turf and repeated plants serve as structure.

The plants chosen revel in the temperate continental climate of southern Germany and are meant to echo an eastern European steppe community, not unlike some chaparral habitats in North America or the Mediterranean. They must tolerate unamended soil, rely only on natural rainfall, present a long season of interest, and require relatively little ongoing care.

While many of the plants offer extended flowering, the majority also look good out of bloom, with interesting growth habits and arresting foliage. The whole garden

OPPOSITE This vibrant garden uses familiar plants—annual cleome, verbena, and cosmos along with maiden grass—that stand out for their mobile grace. Here they join together in a fluid blend of wild-looking flowers and foliage. The display lasts for several months from summer well into autumn. *Verbena bonariensis*, *V. rigida* 'Polaris', *Miscanthus sinensis*, *Cleome hassleriana*, *Cosmos bipinnatus*, Weihenstephan Garten, Freising, Germany.

ABOVE Gardens with plants that engage the senses and fascinate the mind leave their mark on the visitor. Daughter Daphne is lost in a moment of examining ripe seed. *Perovskia* ×*hybrida*, *Euphorbia* sp., *Anaphalis* sp., *Salvia lavandulifolia*, Weihenstephan Garten, Freising, Germany.

RIGHT A group of repeated plants—here natural-looking, unadulterated species—make up this matrix at Weihenstephan. The resulting space is calm and cohesive. This comes as a refreshing contrast to commonly seen overstuffed, visually busy gardens. *Perovskia* ×*hybrida*, *Euphorbia* sp., *Anaphalis* sp., Weihenstephan Garten, Freising, Germany.

seems to flicker and vibrate, sparkling in the manner of distant stars; this distinctive liveliness appears to be a product of twiggy textures and shimmering silvers. The overall effect is soothing and elegant, wild yet not chaotic. Flowers are generally small, giving a natural, serene feel. The choice of cool colors rather than warm adds to the serenity. The colors exaggerate perspective, enlarging the space: perovskia recedes in puffs of blue, while mounds of bright chartreuse spurge, white anaphalis, and silver sage seem to jump forward into view.

Surprise and discovery await despite the flat terrain. Ignoring traditional herbaceous height arrangements of tall in back and short in front, the design interjects diaphanous veils of airy *Stipa gigantea* and Russian sage into the foreground in selected spots, building a sense of mystery. Weaving different species throughout rather than planting in broad, obvious panels tempts one to meander and explore, because one doesn't sense as with panel plantings that the entire garden can be seen and experienced from just one vantage point. Few gardens—especially public ones—so successfully combine intimacy with expansive serenity, nor do they often convey the diversity and power of both wild communities and gardens simultaneously.

Waterwise diversity

Upon entering Denver Botanic Gardens, one quickly encounters an overbearing concrete-and-glass conservatory along a walkway almost the width of a two-lane highway. Between these unfriendly masses of cement, a narrow sloping strip of garden bursts forth, running the length of the conservatory. This is the Water-Smart Garden, whose small size belies its pioneering role in the development of a regional plant palette and style for the mountain West.

Lauren designed this garden in the mid-1990s with the charge to prove that water-conserving plantings, dubbed xeriscapes, can actually be pretty. Before then, public attempts at xeric design generally trotted out a limited palette of poorly combined native plants hopelessly smothered in harsh stone mulches. People wanted to try xeriscape but not give up lushness, floral bounty, or year-round appeal.

The site is small enough to offer intimacy, something not often found in public garden spaces, but its setting is daunting. The overbuilt paving and architecture surrounding the planting roars heat back onto the strip, augmenting the slope's already torrid southern exposure. Nutrient-poor, sandy, alkaline backfill comprises the soil. To succeed here, plants must be truly tough and adaptable. A rich assortment of shrubs, subshrubs, herbaceous perennials, succulents, fiber plants, grasses, bulbs, and self-sowing annuals and biennials have proven themselves up to the task. No longer segregated, western North American natives mingle with Central Asian, Mediterranean, and South African species in a cohesive, informal textural style with unique regional resonance. The garden receives less than one fifth the water a conventional lawn-dominated landscape in the region typically does.

To allow a personal experience up close with the plants, not just from the lower concrete walkway, an understated path of gravel fines—basically compacted rock dust—meanders the length of the garden. Stone, rock, or masonry was intentionally avoided, as there was already an overabundance of this close at hand. Creating an inviting, full, soft garden and giving it human scale were paramount. Small and mid-sized clumping grasses with fine textures, including *Festuca*, *Nassella*, *Stipa*, and *Sporobolus* species, thread through the planting as moving, diaphanous counterpoints to stiff, powerfully structural forms of prickly pear cacti, yuccas, agaves, and sotols. Grasses and other textural plants play with light throughout the day and through the seasons courtesy of the path's east-west orientation, softening the transition between path and planting.

The garden is composed of vignettes to be appreciated up close yet retains an overall unity thanks to repetition of form, texture, and blue and silver foliage. To give the planting instant maturity and scale, Lauren kept previously planted mature pinyon pines that line the conservatory, as well as a massive bank of *Yucca baccata* in the center. Careful color orchestration takes a backseat to form and texture as a design element; in the harsh light of a mile above sea level few hues clash, and even the most ferocious

ABOVE Profuse in spite of little moisture, the Water-Smart Garden blends native and exotic plants adapted to Denver's exacting soil and challenging semiarid climate a mile above sea level. *Centranthus ruber, Nepeta racemosa* 'Walker's Low', *Yucca baccata, Opuntia macrorhiza, Verbascum bombyciferum, Nassella tenuissima, Tanacetum niveum, Salvia cyanescens, Chamaebatiaria millefolium, Pinus edulis,* Water-Smart Garden, Denver Botanic Gardens, Ogden design.

RIGHT A mix of bold and fine textures harnesses low afternoon light in late summer. *Opuntia macrorhiza, Nassella tenuissima, Salvia greggii,* Water-Smart Garden, Denver Botanic Gardens, Ogden design.

LONG-TERM STANDOUTS

Acantholimon spp., spikethrift

Agave parryi, Parry's century plant

Artemisia versicolor, seafoam sage

Ballota pseudodictamnus

Crambe maritima, sea kale

Digitalis obscura, copper foxglove

Ephedra equisetina, blue joint fir

Euphorbia rigida, gopher plant

Marrubium rotundifolium, roundleaf horehound

Oenothera macrocarpa subsp. *incana*, silver blade sundrop

Origanum libanoticum, Lebanese oregano

Salvia dorrii, blue ball sage

Salvia pachyphylla, mountain desert sage

Stachys inflata, silver betony

Tanacetum cinerariifolium, pyrethrum daisy

Tanacetum densum var. *amani*, partridge feather

Veronica incana, silver speedwell

Veronica oltensis, cutleaf Turkish veronica

SHORT-LIVED BUT SELF-SOWING PLAYERS

Alyssum markgrafii

Bukiniczia cabulica

Centranthus ruber, Greek valerian

Dianthus spp., pinks

Eryngium planum, sea holly

Eschscholzia californica, California poppy

Festuca glauca, blue sheep's fescue

Gaura lindheimeri, apple blossom grass

Glaucium spp., horned poppy

Nassella tenuissima, Mexican feather grass

Papaver atlanticum, Spanish poppy

Penstemon spp., beardtongue

Salvia cyanescens

Scutellaria resinosa, Great Plains skullcap

Tanacetum niveum, snow daisy

Verbascum spp., mullein

combinations that would fight in soft light with a brilliant green backdrop are lovely here mitigated by cool silver, sage green, and blue leaves. The Water-Smart Garden is based on such foliage compositions yet blooms with abandon in spring, early summer, and again in autumn. The fullness and complexity of the planting distracts from its harsh surroundings. Its quirky style might be described as cottage-garden abundance meets romanticized chaparral.

Ongoing care is not particularly intensive yet requires deep knowledge of the plants and a strong sense of design. Many species self-sow and the gardener needs to determine which stay and which are exiled. All spent flowers and stems must be cut back at some point, yet this may occur right after flowering or not until the following growing season, a complicated judgment call. A thin mulch of pea gravel retains moisture but is not much good at keeping down weeds; this is accomplished by the density of planting. Late winter is time for an intensive cleanup and cutting back, followed by a couple lesser primpings after floral events as the seasons progress. An added bonus of

this garden is that it holds up better through all four seasons in a cold-winter climate than most traditional garden styles do.

Kaleidoscopic retreat in a small town

The unremarkable street-side view of Tom and Diane Peace's bungalow gives little hint of the enticing garden hiding in back. Longing for privacy in this small-town setting, Tom enclosed the garden on all sides by trees, bamboo, and palms, creating a magical kingdom of sorts. Within the limited space of this secluded, sheltered quarter acre or so, a fantastic abundance of plant species in brilliant color combinations set the stage for an intimate outdoor living space used on all but the coldest and wettest days of the six months each year that the couple resides in Texas.

When the Peaces leave for summer up north, the plants here for the most part must fend for themselves, with a bit of watering by thoughtful friends now and again during the hottest, driest periods. Heavy, rich, alkaline blackland

prairie soil keeps many plants from desiccating entirely but proves challenging when waterlogged at other times of the year. Raised planting areas and a parade of exuberantly stuffed containers—some with seasonal bulb displays, others with year-round denizens—mitigate some of the drainage issues. The matte, chalky white clay pots, unpretentious and stolid in form, are produced regionally. These echo the pale limestone paving of paths and patio, and together identify the otherwise exotically profuse garden as distinctly Texan.

With all focus on garden enjoyment between October and the end of April, Tom fills the space with colorful cool-season annuals and lush edible greens, a soft counterpoint to myriad succulents and fiber plants. Bulbs and South African plants are particular passions and abound throughout. A nurseryman and garden designer by profession, Tom uses this garden as both sanctuary and trial ground.

Plants grow on all planes and obscure much of the house's modest architecture. The small scale and inward

orientation of the garden lend themselves to detailed vignettes: at every turn some new plant is shown off and partnered with another, making a protracted journey of discovery possible without traversing much ground. While the cottage-style layout is traditional, the plants and combinations are anything but. A penchant for adventurous plant possibilities and a painterly, highly personal aesthetic sense combine in an inviting and fascinating kaleidoscope of blossoms and foliage. In a region where gardening is possible every month of the year but still largely seen as a spring and fall event, this garden celebrates horticulturally ignored times.

Ongoing care is sporadically intensive, with the planting of many annuals and lots of deadheading needed to prolong the season. Weeds are minimal, finding little room to prosper amid the dense plantings.

A garden that blends into foothills

On a gentle south-facing slope in the cold, dry foothills of northern Colorado, Lauren blended this garden into natural short-grass prairie and montane chaparral beyond. Compared to working in the framework of linear, often visible boundaries that define garden spaces in urban and suburban settings, designing an unbounded garden into wild surroundings is a complex challenge. Instead of looking inward, the garden needs to reach out and embrace the terrain beyond. Everything about the natural landscape—scale, overall shape, patterns and types of both hard materials and plant species, predominant colors and textures—should be reflected in some way in the garden for a smooth transition that joins wilderness and man-made space into one.

A narrow path of irregular ruddy-colored flagstone, locally quarried and of the same stratum as the foothills canyon where this garden is found, works its way horizontally across the hillside, bisecting the planted area. Its east-west orientation harnesses early and late light effects. Large glacial granite boulders—some already in place, some harvested from other areas on the site, and some brought in from nearby—create structure and echo the tumbled, erratic stone in the wider landscape. They also immediately

OPPOSITE Beckoning from the back door, Tom and Diane Peace's retreat invites exploration. The garden is jam-packed with intriguing plants yet retains a mood of repose. Lockhart, Texas, Tom Peace design.

ABOVE Cloaked in the glowing blossoms of crossvine, the house façade backs a rich planting of early spring flowers. *Hippeastrum* 'Giraffe', *Ajuga tenori* 'Valfredda', *Freesia laxa*, *Anagallis monellii*, *Viola* 'Crown Blue', *Ursinia* sp., *Nemesia strumosa* 'Carnival', and *Bignonia capreolata* 'Tangerine Beauty', the latter a selection found and introduced to the nursery trade by Scott Ogden. Lockhart, Texas, Tom Peace design.

age and settle the garden, connecting it to the ancient geology of its surroundings. These rounded, lichen-encrusted forms—"manatee rocks" as we affectionately call them—anchor the garden slope, harvest water and provide wind protection for adjacent plants, echo the curvaceous roll of the land, give scale and perspective to the treeless space, lend rhythm and purpose to the path, and imbue the scene with serenity. A neutral-toned, tawny mulch of pea gravel helps conserve moisture and moderates temperature swings. The mulch's quiet openness reflects the stark, barren soil and rock spaces found amid the natural plant communities of the region. A garden planted neck to neck with plants, with no soil or stone showing between, would seem too lush in these stark surroundings.

Rounded forms continue as a theme in the plantings: xeric sages, some native to the site, hunker down with Mediterranean santolinas and Central Asian acantholimons. No plants grow above knee height; most are under a foot tall, repeating the scale of the prairie beyond. Fine textures predominate and grasses intermingle throughout; western natives find themselves especially at home, mirroring the wild plant community. All must tolerate drought, wind, strong sun, cold and mostly snowless winters, and a thin, humus-poor mineral soil. A few strong plant forms break the textural tranquility: hardy yuccas and agaves join seasonally present tender potted succulents as accents.

This garden requires no additional water beyond the limited rainfall of the region. During a prolonged, three-year drought many of the short-lived herbaceous perennials such as penstemon, dianthus, and catmint died and there was little flowering, even in the spring. Yet the textures and soft tones of the remaining plants' foliage kept the garden interesting even during its most stressful months. Green is never a major player; silver and tan predominate, with dots of brilliant color in early spring from small drought-tolerant bulbs, and a generous sprinkling of bloom until midsummer, with a small reprise in autumn. Mostly, the garden is not about riotous color at all. It follows the subtle natural cycles of the land of which it is a part, a sere prairie-and-shrub community where flowers come and go in brief, conservative displays.

The garden is quite undemanding in terms of care. It is too dry for most weeds, and the plants look good both in active growth as well as when parched and dried late in the year. Most spent flower heads are left until the following growing season is about to begin. A late-winter cutting back of these flower stalks and grasses makes room for new growth. Debris harvested is minimal compared to most gardens: these plants do not grow fast or large. They, like the wild land they reach out to, have a quiet yet beautiful reserve born of an exacting climate and stingy soil.

An exuberant boreal garden

Carved into a clearing in the wooded Alaskan wilderness near the tiny town of Willow, this one-acre garden bursts forth with unparalleled exuberance. Les Brake, its passionate and singularly energetic creator, tends to its ever-expanding dimensions, a full-time job during the fleeting growing season of these high latitudes. Spilling around and beyond a rustic log home built by Les's partner, the garden blends easily into its natural surroundings.

This is no mean feat, considering the site is home to a dense spruce and poplar forest, whereas the garden is largely composed of herbaceous perennials, biennials, and annuals. Permafrost beneath the otherwise rich, moist soil severely restricts the number of woody plants that can grow, yet massive snow cover allows a large number of

OPPOSITE TOP In severe drought, plants grow to only half their normal size and bloom much less freely. Yet this garden holds its own, thanks to tough native and exotic species that offer good texture and form. Container plants placed outside for the warm months add succulent boldness without needing much water or care. *Alyssum markgrafii, Artemisia versicolor, Santolina* spp., *Yucca baccata, Echium lusitanicum,* agaves in pots, northern Colorado, Ogden design.

OPPOSITE BOTTOM Hues and textures of the dry winter garden have a quiet grace. Without having the previous season's stems removed, plants show improved hardiness and lend the garden their patterns and forms until the return of spring, when they must be cut back to make room for new growth. Same plants as summer image, northern Colorado, Ogden design.

herbaceous perennials to survive the long, cold winters. The garden is loosely organized into graceful asymmetrical beds and borders, with seductive curving paths and small lawns interspersed to guide flow. At forest's edge, an open area covered in native moss visually links the garden's small green lawns to the wilderness beyond.

OPPOSITE In harmony with its surroundings, Les Brake's garden flows easily through a forest clearing. Lush plants, many with strongly vertical forms yet foamy demeanor, echo the mood of the North Woods. *Thalictrum roche-brunianum, Delphinium elatum, Digitalis purpurea, Filipendula glaberrima, Verbascum* sp., Coyote Garden, Willow, Alaska, Les Brake design.

ABOVE Gigglewood latticework made by Les's partner, Jerry Conrad, frames floral abundance with a distinctive Alaskan forest touch. Site, plants, and the gardenmakers join in a unique sense of place. *Papaver somniferum, Verbascum* 'Electric Yellow', *V.* sp., *Thalictrum rochebrunianum, Delphinium elatum, Filipendula glaberrima, Atriplex hortensis* 'Rubra', *Geranium* 'Spinners' seedling, Coyote Garden, Willow, Alaska, Les Brake design.

Tall plants such as delphinium, meadow rue, filipendula, foxglove, and mullein grow in generous groups and repeat informally throughout, as would occur in a natural plant community. Their upright forms echo the verticality of the woodland's trees, which in turn shelter the perennials' vulnerable stature from the worst winds. With Les's attention, good soil, and twenty-some hours of daylight during the summer, these grow taller and more luxuriantly than in perhaps any other place on earth. This, along with the boreal forest as a dark green backdrop and the whimsically gnarled woodwork of gates, fences, and trellises made by Les's partner, gives the garden a unique sense of place. Anyone well acquainted with herbaceous perennials will feel a distinct shift in scale take place here as many of the fantastically vigorous perennials reach, almost treelike, way above head-high. The experience is beguiling and slightly surreal, like entering some sort of fairyland. Les has turned a densely planted floral composition that might easily have become very English or cottage-y in style into a garden with a casual, wild, distinctively Alaskan feel.

The garden revels in floral abandon all summer long thanks to the cool air of the North Woods. Colors glow with a saturation found farther south only at high elevation. Hues never jar in the soft, often diffuse light; turf and woods beyond tie them together in a verdant envelope.

The size and complexity of this garden demand a level of care matched by few unstaffed private gardens. Les follows the rhythms of a unique climate that encourages unbridled, explosive profusion and then retreats into complete dormancy: he gardens tirelessly all summer after months of cabin fever peppered by creative outbursts channeled toward candlelit ice sculptures. His hand is rarely seen, however, as he possesses keen sensitivity and thoughtfulness in orchestrating the dance between spontaneity and control. Fallen petals are left spangling the pathways and lawns; self-sown seedlings of poppies, primulas, mulleins, and of many other happy denizens abound.

With its joyously sensual celebration of boreal summer, this garden, along with the generous and enthusiastic spirit of its unpretentious, optimistic creator, has pioneered a new level of gardening passion in the forty-ninth state.

A garden on a dry limestone ledge

Overlooking a lake from a high bluff, a diverse garden of bold succulents, airy grasses, and low, drought-loving flowers merges romantically with the rough native landscape backed by an ancient limestone escarpment. Scott created this garden in Austin, Texas, as a private hideaway on a ledge above the canyon of the Colorado River. A naturally weathered limestone wall formed a dramatic backdrop for the original wild landscape filled with scruffy native junipers, cedar elms, and weedy undergrowth; an old rusted iron staircase originally provided a way down the steep slope, connecting to more stairs and a boat dock below.

Since this garden has little access to water, it was designed to survive on natural rainfall alone. This guarantees that plants will experience harsh drought during summer and sometimes in winter as well; the shallow soils rest directly on top of lime rock that quickly wicks away moisture. After the old metal stairway was removed, several tons of limestone road base were trucked to the edge of the natural precipice and dumped over to build a small sloping mound. When this loosely crushed limestone absorbed water, it consolidated, binding to the native stone of the site. A shallow layer of crushed granite mixed with a little compost covers this hill along with a few stones gathered from the site to echo strata visible on the escarpment.

To keep in step with the mass and scale of the cliff wall and match its natural feel, colossal stone treads were embedded in the loose limestone base to create a rustic stairway. The path's orientation—it turns and runs parallel to the escarpment—highlights the stone's rugged face and directs visitors toward a mature cedar elm, one of several native trees retained for scale and to keep the indigenous spirit of the site.

The hill's mineral soil provides a friable, well-drained substrate that nonetheless stores some moisture. To play off the bold cliff, powerful plantings that would thrive in the hot sun of this west-facing ledge were called for. Cacti and succulents offered obvious choices but would need to tolerate the summer humidity and hard freezes common to Austin's erratic climate. Staggered columnar cacti create sentinels on the hillside and along the steps, heightening the sense of vertical displacement, while large specimens of tree beargrass and Mexican grasstree give densely leafy rosettes to anchor the plantings, partly hiding views of a small patio at the base of the steps. This irregularly rounded space, a destination for people descending the stairs, reveals choices between further routes down to the boat dock or across the ledge to a shady cliffside sitting area with vistas over the lake.

Detailed plantings include barrel cacti, agaves, and aloes canted at angles along the hillside and steps to show off their geometric form and create the impression that their growth has been responding to the natural slope. A few rosette plants nest in the loose duff along the base of the escarpment, helping tie the succulent-themed plantings to

LEFT The raw bluff before the garden.

BELOW After stairway construction and planting, massive stone treads and mature, sculptural succulents mix with fine-textured perennials to play off the native limestone escarpment. Tree beargrass (*Nolina nelsonii*) and giant cardon cactus (*Echinopsis terscheckii*) create perspective and anchor this unirrigated planting.

HUMIDITY-TOLERANT SUCCULENTS

These take hard frost (15 to 20 degrees F or colder).

large century plants with gray foliage: *Agave asperrima* (syn. *A. scabra*), *A. ovatifolia, A. protoamericana, A. weberi*

large century plants with green foliage: *Agave gentryi, A. salmiana* 'Ferox'

dwarf century plants: *Agave bracteosa, A. mitis* (syn. *A. celsii*), *A. schidigera, A. striata, A. victoriae-reginae*

spotted aloes: *Aloe grandidentata, A. greatheadii* var. *davyana, A. maculata* var. *ficksburgensis, A. prinslooi, A. striata* ×*maculata*

dwarf aloes: *Aloe aristata, A. brevifolia, A. humilis, A. pratensis*

sotols and beargrasses: *Dasylirion berlandieri, D. texanum, D. quadrangulatum* (Mexican grasstree), *Nolina nelsonii* (tree beargrass)

terrestrial bromeliads: *Dyckia platyphylla, D. fosteriana, Puya dyckioides*

barrel cacti: *Astrophytum ornatum* (star barrel), *Echinocactus grusonii* (golden barrel), *Echinopsis bruchii* (syn. *Soehrensia bruchii*), *Ferocactus glaucescens* (blue barrel), *F. hamatacanthus* subsp. *sinuatus* (fishhook barrel), *F. schwarzii*

clustering cacti: *Mammillaria geminispina* and allies (series *Leucocephalae*), *Echinocereus pentalophus, E. viereckii* subsp. *morricalii, Parodia leninghausii*

columnar cacti: *Cleistocactus baumanii, Echinopsis terscheckii* (syn. *Trichocereus terscheckii*), *E. tarijensis* subsp. *totorensis* (syn. *Trichocereus poco*), *E. huascha* (syn. *Trichocereus huascha*) hybrids, *Neobuxbaumia polylopha*

prickly pears: *Opuntia acicularis, O. cacanapa* 'Ellisiana', *O. ficus-indica, O. lindheimeri, O. linguiformis, O. sp.* 'Old Mexico'

succulent spurges: *Euphorbia resinifera* (Morocco mound)

leafy succulents: *Echeveria diffractens, E. lilacina, E. runyonii, E. shaviana, Graptopetalum paraguayense,* ×*Graptosedum* spp., *Lenophyllum* spp., *Sedum confusum, S. diffusum* 'Potosinum', *S. mexicanum, S. palmeri, S. reptans*

the rest of the site, while leafy native subshrubs seed into plantings, and small carpeting succulents and low perennials sheet over the hill and occupy nooks along steps, dotting cliff and hillside with lax greenery that blends into the native landscape.

Floral and textural companions for the mostly architectural composition—shrubby, white-flowered cordia and informal groups of light-catching, blue-leaved ruby grass, creamy white blackfoot daisy, pale blue nierembergia, and vibrant orange bulbine—soften the strong forms of the larger plants with fleeting displays in spring and after summer or fall rains, creating a lush froth of foliage even through punishing drought. Minimal management—policing weeds that sprout during rainy episodes and cutting back dried stems of flowering plants at the end of their cycles—sustains this unirrigated garden; the large, structural succulents hardly require tending at all. Together these rugged, drought-enduring plants romance the ancient weathered face of the cliff, responding to this uniquely beautiful native site.

An English steppe

In the gently rolling terrain of southwestern England, Judy Pearce's estate, Lady Farm, includes a most unusual garden, especially in these parts—a stylized rendition of a tawny grass-filled steppe. Unlike the majority of her countrymen who have only of late begrudgingly noted the beauty of grasses, Judy was naturally drawn to their textures. She called on garden designer Mary Payne to help her create this stunning naturalistic garden.

OPPOSITE TOP Grasslands the world over inspire with their open spirit, supple movement, and diverse plants. High in the South African Drakensberg, kniphofias colonize a moist meadow of grasses. *Kniphofia caulescens, Merxmuellera drakensbergensis,* Tiffindell, southern Drakensberg, Republic of South Africa.

OPPOSITE BOTTOM Seemingly touched by such wild places, the steppe garden at Lady Farm takes on a decidedly non-British air. Tawny sedges and grasses, and bright, warm-hued, dramatic flowers—including many kniphofias—revel on this gentle slope. *Kniphofia* spp., *Coreopsis verticillata, Achillea* spp., *Verbascum* sp., *Eryngium* spp., *Stipa gigantea, Nassella tenuissima,* Lady Farm garden, Somerset, England, Judy Pearce and Mary Payne design.

The sloped area, covering about a quarter acre, is ideal for showcasing grasses, exposing them to breezes and allowing their graceful forms to undulate and flow with the lay of the land. The slope also improves drainage, allowing selected plants to thrive that would sulk and suffer in the otherwise damply verdant acreage of Lady Farm.

The color green—lush, enchanting, and ubiquitous in this part of the world—posed a visual problem for the new garden. How to introduce a garden of browns and tans without jarring? The answer came in the form of gravel, which serves as mulch throughout the planting as well as cover for pathways through and around the garden, separating it visually and physically from the turf beyond. Now when graceful, fine-textured bunchgrasses of varying heights push forth their dusky plumes, and sedge species such as *Carex buchananii*, *C. petrei*, *C. comans*, and *C. testacea* form their fawn and bronze matrix, the garden basks in isolated originality. The tawny tones superbly enhance brightly hued flowers. Once again bucking the British status quo, Judy has a predilection for strong colors over pastels, and nowhere are they more lovely than in the steppe garden. Fiery coreopsis, yarrow, kniphofia, mulleins, and daylilies all glow warm and bright.

Tall grasses form a backdrop and separation at the top of the slope, while shorter sedges and tussock grasses dominate elsewhere, interspersed with *Stipa gigantea* and *Molinia caerulea* that send up veil-like flowers, loosening the composition. Artemisias, eryngiums, and other texturally interesting plants with a dryland feel thread throughout. Upon visiting this garden, we were struck by its power to evoke flower-filled grassy meadows we had seen on the other side of the globe in eastern South Africa. If Judy or Mary has been to those places, their influence on the women's artistry seems obvious; if not, the gardenmakers' creativity deserves even more credit. Strikingly textural and boldly colorful, this garden brings the spirit of some of the earth's most beautiful wild places to the gently domestic landscape of southern England.

An urban oasis

Under the wide canopy of a native live oak, a lush garden offers green respite for a residence on a busy city street. The intimate plantings—set into our small home's equally small backyard in Austin—nevertheless feature a subject of generous scale: a ten-foot-wide Australian cycad (*Macrozamia johnsonii*) makes a fountainlike centerpiece that plays with shafts of light passing through the oak's canopy. Its imposing presence works here because it conveys a sense of nature's power in the city, contrary to conventional design wisdom that would limit small gardens to small plants. Bright green and regal, this elegant plant sets a subtropical mood, anchoring a scene to be enjoyed from a small central lawn and nearby patio.

Although the oak's broadly arching branches shelter plants from the Texas sun, the soil beneath—eight inches of black clay over chalk—experiences drought at times. Its alkaline pH restricts planting choices. Yet this urban garden has become a green oasis with only casual irrigation, a reality made possible by luxuriant yet drought-enduring foliage plants.

Resembling an exotic lotus, giant groundsel (*Farfugium japonicum* 'Giganteum') displays its shining rounded leaves all year, fronting on a soft green lawn of evergreen sedge. Tropical in its leafy spirit, the groundsel reveals temperate affinities in autumn, sending up stalks of yellow daisies that seem unremarkable next to its robust dark green leaves; they earn appreciation mainly by attracting multitudes of showier butterflies. Growing throughout the shaded beds in front of the palmlike Australian cycad, another cycad species—*Zamia pumila*, a small, graceful native of the Caribbean island of Hispaniola—creates ferny effects with loosely arched, glossy green foliage. Subject to seasonal fires in native habitat, these dwarf cycads die back to tough, succulent bulbs following hard frosts, uncoiling lively new fronds when the tropical heat of the Texas summer returns. The leathery foliage stands up to hot, dry air, yet its woodsy appearance lends freshness throughout

The same shaded place follows a procession of bulb flowering events over a period of six months in our Austin garden. Bold subtropical cycads and giant groundsel form a continuous leafy backdrop to the floral divas' performances. *Farfugium japonicum* 'Giganteum', *Zamia pumila*, *Macrozamia johnsonii*, *Ajuga reptans*.

LEFT Hardy Mead Strain hybrid amaryllis in April.

CENTER *Crinum* 'Ellen Bosanquet' after rains in June.

BOTTOM *Lycoris radiata* in September.

summer, sprouting randomly through dark, matte green ground cover provided by heirloom *Ajuga reptans* rescued from an abandoned Gulf Coast garden. Rich green all year, this ajuga sends up short erect spires of blue flowers for a brief show in early spring.

More dramatic blooms explode in spring, summer, and autumn from three different bulbous plants of the amaryllis family, each playing in turn against the backdrop of foliage. April sees elegant white heirloom amaryllis; like the small cycads, these repeat through the garden in groups. Glossy, strap-shaped leaves accompany the blooms, persisting as added summer greenery. Following rains in June and July, *Crinum* 'Ellen Bosanquet' pushes forth stalks topped with succulent rose-red chalices of fragrant bloom. This crinum's opulent but somewhat rank-growing foliage hides behind the groundsel and dwarf cycads to allow prettier foils for its impressive blooms. With cooling September rains, orange-red lycoris send up spidery blossoms on naked stalks against the many lush leaves in this garden. Grassy winter-growing foliage follows after blooms fade.

Casual care—removing spent cycad fronds and bulb foliage—suffices for this garden. The oak sheds small hard leaves annually in spring; these are left to sift into plantings as natural mulch, where they slowly decay to moisture-conserving duff. Anchored by sturdy yet lively foliage plants, this urban garden remains elegantly verdant and inviting all year; gingers, small fan palms, and other cycads—native mostly to regions with similar limy soils in China, southeast Asia, and Mexico—further enhance leafiness along perimeters, enclosing the space in a green, junglelike setting as antidote to city life.

Out in the sun

Peckerwood, John Fairey's garden near Hempstead, Texas —originally begun as a collection of woodland plants grown under tall shade-giving trees—breaks out into the

open in an area across from a small temporary stream. This sunnier garden features many xeric plants gathered during extensive travels into the mountains of northern Mexico. A textural planting here composed almost entirely of woody Mexican plants creates a link between leafy woodland and starker desert components nearby. In doing so this unique area showcases light-sculpting forms with textures and foliage colors that celebrate their environment.

In May several yuccas carry tall spires of creamy bloom and a few self-sown patches of Mexican tulip poppy (*Hunnemania fumarifolia*) top gray, dill-like foliage with lemon yellow goblets; at other times flowers play little role in this composition. Instead, an asymmetrical mix of contrasting and complementary architectural plants assembles into living sculpture to be viewed but—unlike many other areas of the garden—not approached closely from within. Informally grouped Mexican blue palms of varied heights play with sunlight washing over their silvery foliage, reflecting white light or receding into charcoal-toned shadows depending on the time of day. Their potent shapes—joined by olive-colored tree beargrass; gray-leaved, yellow-margined beaked yuccas; and cordlike dusty green Mexican grasstrees—seem lively when backlit, even though the plants themselves remain stiff and still, save when winds blow strong enough to take your hat. Sturdy silver, gray, and gray-green agaves weave into the plantings, while tussocks of Mexican feather grass supply lithe forms to move in the wind. Backing this gallery of architectural plants glassy-needled Montezuma pines glow in the sun, while rugged Mexican pinyon pine and glossy little-leafed ash (*Fraxinus greggii*) mingle, all helping to connect with woodland visible in the distance.

OPPOSITE Winter sun plays on the elegant forms of this dry planting at Peckerwood. Layering and intermingling plants of different heights and habits lends dynamic motion to this grouping of architectural species, rather than the museum-like stiffness with which they are often displayed. *Brahea armata, Nolina nelsonii, Dasylirion quadrangulatum, Yucca rostrata, Agave asperrima, Fraxinus greggii, Pinus cembroides, Pinus montezumae,* Peckerwood Garden, Hempstead, Texas, John Fairey design.

Thanks in part to a tidy mulch of tawny gravel in mixed sizes and tones, this handsome garden asks for little in the way of care, requiring only occasional pruning and weeding. Empowered by light, it presents an intriguing mixture of foliage, form, and color from many angles, merging the spirit of desert and forest with Mexican flair.

A moist meadow through the seasons

This backyard garden covers about an eighth of an acre in a semirural Colorado subdivision. The area is flat and offered no preexisting features but poorly maintained lawn, yet has a good view of the Rocky Mountain foothills. A natural swale runs into the space that collects water after rains, a boon in such a dry climate. Close by, hay fields and old orchards give testament to the unusually rich, fertile, high-pH clay soil and the strong agricultural tradition of the region.

To resonate with this rustic sense of place, make best use of the good soil and seasonally abundant moisture, and preserve a casual, open feeling that takes in the mountain views, we decided to create a romantic orchard and meadow. With the home at some distance and no enforced linearity or hardscape in sight, a bucolic, uncluttered, nonsuburban garden could develop. This meadow transitions from smaller-scale cottage and culinary gardens next to the house; flowers and fruit still play a role here but the overall mood is more spacious and relaxed.

We planted trees in informal groupings of similar species rather than the linear grid typical of an orchard. Those selected have a light and airy deciduous spirit. Spring flowers, fruit, and attractive bark played into our choices. Ornamental and fruiting plums, crabapples and apples, serviceberry, native western birches, hop tree, and two feathery-leaved, fresh-looking deciduous conifers—a dawn redwood and a tough Texas hill country strain of bald cypress—create small copses that visually block neighboring homes and give privacy while leaving mountain views open to the west.

Paths evolved in response to the trees, an organic process rather than drawn ahead of time on paper. In turn, these casual, curving paths—about three feet wide and

covered with a couple of inches of locally quarried, inexpensive, neutral-toned pea gravel—created the shapes of the meadow planting areas.

Bulbs and herbaceous perennials are threaded and grouped informally throughout the meadow, with grass and sedge species forming the main, texturally serene matrix through which more dramatic floral elements come and go. Complex and ever-changing in individual plant palette, the design employs informal repetition and intermingling of plants, colors, forms, and textures that enlarge the space and invite both midrange and distant viewing. The open, flat terrain and western orientation enhance light effects, as do the grassy textures and long-stemmed, wildflower-like demeanor of most of the plants.

Spring, the wettest season, hosts a sea of two thousand daffodils in white and pale yellow. With the grasses and sedges not yet fully emerged, these soft colors keep the serene, expansive mood, unlike stronger colors that would shrink the space and excite the eye. Lime-green and acid-yellow mounds of cushion spurge (*Euphorbia epithymoides*) and moonlight yellow *Thermopsis lupinoides* (syn. *T. fabacea, T. lanceolata*) mingle with the papery-petaled daffodils. Billows of white and pink flowering plums, apples, and crabapples create a delicate vertical framework, harking back to pastoral orchard idylls.

As spring turns to summer, other perennials come to the fore, and grasses and sedges begin to fill in, covering the yellowing bulb foliage. Species and hybrid baptisias bridge the spring and summer seasons in shades of blue, purple, white, cream, and yellow. Summer's strong light welcomes more vibrantly hued perennials, enveloped in a calm green ocean of grasses and sedges. Primary players include bright gold, orange, and rose-red daisies of *Echinacea* species and hybrids consorting with exclamation points of rose-purple liatris and orange kniphofia, and small and midsize globular *Allium* species. Many North American prairie natives join in and continue on to dominate as summer shifts to autumn.

The grasses, now burnished in late-season shades of gold, tan, amber, and orange, create a warm panel against

OPPOSITE TOP This moist meadow changes dramatically over the growing season, thanks to mutable light and the ebb and flow of plants. In spring, grasses are just beginning to emerge in fresh green tufts, and *Thermopsis lupinoides, Euphorbia epithymoides, Iris lactea*, and flowering crabapples and plums take the stage in the pale but bright white light of the early season. Authors' garden, Fort Collins, Colorado.

OPPOSITE BOTTOM By summer, grasses have expanded to their full untamed glory, now dominating the scene. Coneflowers bring staccato notes of color, adding to the wild feeling of the space. Light washes boldly over it all. *Echinacea angustifolia, E. paradoxa, Thelesperma filifolium, Rudbeckia maxima, Allium azureum, Digitalis lutea, Festuca idahoensis* 'Siskiyou Blue', *Taxodium* sp. aff. *mucronatum*, authors' garden, Fort Collins, Colorado.

ABOVE By autumn, green becomes a secondary color player. Grasses have burnished to bronze, amber, tan, and burgundy, glowing in the lower, warmer golden light of the late-season sun. Asters lend a floral note here and there. A ripe, mellow softness pervades. *Symphyotrichum oblongifolium*, red foliage in foreground *Euphorbia epithymoides*, authors' garden, Fort Collins, Colorado.

which Ohio goldenrod (*Solidago ohioensis*), purple and lavender asters (*Symphyotrichum ericoides, S. laeve, S. oblongifolium, Aster sedifolius*), and rose chalices of *Colchicum* species play. Come winter, the grasses and dried seed heads of various composites bring a tawny quiet to the space.

Tending this garden is simple except for an annual late-winter cutting back of the grasses, sedges, and perennials. The feel is casual and not overly tidy. Minimal primping occurs during the growing season—only offensively floppy finished blooms and yellowed colchicum foliage are removed (the other bulbs are relatively inconspicuous during their descent into dormancy). Editing and refereeing of self-sown plants occurs as needed. Additional watering is necessary during the hot summer and early autumn months when there has been no rain; an overhead sprinkler run for an hour and moved to four or five stations gets the job done in less than half a day. Soaker or drip hoses would also work well on this site as it is flat and the plants are tall and dense enough to hide them. Weeds were common early on, as the old lawn contained a large seed bank. After two years, literally only a handful of weeds have found their way through the dense planting. Self-sown goldenrod, allium, and aster seedlings growing in inopportune spots are pulled more often than any weed.

A dry meadow

An extension of the just-described moist meadow responds to drier conditions at the high end of the property. Here a handful of apricots, pears, and apples—drought-tolerant fruiting trees that hail from dry grassland in climatically harsh regions of Eurasia—form an orchard. The openness and western exposure invite cosmopolitan short and mid-size bunchgrasses, together with western native herbaceous perennials, to frolic in wind and sunlight. Most of the bulbs, flowering perennials, and annuals have pliant stems and tend toward wispiness, moving easily in the wind and looking quite untamed. This creates a comfortable, regionally evocative transition between the taller, denser planting of the moist meadow below and a rock garden and strongly xeric perimeter plantings beyond.

OPPOSITE TOP Flowers come and go with the seasons in the dry meadow. Among the first are long-stemmed tulips expanding between the emerging foliage of Junegrass. *Koeleria macrantha, Tulipa clusiana* 'Lady Jane', authors' garden, Fort Collins, Colorado.

ABOVE By late spring grasses have fully flushed, and self-seeding blue and white flax threads through their tussocks. *Linum perenne* subsp. *lewisii*, authors' garden, Fort Collins, Colorado.

OPPOSITE BOTTOM High summer is abuzz with insects attracted by a bevy of flowers, mainly western natives. *Delphinium virescens* and *Echinacea pallida*, authors' garden, Fort Collins, Colorado.

BULBS FOR MEADOWS

These plants are able to compete with grasses and are tall enough to be seen among them and other plants.

Plants needing drier conditions

Allium unifolium
Calochortus spp., mariposa lily
Dichelostemma spp. (syn. *Brodiaea, Triteleia*), blue dicks
Tulipa altaica
Tulipa clusiana
Tulipa montana
Tulipa orphanidea var. *flava*
Tulipa orphanidea Whittallii Group

Plants requiring some moisture even during dormancy

Allium azureum (syn. *A. caeruleum*)
Allium carinatum subsp. *pulchellum*
Allium cernuum
Allium roseum
Allium splendens
Allium stellatum
Allium tanguticum
Camassia spp.
Colchicum spp.
Fritillaria meleagris, guinea hen flower
Narcissus spp., daffodil

Plants tolerant of both conditions

Allium flavum
Chouardia litardieri (syn. *Scilla litardieri*)
Hyacinthoides hispanica, Spanish bluebell
Iris bucharica
Iris cycloglossa
Ixiolirion tataricum
Leucojum aestivum, snowflake
Ornithogalum magnum
Tulipa sprengeri
Tulipa sylvestris

In this dry meadow we experimented with a matrix of underused small to midsize drought-tolerant grasses. The nursery trade has largely ignored these, choosing instead to grow and promote larger ornamental grasses that want regular moisture and much richer soil. Bunchgrasses selected for this garden perform like champions yet have not proven weedy and deserve much more attention in drier parts of the country as ideal components of naturalistic designs and xeriscapes. With a regime of about twenty inches of moisture per year, all grasses planted here remain under eighteen inches in height. Some tolerate even less water. The area is irrigated twice a month in the summer if there is no rain. With less water, the plantings would survive but the trees would drop most of their fruit before it ripened, and grasses would turn brown well before their typical timetable of tawniness.

Instead of mud-loving daffodils, spring bulbs in this drier upland meadow include some of the lankier, longer-stemmed species tulips that can stand up to the grasses. Later, periwinkle-blue *Chouardia litardieri* (syn. *Scilla litardieri*) and *Ixiolirion tataricum*, both much-neglected long-lived charmers that can be bought in large numbers for ridiculously little, thread through the actively growing grasses, along with cream and yellow mariposa lilies (*Calochortus* spp.). Small-headed allium species in blue, lavender, rose, white, and yellow take over come summer.

Many of the garden's nongrassy perennials are remarkably popular with insects. At times, this meadow is so loud with buzzing and humming it can be heard from twenty feet away. Honeybees, solitary wasps, and bumblebees jostle for position on blossoms of locally native white larkspur (*Delphinium virescens*), blue delphinium (*D. geyeri*), and prickly poppy (*Argemone polyanthemos*). Butterflies join in on orange western wallflower (*Erysimum asperum* and *E. wheeleri*), the golden daisies of greenthread (*Thelesperma filifolium*), pale coneflower (*Echinacea pallida*), and a clay-tolerant selection of orange butterfly weed (*Asclepias tuberosa*). During late summer and autumn the action shifts to plains gayfeather (*Liatris punctata*), silky aster (*Symphyotrichum sericeum*), and a self-sowing purple annual from Kansas,

GRASSES AND SEDGES FOR MEADOWS

These grasses are growing in our meadow in northern Colorado.

Grasses in drier areas

Achnatherum hymenoides (syn. *Oryzopsis hymenoides*), Indian rice grass

Blepharoneuron tricholepis, mountain mist grass

Bouteloua gracilis, blue grama

Festuca arizonica, pine grass

Festuca idahoensis 'Siskiyou Blue'

Hesperostipa comata, needle and thread grass

Hesperostipa neomexicana, New Mexico spear grass

Hesperostipa spartea, porcupine grass

Muhlenbergia montana, mountain muhly

Sporobolus airoides, alkali sacaton

Stipa pennata, European feather grass

Grasses in moister areas

Alopecurus pratensis 'Variegatus', striped foxtail grass

Andropogon glomeratus, broom sedge, bushy bluestem

Calamagrostis brachytricha, Korean feather reed grass

Carex grayi, star sedge

Carex muskingumensis, bamboo sedge

Chasmanthium latifolium, wild oats

Deschampsia caespitosa, tufted hair grass

Molinia caerulea, moor grass

Muhlenbergia reverchonii, seep muhly

Grasses growing throughout

Achnatherum calamagrostis, silver spike grass

Andropogon gerardii, big bluestem

Andropogon hallii, sand bluestem

Bouteloua curtipendula, sideoats grama

Carex divulsa (*tumulicola* hort.), European or Berkeley sedge

Carex flacca (syn. *Carex glauca*), blue sedge

Eragrostis trichodes, love grass

Festuca glauca, blue sheep's fescue

Festuca mairei Atlas fescue

Koeleria macrantha, June grass

Melica ciliata, hairy melic grass

Phleum nodosum, Italian timothy

Schizachyrium scoparium, little bluestem

Sesleria autumnalis

Sesleria glauca

Sesleria heufleriana

Sesleria nitida

Sporobolus heterolepis, prairie dropseed

Stipa capillata

Oklahoma, and Texas, *Eryngium leavenworthii*. Alive with sound and motion, and backlit by Colorado's bright sun, this meadow garden draws children and adults alike.

Care is even less than that required for the moist meadow: few weeds grow in the dense, dry planting; plants need no primping during the growing season as they are short and wiry, and the annual late-winter cutting back produces much less debris than from more luxuriant, taller plantings.

A pastoral spring landscape

This landscape shares many elements with the moist meadow garden, on a much larger yet simplified scale. As a prominent display at Chanticleer, a private estate turned public garden in the rolling terrain and temperate climate of the western Philadelphia suburbs, the idyll of pastoral orchard is amplified as mature flowering crabapples, tall conifers, and large shade trees gracefully divide and measure a gentle hillside and transform the front lawn of a dominating manor house at the top of the hill.

Great sweeps of daffodils in pale hues undulate romantically, echoing the roll of the land and adding to the grand scale of the trees and space. Bulbs of smaller stature, such as muscari and squill species, bring blue hues to the earlier-blooming varieties of daffodils in the partly shaded, weaker lawn areas beneath trees where they are able to compete. In the meadow planting of the previously described garden,

RIGHT An old apple orchard and an overgrown, dandelion-studded lawn make a rustic spring picture. Such bucolic scenes are familiar and beloved; gardens that share in their spirit resonate with many people. Laporte, Colorado.

BELOW Daffodils spill sensually in great sweeps over a rolling lawn at Chanticleer, with crabapples as a frame. Varied greens of background trees, along with emerald turf, visually whiten the pale tree and bulb blossoms. *Narcissus* 'Actaea', *Malus* 'Donald Wyman', Chanticleer, Wayne, Pennsylvania.

such short bulbs do not work well because the companion perennials and grasses are too dense and tall.

Predominantly a one-season display, more than fifty thousand daffodils in a variety of selections create a powerful experience for several weeks in the spring. These were selected for slightly staggered bloom times, and for vigor and ability to persist with the competition of lawn grass. The flower-filled hillside recedes into lush verdancy the rest of the growing season, with a few weeks of autumnal tree foliage color and then crabapple fruit to carry on into winter.

Beyond the initial extravagance of planting so many bulbs, the landscape is remarkably carefree. Lawn within the bulb sweeps must be left rough and long until early summer to allow the bulb foliage to ripen; the other lawn areas continue to be mowed regularly. This short period of untidiness is being mitigated by replacing lawn grass in the bulb sweeps with finer-textured, more attractive bunchgrasses, especially fine fescues. These look good and grow best unmown, and remain low enough when uncut to show off smaller bulb species of *Muscari* and *Scilla*. They are also more tolerant of the encroaching shade of the mature trees.

Since Chanticleer offers many acres of distinct garden experiences, this seasonal display works well. Different areas ebb and flow, creating changing interest and making for an exceptionally dynamic public garden. In a much smaller garden, such a stylized event would have to be reduced in size and would not offer the diversity that helps sustain interest over the seasons. Yet for enhancing a monotonous, overbearing lawn, a vignette of this experience—a few spring-flowering trees set into the grass and accompanied by one or two flowing sweeps of daffodils—promises delight.

A hillside garden

On an east-facing slope in the Colorado foothills, plants celebrate the open feeling of the surrounding chaparral. Two hundred feet long and varying in depth from eight to fifteen feet, this garden makes an imposing statement above a curving buff-toned stucco retaining wall and flagstone pathway to the house entrance.

STRONGLY PERFORMING DAFFODILS

In the lawn at Chanticleer
(cool climate, with cool-season turf grass; information courtesy of Lisa Roper):

Narcissus 'Actaea', 'Bravoure', 'Honeybird', 'Ice Follies', 'Ice Wings', 'Salome'
Narcissus gracilis

In our meadow
(cool climate, with both cool- and warm-season bunchgrasses but not turf):

Narcissus 'Actaea', 'Ara', 'Hawera', 'Honeybird', 'Jack Snipe', 'Jamestown', 'Lemon Drops', 'Mint Julep', 'Pueblo', 'Stint', 'Surfside', 'Thalia', 'White Plume', 'W. P. Milner'

In hot climates
(with warm-season turfgrass; species and cultivars marked with ✳ are intolerant of heavy clay soils common in coastal regions of the Southeast):

Narcissus 'Abba'✳, 'Carlton'✳, 'Cragford', 'Erlicheer', 'Fortune'✳, 'Ice Follies'✳, 'Saint Keverne'✳, 'Sweetness', 'Trevithian'
Narcissus italicus
Narcissus jonquilla var. *henriquesii*, *N. jonquilla* var. *jonquilla*
Narcissus ×*odorus*, campernelle
Narcissus papyraceus 'Galilee'
Narcissus pseudonarcissus✳, Lent lily
Narcissus tazetta 'Avalanche', 'Grand Primo', 'Scilly White'

Naturalistic gardens suit wild sites such as this slope. They often present more marked seasonal changes and rhythms than other styles. Northern Colorado, Ogden design.

ABOVE LEFT Spring is heralded by myriad small bulbs set off by evergreen dwarf conifers and ground-covering plants. *Tulipa clusiana*, *T. vvedenskyi*, *T.* 'Princes Irene', *Euphorbia epithymoides*, *E. myrsinites*, *Picea pungens* 'Mesa Verde', 'Hillside', and 'R. H. Montgomery', *Pinus mugo* 'Iseli Whitebud', *Ribes odoratum* 'Crandall'.

ABOVE Summer comes and the hillside fills in with shades of green. Herbaceous perennials and grasses now dominate the scene. *Sporobolus heterolepis*,

Helictotrichon sempervirens,
Achillea 'Moonshine', *Picea*
pungens 'R. H. Montgomery',
Potentilla fruticosa 'Katherine
Dykes', *P. fruticosa* var. *davurica*
'Prairie Snow', *Stachys byzantina,*
Alchemilla mollis, Penstemon
pinifolius 'Mersea Yellow',
Allium sp., Mimi the dog.

ABOVE Autumn transforms
the garden, both by light and
by plant colors. Dwarf conifers
come to the fore, their cool
greens and blues contrasting
with the ruddy and tawny
senescence of deciduous plants.

ABOVE RIGHT As winter
descends, conifers take pride
of place. They hold our interest
while all else sleeps, as we wait
for the cycle to begin anew.

Natives to the site—three-leaf sumac, golden currant, and mountain mahogany—intermingle and feather into untended territory. Compact selections of conifers include common prostrate juniper cultivars and both Colorado and Serbian spruce. Pines represented are semi-dwarf forms of Scots, mugo, Swiss stone, bristlecone, red, Austrian, and jack pine. All echo the Rocky Mountain junipers dotting the rolling hills beyond and the ponderosa and lodgepole pine forests on the slopes above. These small evergreens enliven the garden through the long dormant season. Come early spring, thousands of small bulbs—squills, grape hyacinths, puschkinias, alliums, fritillaries, colchicums, dwarf daffodils, *Iris bucharica*, and short-statured tulips—bloom against the soft greens and blues of the conifers.

Spreading, mat-forming, and cascading herbaceous perennials, many with evergreen foliage, knit the slope together visually, spill over the stucco wall, and work to control erosion on the steep hillside. Many of these plants are typically found in rock gardens; here they grow without rocks, benefiting from elevated placement to show them off.

By early summer the conifers have receded into the perennials' greenery, and low mounding grasses and sedges come into their own, tying the garden texturally with the short-grass prairie and chaparral matrix beyond. Most nonwoody plants are less than eighteen inches tall, in keeping with surrounding native vegetation and preserving views of the wild landscape that extends beyond the garden. As autumn sets in, ruddy hues transform the hillside and once again the conifers take center stage, their cool tones silhouetted against fiery deciduous foliage.

This garden presented many horticultural challenges for Lauren. Seeping with snowmelt in the spring yet dry the rest of the growing season and populated with a hearty stand of Canada thistle, the site had issues. Plants selected needed to tolerate periodic inundation in sticky mud and then hardpan, as well as constant wind. Fall planting proved a mistake, as plants suffered wind and cold desiccation before they could establish and most died. Spring planting was crushed into a small window when early-season waterlogging had passed and summer drought had not yet set

BEST STABILIZING PLANTS IN THE HILLSIDE GARDEN

Achillea spp., yarrow
Antennaria spp., pussytoes
Anthemis biebersteiniana (syn. *Anthemis marschalliana*)
Cerastium candidissimum, dwarf snow-in-summer
Delosperma spp., hardy ice plant
Eriogonum spp., buckwheat
Gypsophila repens, creeping baby's breath
Penstemon procumbens, creeping penstemon
Phedimus spp., creeping stonecrop
Phlox nana, Santa Fe phlox
Phlox subulata, cushion phlox
Saponaria ocymoides, rock soapwort
Satureja spp., savory
Sedum spp., stonecrop
Thymus spp., creeping thyme
Veronica pectinata, woolly veronica

in. Many southwestern or Great Plains natives that thrive in the hotter, lower elevations of the region could not be counted on in the cool higher-elevation climate and eastern exposure of the space, so tough clay-tolerant plants from the Old World were called upon to join montane native penstemons, lupines, buckwheats, fleabanes, and phlox.

The thistle was sprayed with herbicide for a year before planting, and from then on periodic "hot spots" of surviving resprouting shoots were treated. It never disappeared entirely; rather it was kept at bay in a truce of sorts, as it lived in brush thickets above the planting and also blew in from ravines closeby.

The garden's steep terrain made for potential erosion problems. Lauren opted against incorporating any amendment and chose the smallest sizes available of the plants to be used, to minimize the destabilizing effects of digging and loosening the soil. Watering was accomplished by gentle overhead sprinklers twice a month during the growing season in the absence of rain. Plants were spaced extra closely to accelerate coverage since wind and gravity made mulches impossible. All spring cleanup had to be done during the frozen months because once the ground thawed, it was impassable muck until well into May. Weeding and deadheading occurred annually in one intensive midsummer session, keeping trampling and erosion to a minimum.

Despite all these challenges, the space grew into a spirited composition where plants that are typically relegated to their own horticultural "ghettos" are allowed to mingle and coexist. Rock garden perennials, small conifers, natives, and common landscape junipers all join in this novel garden made for an unconventional site.

Into the woods

Along a gentle wooded slope banking a meandering small stream, the otherwise dramatic, effusive, and often avant-garde mood of the public garden Chanticleer shifts to one of subtlety, contemplation, and reverence of site.

Horticultural and artistic prowess spill from almost every turn at Chanticleer, yet one of its most special places downplays these aspects of human control. Along this stream the natural site and the region's rich woodland heritage take the lead rather than the more obvious hand of designer and gardener.

As with most successful naturalistic gardens, this seemingly untouched appearance is really an illusion—similar to the effect of dragging a stick in the snow to erase one's footprints. Gardening and designing here are just as intensive and involved as with the most obviously manipulated plantings, yet arguably require more knowledge and skill to accomplish such subtle, natural effects.

The woodland garden was among the first areas to be developed at Chanticleer, with redbuds, stewartias, halesias, styrax, fothergillas, deciduous azaleas, and other woody plants brought in for understory before the garden became public. Wildflowers and ferns native to the site were divided and spread throughout once the poison ivy, brambles, and other unwanted vegetation were cleared. Other regionally native woodland plants were added in comfortable groupings and generous sheets. Simple combinations, such as golden wood poppy (*Stylophorum diphyllum*), ostrich fern (*Matteuccia struthiopteris*), and Virginia bluebells (*Mertensia virginica*) in one area, and golden groundsel (*Senecio*

Ostrich ferns and Virginia bluebells fill this rocky slope with delicate, fresh color and growth in spring. *Mertensia virginica,*

Matteuccia struthiopteris, *Thalictrum* sp., Chanticleer, Wayne, Pennsylvania.

aureus) with creamy foamflower (*Tiarella cordifolia*) elsewhere, give the area beneath the trees a calming cohesion typical of naturally occurring plant communities and also offer more visual drama when in bloom than if the plants grew in smaller numbers.

Later, adjacent native woods were developed as a woodland garden featuring Asian plants, in contrast to the mainly North American piedmont natives that dominate in the first garden area. The spirit is similar but distinct, as many of the plants have bolder texture and offer a more varied season of bloom, such as elegant late-blooming *Begonia grandis* and species of *Deinanthe*, *Ligularia*, *Hosta*, *Hydrangea*, *Rodgersia*, and *Kirengeshoma*.

The stream runs along the bottom of the Asian Woods garden, and one can cross it by way of a small bridge at the base of a pond, walk alongside the pond in sunlight for a brief spell, and then reenter the woodland and join

LEFT Generous sheets of trilliums and ferns give a settled feel to the woodland floor. *Trillium grandiflorum*, *Matteuccia struthiopteris*, Chanticleer, Wayne, Pennsylvania.

BELOW Though subtle, woodland light is mercurial, intimate, and dynamic. A scene changes dramatically over a day and over the seasons. What was hidden in morning shadows may jump into view as afternoon sun dapples a space. Perhaps this is what makes discovery so commonplace yet still compelling when walking beneath trees. *Matteuccia struthiopteris*, *Phlox stolonifera*, Chanticleer, Wayne, Pennsylvania.

the stream once again to continue along its course. All of Chanticleer plays with contrasts of open and closed spaces, be they courtyard, lawn, ruin, meadow, water, or woodland. After crossing several open areas, one can move into a canopy of trees and walk the length of most of the property along this steam bank, immersed in the quiet intimacy of deciduous woods.

Chanticleer makes a strong point of stating that its mission is that of a pleasure garden. Yet beyond the sensual joy of the place, its woodland areas take the garden one step further. While the majority of areas are not particularly congruous with what's possible in most home gardens, the woodland's intimate spaces have much to offer garden visitors from the heavily forested East Coast in the form of visual inspiration and specific ideas for plants and their combination. Here we can rekindle our love of the woods, experience their unique essence, and bring a bit of them home for our own interpretation.

Succulents in the cold

Since both of us love succulents, we dedicated our home's south-facing foundation—the warmest, most protected part of our garden—to these sculptural plants. At five thousand feet elevation, our northern Colorado garden falls in USDA zone 5a: annual winter minimums of −15 to −20 degrees F. Periodic bouts of bone-chilling cold, brutally dry blasts of arctic air, and several snows visit each winter, yet our sunny strip of well-drained soil accommodates numerous hardy cacti, agaves, ice plants, and drought-loving companions.

This lush yet xeric garden fronts on a narrow side yard with little in the way of views. The bed near the foundation mounds one to two feet above grade, sloping gradually down to a flagstone path. This sunny south-facing slope, top-dressed with a thin layer of pea gravel, is the most protected area for plants and elevates them for display. Defining a visual corridor where succulents dominate, this garden focuses interest on diverse shapes and textures, distracting from a window-filled but otherwise uninteresting façade of our passive solar home.

Several mature century plants of *Agave havardiana*, a species from the Davis and Chisos mountains of Texas, punctuate plantings at intervals. Their large gray rosettes —edged defiantly with formidable black spines—tilt gently south, creating the impression that their growth has responded to the sloping beds for some time. This canting also discourages snow and ice from collecting in their channeled leaves. Although stiff looking by nature, large and small specimens of century plants huddle together like mother and child, relaxing the composition with a sense of natural process.

Other structural plants—cold-tolerant yuccas such as *Yucca harrimaniae*, *Y. nana*, *Y. thompsoniana*, *Y. baccata*, *Y. elata*, and *Y. schottii*, as well as shrubby chollas and large- and small-padded prickly-pear cacti—mingle with the agaves. Positioned so that passersby will avoid unhappy encounters with their unfriendly but often attractive spines, these alternate a few feet back from the path on either side. In early summer the prickly pears sport blooms in luscious colors, briefly rivaling any flower for beauty. Some species, especially forms of *Opuntia macrorhiza*, later ripen showy maroon fruits that last well into winter.

Leafy companions highlight the spiky silhouettes of cacti, agaves, and yuccas with contrasting textures and varied foliage colors, creating an interesting composition all year. *Tanacetum densum* var. *amani* forms boulderlike mounds that move rhythmically back and forth across the path, leading the eye. Its silvery, feathered leaves remain evergreen, as does the olive-toned waxy foliage of several manzanitas (*Arctostaphylos nevadensis* and *A. patula*) that wedge between rocks, sprawling down the slope. Wispy dryland grasses—*Nassella tenuissima*, *Achnatherum hymenoides* (syn. *Oryzopsis hymenoides*), and *Stipa pennata*—move with breezes and create daily lighting effects with feathery tufts against the stonelike agaves.

Penstemons; self-seeding and somewhat weedy California poppies; desert mountain sage (*Salvia pachyphylla*); hardy blue sage (*Salvia farinacea* 'Texas Violet'); and several species of eriogonum all add floral notes to this dry garden, joined in spring and early summer by xeric bulbs:

Crocus ancyrensis, *Allium coryi*, and *Calochortus* spp. Arching gently away from the house wall, multibranched desert willows (*Chilopsis linearis*) create open shrubs, tipping wispy summer branches with white or purplish-pink trumpets and shading and cooling the house when clothed in foliage during the summer.

Clustering hedgehog cacti (*Echinocereus* spp.)—special favorites—nest near boulders: mound-forming claret cups (*E. triglochidiatus* and *E. coccineus*) crowned in spring with long-lasting red blooms, and two glassy-spined Oklahoma species (*E. baileyi* and *E. albispinus*) that shimmer when backlit each afternoon and push out oversized purple flowers sporadically throughout summer. Near stones other dwarf cacti like the white-spined, globular *Escobaria orcuttii* join low-creeping desert phloxes, dryland ferns (*Cheilanthes* spp.), miniature *Eriogonum ovalifolium*, and tufted succulents of the ice plant family: *Titanopsis*, *Aloinopsis*, *Rabiea*, *Chasmatophyllum*, *Nananthus*, and *Stomatium* species. Showy *Delosperma* species range from the tiny fuchsia-flowered mounds of *D. sphalmanthoides* to California-style sheet-forming ice plants like golden *D. nubigenum*, apricot-pink *D.* 'Kelaidis' (sold as Mesa Verde), and rich magenta *D.* sp. 'John Proffitt' (sold as Table Mountain). These offer satiny blooms in spring and, in some types, well into summer. Especially good performers for our small garden, *Delosperma* spp. 'White Nugget', 'Gold Nugget', and 'Lesotho' make tidy mats topped each spring with lavish blooms in cream, white-centered yellow, and white-centered pink, respectively.

Big blue spruce stonecrop (*Sedum sediforme*), mat-forming pussytoes (*Antennaria parvifolia* 'McClintock'), and low-creeping xeric daisies (*Heterotheca jonesii*) spread along the path and sometimes between stepping stones, finishing this diverse garden with carpets of ever-gray foliage.

Work is minimal in this garden: unwelcome weeds are rare because of the site's dryness and the gravel mulch, while self-sown seedling cacti, poppies, penstemons, and eriogonums need occasional moving and policing. The area receives at most about three waterings per year, and only if there has been no rain for a month or more in the summer.

Combining intimate views of plant miniatures with bigger, bolder forms, colorful flowers, and light-catching spines and foliage, this succulent-themed garden offers both large- and small-scale beauty, maintaining lively textural appeal even when dusted in snow. In our zone 5a garden this Arizona dream offers the most handsome landscape of winter.

A cottage rose garden

More than the predilections of the owner, a house and its neighborhood sometimes determine the aesthetic direction of a garden, as happened here. In the end, this often results in a happy arrangement. While individualistic gardens and horticultural creativity are a pleasant surprise amid the mind-numbing sameness of American landscapes, when gardens refuse to take their surroundings into account they can feel dissonant and self-important.

Lauren bought a simple 1921 Craftsman bungalow as her first home. Situated on a corner lot in a small Colorado plains town, the house cried out for a classic cottage garden; the quiet tree- and lawn-dominated neighborhood of older homes seconded this.

Sunny days, cool nights, and low humidity allow hardy roses, most herbaceous perennials, and many annuals to luxuriate in the high-elevation West. Some additional irrigation is usually necessary for all but the most xeric species, and soil amendments, mainly in the form of organic matter, are helpful except in the case of the most drought-

OPPOSITE TOP As in much grander wild deserts, sculptural cacti and succulents mingle with ephemeral flowers, fine grasses, and scruffy subshrubs in this small south-facing dryland garden. The bright light at five thousand feet elevation has the clarity of desert sun, saturating brilliant flower colors and flattering strong textural contrasts. *Agave havardiana*, *Yucca harri-* *maniae*, *Arctostaphylos ×coloradoensis*, *Opuntia macrorhiza*, *Cylindropuntia whipplei*, *Nassella tenuissima*, *Eschscholzia californica*, *Penstemon purpusii*, authors' garden, Fort Collins, Colorado.

OPPOSITE BOTTOM *Eriogonum jamesii*, *Cylindropuntia* sp., *Heterotheca* sp., *Eschscholzia californica* 'Tequila', authors' garden, Fort Collins, Colorado.

ABOVE A cottage-y house welcomes a cottage-style garden. Billowing floral abundance, old garden roses, and soft colors hark back to traditional English border style, done in a more casual, comfortable American scale here without help of staff. *Phlomis russeliana*, *Campanula latifolia* 'Alba', *Penstemon digitalis* 'Husker Red', *Alchemilla mollis*, *Epilobium angustifolium* 'Album', *Geranium* spp., *Aquilegia chrysantha*, *Cornus alba* 'Elegantissima', roses, northern Colorado, Ogden design.

RIGHT Roses deserve companions. Larger shrub species and old garden roses don't seem to mind competition from other plants for water and food. Northern Colorado, Ogden design.

TOUGH AND BEAUTIFUL OLD-FASHIONED SHRUB ROSES USED IN THIS GARDEN

Unless noted otherwise, these are all once-blooming and intensely fragrant.

'Blush Damask' (pale pink)

'Celestial' (pale pink)

'Charles de Mills' (magenta purple)

'Complicata' (pink)

'Great Maiden's Blush', syn. 'Cuisse de Nymphe' (pale pink)

'Königin von Dänemark' (pink)

'Louise Odier' (rose pink, repeats bloom)

'Madame Hardy' (white)

'Madame Plantier' (white)

Rosa ×alba 'Semi-Plena' (white)

'Stanwell Perpetual' (pale pink, repeats bloom)

'William Lobb' (violet-rose)

loving species that thrive on mineral soils. This site, unlike most in the region, is blessed with deep, friable river-bottom loam. A cottage garden here supports not only a rich assortment of billowing border favorites but also roses and other flowering woody plants that so strongly figure in this traditional style.

A narrow ten-foot-deep by forty-foot-long area running along the east side of the house was chosen as home for a lawnless rose garden in the cottage spirit. The exposure offers protection from prevailing northwest winds as well as from fierce afternoon sun that bleaches soft floral colors and ages petals before their time. It stays moist longer than south- or west-facing sites, yet affords roses and many perennials enough sun to bloom well. Scents also carry better on this sheltered side of the house; the narrow bed, fronting on sidewalk and backing up to windows, offers intimate olfactory as well as visual encounters for passersby and for those inside.

A dozen highly fragrant old garden roses—albas, damasks, gallicas, and mosses—went in first. These large, hardy,

easy-care shrub roses quickly gave the planting scale and determined the colors and textures of companions chosen for them. For the most part once-blooming, the roses needed seasonal support from other shrubs: traditional white-flowered lilac, purple-leaf sand cherry, variegated red-stem dogwood, and opulent 'Annabelle' hydrangea hold up the back of the garden spring through autumn. These shrubs and the roses seem to swallow the small house in charming profusion.

Spring daffodils are followed by several months of English-style perennial abundance: cranesbills, lady's mantle, lamb's ears, columbines, fragrant lilies and nicotiana combine in a frothy melee, blending with the roses in pastel hues of yellow, chartreuse, cream, pink, peach, and lavender-blue. The putty-colored house serves as a structural backdrop to the somewhat amorphous planting. The deciduous rose-based planting is entirely geared toward the period from April until October—winter is uninteresting. Other areas with evergreen plants pick up the slack during the off-season. Word spread beyond town and in a few years this ebullient garden became a popular destination, as no one in the region had filled an entire yard with flowers. Though not in the least bit novel in style, the romantic pairing of house and garden strikes a deep chord and enchants many.

Tending this garden includes an annual cleanup in late autumn rather than the late-winter cleanup more customary in other gardens, because the bulky brown remnants of the perennials look especially unkempt viewed up close from the sidewalk and against the prim house. Deadheading is done regularly throughout the growing season to keep the planting in bloom and fresh looking for as long as possible. Weeds are not a problem. Watering is accomplished weekly with soaker hoses that are hidden from view by the lush plants. A drip system would also work well, but not any sort of overhead irrigation, whether sprinkler or microjet. Roses are more likely to get foliar diseases with water regularly sitting on their leaves, and the soft flowers and plant forms of their companions are easily disfigured or flattened by irrigation coming from above or the side.

A tropical wedding garden

Glowing in luminous hues of copper, orange, and yellow, a shining wave of bromeliads swells beside a formal allee of palms along a processional walkway. Behind plantings an undulating wall in blue tile screens street noise and views, while its glassy mosaic surface offers a reflective backdrop for equally glittery foliage. At once grand and intimate—part flamboyant modern Brazil, part romantic Spanish patio—this lush tropical display greets visitors at a public garden in southwest Florida.

Scott was asked to co-design these gardens for the Naples Botanical Garden. The unpromising site—the parking lot of a former strip mall near a busy intersection—needed to become lush space for outdoor gatherings and weddings. This new public garden called out for plantings that would "wow" first-time visitors with color, but these needed to be essentially self-sufficient as the young institution did not yet have horticultural staff. In this fast-growing community—set in a humid climate that nonetheless sees water shortages—unthirsty plantings would set a good example.

Fluorescently colored bromeliads native to semiarid coastal Brazil, *Aechmea blanchetiana*, fill sunny beds south of the blue-tiled streetside wall. Here the intense Florida sun heightens their strong natural colors: warm tones that create a scene reminiscent of a coastal sunset for instant drama. Reddish blooms add interest at times, but the leathery leaves of these lush yet tough plants provide most of the color. A modern mosaic on the gently undulating wall uses smashed tile shards in the style of Brazilian designer Roberto Burle Marx; patterns playfully echo shapes and colors of the bromeliads in places. Informal crushed shell paths front the plants, placing this exotic scene in a distinctively Florida context.

Palms in the allee are sugar dates (*Phoenix sylvestris*). Visually similar to the palms of Moorish patios, these iconic plants—formally placed as in ancient Mediterranean gardens—connect this part of the design to the Spanish style of old Florida homes. Not a true date palm, the sugar date belongs to an Indian species better adapted to Florida's humid climate. Bold cross-hatched patterns on their

thick trunks left by trimming the palm's enormous leaves repeat in the walkway where paving tiles are set on a bias. Columns interspersed among the palms support climbing fig vines and are topped, palmlike, with potted rosettes of giant bromeliads, *Alcantarea imperialis*.

Along the allee low ground covers lap against the walk, contrasting with lush cycads and orange-red firecracker ferns (*Russelia equisetiformis*) that show off feathery stems and shining green leaves, arching like jets of water to echo

BELOW The mosaic wall includes smashed dishes donated by Naples Botanical Garden members, fanciful ceramic sea creatures, and—as here—playfully tiled echoes of the plants themselves. *Aechmea blanchetiana* and *Macrozamia moorei*, Naples Botanical Garden, Florida, Ogden and Smith design.

OPPOSITE TOP An allee of date palms intersperses with columns and underplantings of palmlike, arching cycads in a walled courtyard. *Phoenix sylvestris*, *Encephalartos ferox*, on top of columns *Alcantarea imperialis*, Naples Botanical Garden, Florida, Ogden and Smith design.

OPPOSITE BOTTOM Like a colorful sunset, an undulating blue and mauve mosaic wall provides a foil for giant bromeliads that glow with orange tones when planted in strong sun. Cycads with *Aechmea blanchetiana*, Naples Botanical Garden, Florida, Ogden and Smith design.

Shaggy with native Florida maidenhair ferns, a cool, dripping fountain built from locally quarried coral rubble creates a green destination. *Adiantum capillus-veneris* on dripping wall, *Nephrolepis cordifolia* 'Kimberly Queen', *Microsorium scolopendrium*, Naples Botanical Garden, Florida, Ogden and Smith design.

built of rough native limestone—quietly drips water, sustaining pendant maidenhair ferns. This creates a cool green backdrop for weddings that imitates a fern-draped sinkhole, a common natural feature in Florida. The tiled basin at the base of this grotto, faced on the outside with bulging heads of fossil coral, gives an old Florida feel in keeping with the rest of the garden.

Although flowering plants here demand relatively little deadheading, fast growth in this near-tropical climate results in frequent trimming to remove old leaves of palms, bromeliads, and others. Fertilizers—although not needed—are welcomed by the palms and their underplantings; excess feeding spoils the colorful leaves of the bromeliads, turning them green.

A palm-crested island

Not far from the allee and its tropically themed mosaic garden, another planting at Naples Botanical Garden plays up the unique beauty of a spectacular plant: *Bismarckia nobilis*, the giant silver-leaved fan palm of Madagascar. In most Florida gardens this architectural plant features as a staid solitary specimen or in matched pairs and regimented lines along boulevards; here Bismarck palms in mixed sizes crest a mounded oval garden, gently tilting this way and that. The resulting explosion of silvery foliage at many angles exaggerates the already potent form of these noble plants, creating natural sculpture to play against buildings and more formal plantings nearby.

On its western side the *Bismarckia*-dominated bed fronts a lawn used for meetings and events. A simple underplanting—a dwarf selection of Florida native *Viburnum obovatum*—creates a billowing mass of fine-textured evergreen foliage, contrasting with the jumble of silvery palms. The silver and dark green foliage reads strongly black and white when illuminated during evening gatherings that take place nearby among plantings devoted to sweet-scented nocturnal flowers and under an arbor overhung in night-fragrant vines.

Out of sight of this area on the east side of the palms a collection of succulents—many native, like *Bismarckia*, to

the arched canopies of the palms up and down the walkway. Tangerine-flowered bulbine (a South African succulent) and Bolivian sunset (a winter-flowering *Gloxinia* species with water-storing tubers) ensure added color with little irrigation; their flowers come in orange tones that pick up the warm bromeliad colors along the wall.

The allee's destination—a tall semicircular fountain

ABOVE Planted in a loose, slightly canted group, the spectacular silver fans of Bismarck palms crest an underplanting of rich green foliage. The composition reads black and white when viewed at dusk. *Bismarckia nobilis, Cycas taitungensis, Viburnum obovatum* 'Mrs. Shillers', *Kalanchoe grandiflora*, Naples Botanical Garden, Florida, Ogden and Smith design.

RIGHT On the opposite side of the same planting a collection of oddly shaped succulents joins the Bismarck palms to provide a different experience of color and texture. Like the overarching palms, many of the plants in this island bed are Madagascan natives. *Bismarckia nobilis, Kalanchoe beharensis, Euphorbia millii, E. millii* subsp. *hislopii*, Naples Botanical Garden, Florida, Ogden and Smith design.

Madagascar—compose a planting with weird shapes and bright colors, playing against the silver palm backdrop. This xeric underplanting includes Florida-friendly species of kalanchoe, euphorbia, adenium, and aloe mingled among irregular limestone boulders. Removal of old leaves from the palms and occasional pruning of spent blooms from the succulents keep the plantings in shape. Dramatic day and night, this small garden presents a commonly used tropical landscape plant in a novel setting, rescuing it from cliché to awaken and expose its astonishing character.

A bold front garden in suburbia

Our house in northern Colorado is an unassuming wood-sided box in an equally unremarkable suburban neighborhood. Were it not for spectacular foothills views to the west, this could be Anywhere, USA. The yard offered a blank slate of lawn and one bodacious purple smokebush by the front door. The rest was up to us—just how we like it.

After Lauren's experience with her first garden where she unwittingly became a destination for garden gawkers, the most important thing was to create privacy from street and neighbors. Disguising the house itself wasn't a bad idea either: unlike the charming Craftsman cottage and lovely stucco home of former gardens, this building had little to contribute.

The front takes up a tiny part of the half-acre lot; most of the land hides out back, one of the reasons we bought the place. Flat, east-facing, less than an eighth of an acre, and visually cut off by the house from the backyard and mountain views, this offered a sheltered, limited space to grow plants we covet that look the least western and need more water and soil amendment than the rest of the garden.

A casual buff-toned sandstone path ambles to the front door; another curves through the garden and heads out back. These bisect the space into distinct planting areas. Contrary to common assumptions, big plants don't shrink small spaces—they make them feel larger. We indulged ourselves in the wildest looking, tallest, most texturally bold plants possible in Colorado's climate. Eight trees of varied ultimate sizes went in first, a large number for the

space. Western catalpa, white-flowered eastern redbud, and a multistemmed goldenrain tree form the primary screen, lending a leafy, almost tropical backdrop to the planting. Eventually they will force us to embrace a quite shaded situation, but for the next half-decade or so, sun-loving plants make up the main menu. Rosemary willow (*Salix eleagnos*) and threadleaf buckthorn (*Rhamnus frangula* 'Asplenifolia') anchor the perennial planting with amorphous billows.

A number of larger grasses and sedges add to the somewhat out-of-control feel and further screen the house from view. With herbaceous perennials, foliage and form is also our priority, and rich flower colors rather than pastels dominate. Aside from the grasses, most of these leafy plants have little or no winter interest and don't look like much until late spring and early summer. Evergreen rounded boxwood and a compact selection of Japanese red pine (*Pinus densiflora* 'Globosa') dress up the walk to the front door in the off-season. To counteract springtime baldness, hundreds of tiny squills (*Scilla sardensis* and *S. luciliae*, both formerly *Chionodoxa*) bloom in pools of lavender blue, while many small groups of short cyclamineus, triandrus, and jonquilla daffodils unfurl their demure yet sturdy blossoms. Dependably perennial kaufmanniana, fosteriana, and lily-flowered tulips follow in procession over six weeks of bloom time in shades of orange and yellow.

Come late May, perennials vibrantly take over until the hard freezes of late October and November. Species and selections of *Baptisia*, *Liatris*, *Euphorbia*, spuria iris, *Echinacea*, *Kniphofia*, *Acanthus*, and *Sanguisorba* dominate; above our heads hover garden giants *Persicaria polymorpha*, *Thalictrum glaucum* and 'Elin', *Veronicastrum*, *Eutrochium*, *Rudbeckia maxima*, *Eryngium yuccifolium*, and altissima daylilies. Self-sowing annuals and biennials form a blue and lavender haze over the bright colors through the seasons beginning with nigella and *Papaver somniferum* 'Lauren's Grape'; on to larkspur, *Echium lusitanicum*, and *Anchusa capensis*; then *Eryngium planum*; finishing with *Verbena bonariensis*. Corm- and bulb-forming large alliums, trumpet lilies, and hardy gladiolus species and selections bring exotic flower power to the scene. Ornamental asparagus

LEFT Planted closely, large, sturdy herbaceous perennials fill this small front garden seven months of the year. *Sanguisorba menziesii, Eryngium planum, Echinacea* 'Evan Saul' (sold as Big Sky Sundown), *Alopecurus pratensis* 'Variegatus', *Kniphofia stricta, Solidago* sp., *Consolida ajacis, Echium lusitanicum, Eutrochium dubium* 'Little Joe', *Helianthus salicifolius, Iris spuria* 'Fontanelle', *Rudbeckia maxima, Rhamnus frangula* 'Asplenifolia', authors' garden, Fort Collins, Colorado.

BELOW The path to the front door fluoresces in autumn as deciduous perennials, grasses, shrubs, and trees go out with a bang. *Symphyotrichum lateriflorum* 'Lady in Black', *Diascia integerrima* 'Coral Canyon', *Salvia azurea* 'Nekan', *Verbena bonariensis, Pinus densiflora* 'Globosa', in fall color *Sporobolus heterolepis, Cercis canadensis* 'Alba', *Koelreuteria paniculata, Euphorbia palustris*, authors' garden, Fort Collins, Colorado.

(*Asparagus officinalis* subsp. *pseudoscaber* 'Spitzenschleier') and a willow-leaf sunflower from Kansas (*Helianthus salicifolius*) deliver the coup de grace, hiding the mailbox and house number in their wild foliage, with hardy South African *Crinum bulbispermum* expanding its exotic chalices at the base.

Care is intensive from midsummer on through autumn, in the form of deadheading and selective cutting back to keep profusion from descending into chaos. Some neighbors enjoy this distinctly unsuburban front yard, while others (to our amusement) make a beeline to the other side of the street, as if the garden might attack them at any moment. As proof that we have succeeded in our mission, not only has the house seemed to shrink behind a sea of gorgeous plants, we can be deeply immersed in and enjoying the planting yet remain hidden from view.

A romantic overgrown wall

Fronting a street in an old neighborhood, a twelve-foot wall built of rough stones disappears beneath greenery. Vines ramble along a balustrade at the top; other plants sprout from terraced compartments along the wall, spilling downward with pendant stems and flowers; more grow up from below, mixing in random profusion. Scott created this garden in Austin to soften the overly high wall and create the mood of an old semi-abandoned estate, a theme in keeping with the property's large stone house and immense native oaks.

Despite its east-facing exposure, this garden suffers scorching conditions in summer as a result of the reflective masonry, mandating heat- and drought-tolerant plantings. Beds in stepped tiers along the wall receive drip irrigation but are filled with lean mineral soils to discourage overly lush growth. Retained with dry-stacked stones, plants along the foot of the wall grow in a mix of crushed granite and native limy soil.

Antique garden plants suggestive of an aging villa—fruiting grapevines and the climbing rose 'Souvenir de Madame Léonie Viennot'—entwine the balustrade, while

A casually mixed planting colonizes and partly obscures a stone wall, creating a romantic sense of age. *Chamaerops humilis, Sophora secundiflora, Parthenocissus* sp. 'Hacienda Creeper', *Muhlenbergia lindheimeri, Russelia coccinea, Taxodium mucronatum, Leucophyllum frutescens* 'Alba', Austin, Texas, Ogden design.

a shrubby Mediterranean fan palm sprawls from the narrow planting terrace. These rugged Old World plants consort with Texan and north Mexican natives that revel in hot sun. Lush coral blow (*Russelia coccinea*) cascades from the wall with rich green asparaguslike whorled stems that bear red tubular blossoms following summer rains, drawing hummingbirds.

A Texas mountain laurel (*Sophora secundiflora*) glistens near a small wrought-iron gate. Its densely cloaked evergreen branches shelter this private opening from street view and carry grape-scented trusses of purple pea blossoms in spring. Felted silver-gray ceniza; Texas redbud, with dark green heart-shaped foliage; and a Mexican orchid tree, with matte, pale green, butterfly-shaped leaves, offer contrasting leafy texture and color, along with varied flowers in season.

Beneath the sheltering mountain laurel, Mexican stonecrop (*Sedum palmeri*) and ghost plant (*Graptopetalum paraguayense*) fill the dry shaded bed with succulent sage-toned foliage, spilling over the stacked rocks. Nearby, grayish tussocks of muhly grass (*Muhlenbergia lindheimeri*) and dwarf ruby-flowered amaranth (*Gomphrena haageana*) self-seed along a short stone path by the narrow gate. This doorway and the wall surrounding it are romantically draped in hacienda creeper, a small-leafed Mexican *Parthenocissus* species that veils the wrought-iron gate, allowing a half-hidden glimpse to curious passersby. The fast-clambering vine gives vigorous cover, cooling the wall's hot stones, yet allows the powerful architecture to read through its bright green, leafy veneer. Its leaves turn crimson in late autumn and drop briefly in midwinter, revealing the stone.

Plants in this garden demand little care beyond occasional trimming and annual policing of the more aggressive vines and coral blow. Playing against the rough stone, this unstudied composition takes advantage of elevated positions to show off diverse habits, colorful blooms, and varied textures. Against ponderous masonry the plants convey a sense of age, romance, and the power of nature.

First steppe

Where a thirsty sheet of Kentucky bluegrass once occupied our flat, sunny backyard, low tufts of blue and green grasses wave in hazy afternoon light, flowing among mats of silvery foliage and small but bright flowers. Vastly more diverse than lawn yet still serene, this grassy garden draws interest over the four seasons while retaining restful openness in contrast to profuse plantings on all sides. Inspired by short-grass prairies of the semiarid West and similar steppes of central Asia, we developed this naturalistic garden—just a few years old and still experimental—at our northern Colorado home.

A drought-tolerant grass matrix provides the essential framework. As in native grasslands this includes both cool- and warm-season species; all are selected to remain below a foot in height, even when in flower. This low stature—important for the steppe's calming open feel—has proved hard to predict on our rich clay, which sometimes stimulates unduly tall growth. We have exiled species violating height regulations to other parts of the garden. Grasses in the planting—tufted rather than running species—form discrete tussocks rather than making unified turf. Dark green, bright green, gray, and silvery-blue species, some with stiff, wiry blades, others with graceful arching habits, intermingle; these grasses warm with ripe seed heads at times and continue to show individual character and texture as they turn varied tawny tones at the end of the growing season. Composed entirely of species with especially fine textures, this small version of a steppe repeats separate tufts of grass. These visually layer one upon another to enlarge the sense of space. Bordered in places with gravel and stone paths, this garden nevertheless merges visually with taller mixed plantings around it, all of which include grassy components. This avoids an abrupt or obvious interface in conflict with the steppe's wild spirit.

Even before the grasses begin spring growth, pasque flowers, crocuses, grape hyacinths, snow irises, miniature daffodils, squills, and species tulips brighten the otherwise dormant steppe with colorful, translucent blooms, brightly

OPPOSITE TOP Small daffodils and early low-growing perennials respond to spring moisture before the steppe's grasses have filled in. *Narcissus* 'Segovia', *N.* 'Hawera', *Pulsatilla vulgaris, Geum triflorum, Geranium multisectum, Cotula hispida, Sisyrinchium* sp., *Festuca glauca,* authors' garden, Fort Collins, Colorado.

OPPOSITE BOTTOM Late-spring warmth and moisture allow grasses to expand to their lushest, greenest moment. Small wild-looking perennial forbs dot the serene scene with spots of color. *Dianthus carthusianorum, Bouteloua gracilis, Festuca* spp., *Artemisia frigida,* authors' garden, Fort Collins, Colorado.

TOP LEFT By midsummer cool-season grasses have flowered and gone to seed, their spent stalks a tawny contrast to the blues and greens of the grass foliage. This subtle foliage composition is the antithesis of the overwrought, flashy, so-called contrastifolia style. *Festuca* spp., *Artemisia frigida, Gutierrezia sarothrae,* authors' garden, Fort Collins, Colorado.

LEFT In autumn, all grasses go beige; dried seed heads and senescing foliage play in the amber sunlight of the season. *Festuca* spp., *Bouteloua gracilis, Gutierrezia sarothrae, Liatris punctata, Artemisia frigida, Antennaria parvifolia,* authors' garden, Fort Collins, Colorado.

backlit in the western sun. Most of these early flowers prefer summer drought, but the daffodils enjoy damp soils; these are fortuitous choices for low-lying portions of the steppe garden that stand in water during the spring thaw and briefly following infrequent summer showers. South African species of *Cotula* and *Geranium*, and native perennials like *Phlox kelseyi* 'Lemhi Purple' and prairie smoke also enjoy these occasionally wet areas; after bloom the latter's small flowers ripen rose-tinted tufts of seed that glow in late-day sun, matching the equally feathery ripening heads of pasque flowers in drier parts of the steppe.

Several fescues are among the first grasses to flush in spring, sending up wiry leaves in tones of green, gray, and silver. These blend with spreading mats of *Dryas drummondii*, pussytoes (*Antennaria* spp.), and dwarf species of sage (*Artemisia caucasica*) in equally subtle but varied hues. As early summer arrives, cool-season grasses flower, turning the steppe into a mesmerizing pool of motion; their silken textures play gently with breezes and sunlight. Bright but small flowers of *Dianthus carthusianorum* and dwarf, tufted daisies match the grace of the grasses, sitting loosely atop slender stems, while grasslike alliums and dwarf members of the iris family, *Sisyrinchium* species, spangle white, blue, and yellow blooms among tufts of grassy foliage.

As summer advances, warm-season grasses bloom; in native blue grama and South African caterpillar grass (*Harpochloa falx*) flowers resemble small insects floating over the leaves on airy stems. At the same time, cool-season grasses ripen their seed heads and the entire steppe assumes a mature, tawny aspect. Purple spikes of xeric, compact *Liatris punctata* and shrubby golden mounds of dwarf rabbitbrush and broomweed play against this warm brown backdrop. As the last grasses ripen in fall, more purple and lavender flowers thread through fading leaves: late-blooming *Allium thunbergii* and autumn crocuses.

Our steppe garden resembles a wild, uncared-for prairie yet demands more attention and care—especially weeding—than most other areas of our garden. We leave the browned grasses to overwinter, but these must be hand cut and removed before bulbs sprout in spring. Aggressive

GRASSES, SEDGES, AND RUSHES IN THE STEPPE

Aristida purpurea, purple three-awn
Bouteloua gracilis, blue grama
Carex muskingumensis 'Little Midge', dwarf bamboo sedge
Festuca amethystina, purple fescue
Festuca glauca, blue sheep's fescue
Harpochloa falx, caterpillar grass
Juncus tenuis, dwarf rush
Koeleria brevis
Koeleria macrantha, June grass, dwarf western form
Sesleria caerulea
Sesleria glauca

seeders like blue grama require shearing before their seed heads shatter. In return for the many hours spent managing this complex yet simple-feeling matrix, we are rewarded with never-ending interest that varies over the seasons and over each day as the sun plays across its serene textures.

Plants over patterns in an exotic land

South Africa's second largest city, Durban, lies beside the warm waters of the Indian Ocean. With a tropical climate similar to Miami, this capital of Kwazulu-Natal Province served as a center of colonial life during the days when this country was part of the British Empire. English heritage shows itself at the Durban Botanic Gardens in a small area with neatly patterned paths and symmetrical planting beds. Familiarly English in layout, the garden nonetheless takes on a decidedly African flavor: exotic shapes of tropical succulents overwhelm its tame period formality.

Bisecting paths forming four quadrants with a central sundial recall a medieval knot garden. Yet where one expects to see sheared herbs and flowers set in dainty parterres, the playful designer of this planting refused such a predictable impulse, instead substituting plants with powerful forms and robust constitutions that better suit and express the African climate. Backed by tall native palms—*Hyphaene natalensis* and *Phoenix reclinata*—several branched specimens of indigenous *Euphorbia triangularis* make cactuslike candelabras of waxy green four- and five-angled stems. These weird plants—quirky sculptures invading the erstwhile formal beds of the garden—mix among other striking shapes: rosette-forming aloes and agaves, shrubby jade plants, spiky rhino-horn *Sansevieria,* and branching prickly-pear cacti. Although they hardly resemble typical floral bedding of a parterre garden, spiny crown of thorns and fat-stemmed gout plant (*Jatropha podagrica*) offer colorful scarlet blooms while seeding through the plantings. A dense ground cover of succulent *Plectranthus*—yet another indigenous African plant—gives the drought-tolerant composition a soft green foil,

BELOW Instead of roses, sheared box, and herbs, this South African garden fills its formal lines and spaces with energetic succulents. *Agave attenuata, Euphorbia triangularis, Aloe arborescens, Cereus hildmannianus* var. *uruguayanus, Jatropha podagrica, Asparagus asparagoides, Opuntia* sp., *Sansevieria cylindrica,* Durban Botanic Gardens, Durban, Republic of South Africa.

RIGHT Slightly incongruous yet mirroring the blended cultures of the place, a vigorous tropical planting surrounds a central sundial. The quaint object recalls England, where many of South Africa's people and their gardening traditions have roots. *Agave attenuata, A. americana* 'Marginata', *Crassula ovata, Euphorbia triangularis, Aloe ciliaris, Plectranthus* sp., Durban Botanic Gardens, Durban, Republic of South Africa.

while native asparagus vines are allowed to clamber over the stiffly branched succulents to provide rampant notes of tropical vigor.

Showing indigenous spirit and a sense of humor, this small garden juxtaposes an overtly traditional context with novel planting. The bold botanical palette—randomly naturalized, not formally bedded—turns the design on its head, redeeming this foursquare garden from its otherwise predictable fate. While offering a nod to colonial heritage, this Anglo-African planting aptly expresses the vitality of the tropics: potent rum rather than polite tea.

A place among plants

At the heart of our backyard garden a rustic sandstone patio with four raised stone slabs for benches offers places to sit, enjoy an occasional evening fire, and simply lose ourselves in nature. Surrounded by wild-inspired steppe and meadow plantings, a gently sloped rock garden, and views to our rugged perimeter and distant foothills, this decidedly human space nevertheless melds into the naturalistic spirit of our garden. It organizes and defines space while inviting people in to experience plants.

The original backyard—a drought-stricken lawn—concealed an ever-so-slight change of grade. We wanted to create a rockery that would accommodate dwarf conifers and other choice plants but were determined to avoid the grand escarpments favored by alpine enthusiasts. Instead of resting on an artificial mound, our rock garden simply plays up this very modest natural rise with scattered stones and plants. Encrusted with lichens, a few dozen flat-topped boulders lie in gentle arcs along the barely perceptible slope with wide spaces left between for dwarf pines and spruces, spreading junipers, and other small plants. Together these create the impression of a low rock shelf filled with stunted trees, an illusion continued by perimeter plantings behind the rockery; these include bristlecone and pinyon pines interspersed with coarsely branched New Mexican olives (*Forestiera neomexicana*). Placed to screen and distract from

nearby houses, these naturalistic groupings echo the conifers in the rock garden, helping the spaces flow together visually.

After a little excavation, a low spot—actually, the lowest on the property—now provides space for a fire pit and seating next to the rockery, which curves gently nearby, embracing the space like a plant-filled amphitheatre. Built with local buff-colored sandstone slabs, paving and benches match the lumpy stones of the rock garden in color. Open to the sky and surrounded on all sides by plants, this circular seating area terminates a path leading from the house. Simultaneously prime destination and a sort of switchyard, this is where one chooses between varied routes through adjacent meadow, orchard, and other experiences. The fire pit offers full views over steppe, rock garden, and perimeter, especially satisfying when late afternoon light streams across these plantings.

Although each area of the garden offers distinct moods —the steppe with its low grasses and open feel; the rockery with weathered stones and ancient-looking dwarf and mounded plants; and the perimeter with wild mixtures of western trees, shrubs, and perennials—these spaces don't read as an unrelated, jumbled patchwork of separate garden rooms. Instead, the disparate plantings merge comfortably into a larger composition, fused by shared leitmotifs—grasses and feathery seed-bearing plants especially flattered by western light. Allowed to seed or placed so that they suggest spontaneity, these fine-textured plants repeat as varied species through the garden, uniting the spirits of steppe, rockery, and perimeter into a single rich whole.

Native landscapes don't formally divide between riverside and meadow, cliff and prairie, or hillside scrub and forest's edge. In a small suburban garden one way to have diverse plantings yet still enjoy a unified garden experience is to mirror this natural blurring. By understating a garden composition, at times partly erasing our own hands, we leave space in nature for ourselves. Our reward is a place among the plants.

Steppe, meadow, rock garden, and perimeter plantings all converge at our fire pit. What its indoor cousin the hearth is to a house, the fire pit is to our garden: the heart and center where plants, stone, sky, fire, friends, and family can all come together.

INDEX

Pages with numbers in **boldface** include photo captions.

OPPOSITE *Tulipa vvedenskyi, Pulsatilla vulgaris, Phlox bifida*, Edie the cat, authors' garden, Fort Collins, Colorado.